THE TIMES OF
MY LIFE

THE TIMES OF MY LIFE

Sportswriting in the 20th Century

Michael Strauss

Edited by
Ellen Strauss Boer and Peter Boer

Library of Congress Control Number:		2018914568
ISBN:	Hardcover	978-1-9845-7151-9
	Softcover	978-1-9845-7150-2
	eBook	978-1-9845-7149-6

To order additional copies of this book, contact:
Xlibris
1-888-795-4274
www.Xlibris.com
Orders@Xlibris.com
785790

CONTENTS

FOREWORD

Michael Strauss was a sportswriter and a sports editor for the *New York Times* for fifty-three years. Equally remarkably, he continued as a sports columnist for the *Palm Beach Daily News* for another twenty-five years until his death at age ninety-six. It is thought that he covered more sports than any other writer, making him an expert on less well-known sports, those driven more by the love of competition and personal glory than financial gain. He made his mark in covering skiing from its earliest days, and a weekly story on prep school football. His book covers a unique period in American history, with a focus on sports as a mirror of its society. The period marks the transition from the amateur sports and the relatively impoverished professional leagues of the 1920s to the mass television entertainment of the 1980s.

Around 1990, Michael assembled a hand-typed manuscript of his reminiscences over a period beginning with his first byline in 1928. It was never published. We, the editors, his daughter and son-in-law, believe the contents are so unique and interesting that publication is warranted, if only to serve as a firsthand record of changing times. Some readers may enjoy his recollections of famous sports figures. Others will enjoy his breezy, but disciplined, style. Finally, there is an underlying thread of how Michael, born in 1912 in Brooklyn, became acquainted with circles of American society then not normally accessible.

He worked in the newsroom and played poker until the first edition was published sometime after midnight, in order to proofread his stories. He lived through the Depression, World War II, and the Holocaust, and his three younger brothers served in the US Army. Daughter Ellen recalls heated family discussions at the time President Truman fired General MacArthur. Michael worked at the intersection of the WASP (white, Anglo-Saxon, Protestant) establishment, the Irish-Italian personalities then dominating big-city culture, and Jewish businessmen and intellectuals. He touches on race lightly, with a few anecdotes about his interactions with Jackie Robinson, Elston Howard, Muhammed Ali, and Kareem Abdul-Jabbar. Above all, he discusses a newsroom culture that was overwhelmingly male, with very different values and issues from those of a modern workplace. Importantly, he was respectful of the private lives of sports personalities.

The following is excerpted from his obituary in the *Palm Beach Daily News*. The contributing writers were Frank Houston, Andrew Davis, and Michele Dargan.

> One of the most durable and fascinating careers in journalism came to a close Saturday, October 11, 2008, with the death of Michael Strauss, the Palm Beach Daily News' sports editor since 1983, who came to Palm Beach after spending half a century at the New York Times. He was 96. In his extensive and remarkable 75 plus years as a sports journalist, Mr. Strauss covered everything from archery to yachting and he prided himself on never having missed a deadline. His dry wit, wry smile and extensive knowledge of history and geography were inescapable for anyone who'd ever gotten to know him. In Palm Beach, Mr. Strauss was a regular presence at events at the Palm Beach Recreation Center, the Phipps Ocean Park Tennis Center, the Breakers and Mar-a-Lago. He was well-known to the athletic directors of Palm Beach Day Academy, St. Ann's and Rosarian Academy as well as officials at Trump International, the Kennel Club and the Croquet Center in West Palm Beach. He first was published in the New York Times about 70 years ago, and his last published article was published in the Daily News last month. About two weeks ago, Mr. Strauss suffered a fall in his South Palm Beach condominium and was hospitalized at JFK Medical Center in Atlantis. Earlier this week, he was transferred to Hospice by the Sea in Boca Raton. At the Times, he served as winter sports editor and a sports writer and traveled with his hometown Yankees and Mets for 14 seasons. He had a seemingly inexhaustible reserve of personal anecdotes about everyone from Babe Ruth to Pete Rose, Sonny Liston to Joe Namath, Calvin Coolidge to Richard Nixon. As the Times ski editor from 1963 to 1982, Mr. Strauss wrote more than 1,000 articles on the sport. He was inducted in 2001 into the U.S. National Ski Hall of Fame, in Michigan,

because of his prolific coverage. Mr. Strauss did not limit himself to journalism; he managed his high school baseball team, and later managed women's professional basketball and baseball teams in the 1940s and 1950s. He also owned a public relations firm and earned a law degree from St. John's. Mr. Strauss was born July 13, 1912 in Williamsburg, Brooklyn. When he was 10, he caught a glimpse of his first professional baseball game at Ebbets Field, home of the Brooklyn Dodgers. As the 13-year-old manager of his high school baseball team, Mr. Strauss called in the details of his team's games to the New York Times' sports desk. Soon his editor, Joe Gephart, invited Mr. Strauss to write the stories himself. The following summer, he covered New York City boxing club matches for $3 a night. At 18, Mr. Strauss officially joined the staff of the New York Times, covering semipro baseball on Sundays. He was a college freshman, earning 40 cents an inch, or $8 a column. From there his 50-year career at the Times blossomed. He covered hundreds of college and professional football games, from Dartmouth, Harvard and Notre Dame to the New York Giants and New Jersey Jets. He covered thoroughbred and harness horse racing. As the ski editor for the Times from 1963 to 1982, he covered Winter Olympics in Squaw Valley, Grenoble, Innsbruck, Lake Placid and Alberta. He covered dragon boat racing in China, Gaelic football in Ireland, and harness horse racing in Macau. He may have been the first sportswriter to take notice of a 12-year-old basketball player named Lew Alcindor later known as Kareem Abdul-Jabbar when he attended an athletic awards ceremony at a New York City Boys Club in 1958. When he wasn't covering sports in exotic locales, Mr. Strauss frequently wrote stories and took photographs for the Times' Travel section. He also contributed articles to Readers Digest, Esquire, Playboy, Travel and Leisure and other magazines, as well as annual entries in *Encyclopedia Britannica* and *Collier's Encyclopedia Yearbook*. And for about a decade Mr. Strauss also had his own radio broadcast, on WQXR in New York, which covered the subject of skiing. Mr. Strauss had such an appetite for winter sports that he once covered three stories in three states, Maine, New Hampshire and New York, in one day. His second career began in Palm Beach after a brief, untenable retirement from the Times in 1982. Mr. Strauss had settled in South Palm Beach with his wife, Cecilia. The couple, who married in 1938, also shared a home in Danby, VT, where they spent summers. Mr. Strauss credited Cecilia, who died in 2002 at 86, with landing him his job at the Daily News. Cecilia called then-publisher Agnes Ash, who hired Mr. Strauss on the spot. In Palm Beach, Mr. Strauss covered sporting events at a dozen venues and schools, from the Rec Center to Mar-a-Lago. "I worked with him for 25 years," said Rick Dytrych, head pro at the Par 3 golf course. Tim O'Connor was stadium manager for the now defunct polo stadium at Palm Beach Polo & Country Club during the early days of polo in Wellington in the mid-1980s. That's when O'Connor, now spokesman for the Palm Beach County Health District, met Mr. Strauss who was covering the sport for the Daily News. Rose Carnicelli, supervisor at the town tennis courts, said Mr. Strauss was the second person she met when she came to work at the town's Palm Beach Par 3 10 years ago. Carnicelli said that she became close to Mr. Strauss after his wife died and she would cook him breakfast and help him around the house. Russ Bitzer, the former head of the Palm Beach Recreation Department who retired in 2005, once said of Mr. Strauss, "He wrote hundreds of articles for us about the kids and the programs. I would credit him in large part with many of our successes over the years." Mr. Strauss also found time to write light verse, and in 1994 published "Rhymes of My Times." Mr. Strauss was a member of the Newspaper Guild; the Baseball Writers Association; the U.S. Ski Writers Association, for which he founded the Eastern chapter; the U.S. Harness Writers Association; and the New York and U.S. Turf Writers Associations. He is survived by daughters Ellen of Alexandria, VA, and the Village of Golf, and Sharon Parker of Boca Raton; four grandchildren; Dr. Alexa Boer Kimball of Boston, Andrew Boer of Greenwich, CT, Amy Sumida of Syracuse, NY and John Parker of Kansas City, and eight great-grandchildren.

Technically, in digitizing his book, the editors learned that OCR (Optical Character Recognition) still lacks the artificial intelligence to make it superior to manual data entry. So we thank Dina Ligatino and Frederica Galloway for helping with this task.

We are especially appreciative of the support of Elizabeth Clarke of the *PBDN* for giving us access to some of Mike's editorial and photographic materials. We also thank the Nixon Presidential Library, and especially Ryan Pettigrew, for the photographs of Mike visiting the White House with the New York Yankees in 1969. We appreciate the help of Amanda Miller of the Trump Organization for permission to use Donald Trump's picture.

Ellen and Peter Boer

PREFACE

There I was turning the busy corner of Third Street and Seventh Avenue—something I had done thousands of times for half a century—heading down the block to the New York Times building. This time I was going there to attend my retirement party after fifty-three years as a sportswriter for that estimable journal.

The brightly designed decals were still on my Buick back home. These were the tags that had given me such easy entry to privileged parking at Shea and Yankee Stadiums and to such race tracks as Belmont Park, Aqueduct, Roosevelt, and Yonkers Raceway. In the days that preceded the party, I had found myself reluctant to admit it was all over as far as my lifetime adventure in the news media was concerned. And so it was small wonder that after sitting around a pool in Florida to find myself continually thinking, "Is that all there is?"

I decided to try and start all over again.

It was my wife Cecilia, who originally had come from a town of three hundred in Vermont and loved Florida's weather, who got me back on track. She knew from our repeated conversations that I was not prepared to loaf around a swimming pool every day just waiting for my time to come. Finally, she phoned Agnes Ash, the well-known publisher of the *Palm Beach Daily News*, the colorful newspaper known as "the Shiny Sheet" which focuses on Palm Beach social life and local news.

"My husband is a retired New York newspaperman," Cecilia told Mrs. Ash. "He's thinking of giving up on our condominium here on the ocean and returning to New York to look for something to do."

"What's his name?" Mrs. Ash questioned.

"It's Mike Strauss," my wife replied.

"Not Mike Strauss of the *New York Times*?" asked Mrs. Ash.

"He's the one," my wife replied.

"Tell him to come and see me tomorrow. I think we can work something out" was the happy word.

Within a short time, I found myself with the title of "Sports editor" of the *Palm Beach Daily News*.

What do I think of my second career now that I've written sometimes daily features on the new job for six years? It's the best thing that ever happened to me. I'm back in the mainstream. I couldn't be more content. I have been writing about sports—polo with Prince Charles, thoroughbred racing at Gulfstream and Hialeah, golf and tennis featuring top stars, greyhound racing, international croquet, and even big-league baseball—during spring training, featuring the Mets, the Yankees, the Expos, and the Braves, plus other sports. This all came at a time when I had begun thinking of only memories. There were many:

My visit to the Rose Garden of the White House with President Nixon and a few members of the New York Yankees. The president discussed baseball with them and poker-playing with me. Back in the early days of the Great Depression, the great Babe Ruth set the groundwork for me for a touching human interest story that never has been told.

There was that day in Italy—in Terminello—listening to Mussolini's one-time ski pro tell me about the former dictator's ability as a skier. In Ireland, I lunched on leg of lamb with Dr. Desmond Guiness, of Guiness Ale fame—just the two of us in his castle in County Kildare—to discuss one of his favorite topics: the Irish Georgian Architectural Society.

At Yonkers Raceway in New York, I *broke* bread twice with the dynamic Jackie Robinson, the first black athlete ever to play major league baseball. At four international Winter Olympics, as the *New York Times* ski editor, I watched many of the world's greatest athletes—skiers, skaters, and bobsledders—in action at Squaw Valley, Grenoble (France), Innsbruck (Austria), and at Lake Placid.

Then for the *Palm Beach Daily News*, I visited Calgary, Alberta, in 1988, for my fifth Winter Olympics. It was there that I stayed with my old friend, Ivor Petrak, vice president of the Canadian Pacific Railroad and the director of the famous Banff Springs Hotel and the nearby Lake Louise Resort.

Surprisingly enough, the one experience that gave me my greatest satisfaction was my first meeting with Lew Alcindor, who eventually became known as the Kareem Abdul-Jabbar when he was only twelve years old. I believe I was the first sportswriter from a major newspaper, by at least several years, to have his potential brought to national attention.[1]

---

[1]   See Chapter 22 for more details.

And then there was Lowell Thomas. Lowell was a famous radio and newsreel commentator. His dynamic presence was a source of pleasure to all who were his friends. How we enjoyed skiing together at Loveland Basin in Colorado even though he was wearing rental boots that were too tight.

I was on hand to write about the loquacious Muhammad Ali, then known as Cassius Clay, when he made his first New York appearance—at a luncheon held at Madison Square Garden. As a tune-up before his first bout in the Big Apple, he recited some of his familiar poetry. Among many others whose trail I crossed were Jack Dempsey, Gene Tunney, Casey Stengel, tennis' Big Bill Tilden, skiing's amazing Jean Claude Killy, and just about all of America's top jockeys.

"How does one become a sportswriter for a major American newspaper?" Through the years, that's been the question most often asked me by youngsters. I really have no answers. For me, it was merely luck. It was the year of the big crash—in 1929—that I became the manager of my high school varsity baseball team in Brooklyn. Part of this job was the phoning of a short report and the score of each game to the Long Island section of the *New York Times*. Toward the end of that baseball season with the school year ending, the Long Island sports editor—Joe Gephart—asked, "What are you doing for the summer, Mike?"

"I have no plans at this point," I answered. "In September I plan to go to St. John's College. After that, probably law school."

"But what about the next two or three months?" Mr. Gephart asked.

My eyes widened as I awaited the next question.

"How would you like to cover some sports assignments for us during your vacation?"

"That would be just great," I answered, trying to control my excitement.

I never did find out why Mr. Gephart had chosen me because there had been at least fifty freelance high school correspondents calling in with their games. Many of them, it later developed, had asked him for summer work.

And so there I was, starting on my journalism career at the *New York Times* that was to last for more than five decades. I did attend St. John's College and graduated from its law school. During this entire time, I kept writing for the paper.

In those early days, it was go-go-go for me all the time—taking elevated and subway trains to my early morning classes at St. John's and then to my assignments for the *New York Times*.

During my career at the *Times*, I've visited scores of college campuses, dozens of race tracks, golf courses, and baseball and football stadiums all over America. I've traveled in deluxe style in large planes with big-league baseball teams, and sometimes in small chartered planes, all paid for by the New York Times. I've wired stories from four continents.

The thought always uppermost in the minds of reporters is "making the deadline" because if the deadline is missed, the story doesn't get into the paper.

At the *Palm Beach Daily News*, the deadline is almost three hours earlier than it was for the *New York Times*.

But I'm still making them.

CHAPTER 1

Doing Things in Style – Ebbetts Field

Take me out to the ball game
That's where I long to be
That's all that's dear to me
See those sluggers, watch them hit;
And the pitchers do their bit.
Country fair? I don't care—anywhere!
Baseball games?—I'll be there.

There I was, lying on my stomach beneath a high fence, a nine-year-old watching my first big-league baseball game at Ebbets Field in Brooklyn. The year was 1922. There were no make-believe aspects to that notable afternoon. For there they were, in real life, the Brooklyn Dodgers, in action on their home diamond.

I was lucky to be there to see them. I didn't have the fifty-cent admission price for one of the ball park's backless bleacher seats.

"You don't need any money to watch a game," Alex Nacht, a friend had told me a few days earlier. "All you have to do is to get there about an hour before game time and head for the center field exit on Bedford Avenue. There's a good guy there, a friendly policeman. He lets six kids lie on the sidewalk at that green gate so they can look under it and watch the game."

I didn't tell my mother where I was going. She never would have understood. I told her that I was heading for the public library on Division Avenue, eight blocks away.

"And I may be a long time," I explained. "There's a book there that I've been reading. They won't let me take it home. I want to finish it today."

I lied. The only bit of truth to my story was that I was going to do lots of walking. The distance to the library was just about as long a walk as to the Franklin Avenue trolley car line that went to Ebbets Field.

And so I proceeded up Roebling Street, past the statue of George Washington on a horse at the Williamsburg Bridge Plaza, and boarded the open-air trolley which delivered baseball fans to Ebbets Field. It was a half-hour ride.

After all that trouble, I almost didn't see the game. When I arrived, there were four boys already sprawled out, peering under the gate. I got spot No. 5. Two youngsters showed up within five minutes, but only one of them was allowed to lie down.

"There's only room for six," the cop told the disappointed seventh boy. "I can't let seven get down there because then it becomes too congested. Come back tomorrow but get here earlier."

There was only one requirement to get one of the six vantage points. You had to have a newspaper to lie on. The policeman didn't want angry parents complaining about dirty kids. I laid on the spread out front and back page of the *New York Daily News*, which was then a fairly new tabloid.

Watching a game in this style was a far cry from sitting in a box seat behind the Dodgers' dugout. From where we were, you couldn't see right field. The center fielder? He was the only one that could really be identified. He was positioned close to our game. The rest of the team's players were just dim figures in the distance. Ball parks didn't have public address systems in those days. There was no way of telling who else was playing.

Just before the game's start, we would spot the team's announcer—in the far distance around home plate—with a large megaphone in hand, calling out to the crowd that day's batteries (the pitchers and catchers). His announcement would be brief. But we were too far away to hear him.

"For Brooklyn, Grimes pitching and Miller catching. For New York, Nehf pitching and Snyder catching," I heard him bellow one day much later in the season, when I had the good fortune to be treated to a grandstand seat by my father's friend.

Then the announcer would walk halfway between first base and home plate and shout the batteries again. He would make three more such reports before ending up at third base. As for the rest of the fame's players, most spectators referred to their scorecards to identify them. The cards were only ten cents. Players wore no numbers on the backs of their uniforms, as they do today. But their numbers, as each came to bat, were inserted on the scoreboard high up in center field.

That was the reason, hawkers, wearing caps and white cotton pants and jackets, would shout to fans as they approached the turnstiles in Ebbets Field's rotunda. "Only ten cents. You can't tell a player without a scorecard." Hot dogs incidentally were a dime. However, they could be bought for a nickel at the stands on Sullivan Place, across the narrow street from the field.

But to get back to my first live encounter with the national pastime. After all, it was frustrating to be stretched out on the sidewalk without at least knowing who was pitching for the Dodgers. And so on the day of that first game, as the Dodgers' center fielder came out to play his position, I shouted under the gate, "Who's pitching for Brooklyn?"

Bernie Neis, a utility outfielder, occupying center field that afternoon, showed no hesitancy in informing us.

"Dickerman," he shouted, as he went into his bent knee crouch prepared to field the ball if it came his way.

I can't for the life of me understand how, after all these years, I remember the name "Dickerman." Leo Dickerman lasted only three years in the big leagues as mostly a part-time starting pitcher, and never approached anything resembling stardom.

I saw only four games from the sidewalk that summer. The main reason was that getting to Ebbets Field from where I lived in the Williamsburg section of Brooklyn wasn't easy. It was a long walk from my home just to get to the open-air Franklin Avenue trolley.

Open air? In the summer, that trolley line—its final destination was fabulous amusement parks-oriented Coney Island—was serviced by cars that were open on both sides. Seats, placed right behind each other, ran the entire width of the cars. On game days they were jammed.

The conductor, collecting fares from a narrow running board which ran the length of the trolley, would hang on for dear life as he moved from one end of the car to the other. When all of the car's seats were occupied, he often had to worm his way around passengers who were also standing on the running board, to receive the fares—a nickel for adults, three cents for kids.

He failed to collect mine at least twice when I was sitting on the far end of one of those long seats. I was small for my age and it was very crowded. He probably never saw me and I never saw him as the trolley kept clattering along Franklin Avenue on its way to the ball park.

Alex Nacht? He would get to one of those privileged fence spots regularly. He thought nothing of playing hooky from school. And even at that early stage in his life, he was a gambler. Somehow, he played in sidewalk dice games in which kids would bet as much as a nickel at a time.

"I went to a game yesterday and for the first time, I bought a ticket," he told me. "I sat in the bleachers and you know what? It's no better watching a game from there than seeing it lying on the sidewalk underneath the gate. You even see the batters at home plate from there better than from the bleachers. And," he concluded with a toss of his hand, "you save fifty cents."

In those days, youngsters became interested in baseball primarily because of the attention paid to the sport by New York's newspapers. The *New York Telegram*, the *Globe*, the *Mail*, the *Brooklyn Eagle*, the *Brooklyn Times*, the *Sun*, the *Journal*, and the *Evening World* would print a few extra editions each afternoon with the latest scores by innings on the front pages of games played in both the National and American leagues.

There was no such thing as radio. Television, of course, was just a dream. Afternoon papers were the only source of hot-off-the press baseball information unless one was attending a game. In some cities, however, there was one other way of keeping informed with live information.

Enterprising shopkeepers, eager to have their stores come into greater focus, would lease ticker tape machines from Western Union. That company provided a special wire that offered scores at the end of the each of the innings of games being played. The shopkeepers would display these up-to-date scores by innings in their store windows.

During World Series time, play-by-play descriptions would be offered at many of these shops, but on much larger boards on which baseball diamonds were displayed. When the season reached that stage, hundreds of fans would be seen clustered in front of these stores.

It was almost like being at the ball game itself. Loud cheers could be heard whenever the favorite team came through with a key play. The old *Brooklyn Citizen* daily paper at Brooklyn's Borough Hall, I recall, was one of the best spots in town to watch the progress of these games.

By the next season, and I was a year older, I was a confirmed Brooklyn Dodgers baseball fan. I knew the player's names just as well as I knew such names as President Harding, Calvin Coolidge, Woodrow Wilson, General Pershing, Jack Dempsey, Babe Ruth, and Big Bill Tilden, the tennis star.

One day, I said to my mother. "I know all the names of the Dodger players. Jimmy Johnston's at third base, Ivy Olson is the shortstop, and Zach Wheat and Tommy Griffith are in the outfield. That team has some great—"

I was about to utter the word "pitchers" when she stopped me.

"Aren't you supposed to have the first stanza of "The Village Blacksmith" memorized by tomorrow?" she asked somewhat dryly. So I forgot about baseball for the next hour or so and took out my book to tune in on what was under a spreading chestnut tree.

The most exciting player for me in those days was the fiery Ty Cobb of the Detroit Tigers. He was to baseball what Red Grange later became to football—a major, hard-hitting drawing card. And so when the aggressive Cobb, who it was said always slid into bases with "spikes high," was scheduled to appear at Yankee Stadium I made sure I had the necessary $1.10 for a grandstand seat to see him.

It was said that Cobb, a great base runner as well as batter, frequently would sit on his dugout's steps and file the metal spikes under his shoes while a game was in progress. I had read that the great Cobb would go through this routine to intimidate rival infielders who might be called upon to tag him as he slid into bases.

I watched Cobb closely that afternoon, even more closely than I watched Babe Ruth who hit one of his typical home runs into the right field stands.

Imagine! Babe Ruth of the Yankees and Ty Cobb of the Tigers on the same ball field and on the same afternoon! But I never saw the Detroit star work with a file on his spikes. He sat on the bench in his dugout apparently as relaxed as any of his teammates.

The Tigers' manager, little Hughie Jennings, in contrast, was something to behold. He would station himself in the coaching box behind first base. Every time the Tigers came to bat, he would give the grass around him a plucking. He kept pulling out blades of grass—one at a time—while yelling encouragement to his hitters. He must have yanked about 200 blades by the time that game was finished.

It took less than ten years for a marvelous transition to take place in my game-going habits. Soon after being asked to do some stories for our *New York Times*' suburban sports section, I learned that our sports editor, Col. Bernard Thompson, a retiree from the Canadian army, received free season passes from the Dodgers, the Giants, and Yankees.

Baseball fan that I was, I proved his best customer. I would use one of those passes—made out to members of our sports staff—present it at the ball park's press gate, and go to an unreserved grandstand seat. I rarely stayed for the full game because I didn't have that much time. But the price was right and I didn't mind leaving early. I was due at the office.

In 1953, I became the ski editor of the *New York Times*. And since I had spent most of my earlier years as a "swing man," being asked to cover a variety of sports, I lost some of my interest in baseball and basketball. I now found myself involved with such events as the Penn Relays, the historic Yale–Harvard crew race, the opening days of major tennis tournaments, yacht racing on Long Island Sound, and "Field and Stream" columns.

Suddenly, in the late 1960s, Phil Burke, our afternoon sports editor, said, "Mike, how would you like to cover some major league baseball for us? It will mean covering some home games as well as traveling with the Yankees and Mets. You may have to be gone for a couple of weeks at a time."

"Sounds great to me," I replied. "Baseball always was my first love."

I had covered some big-league games earlier but not on a large scale. Now, I suddenly found myself reporting about seventy games each season and making coast to coast with the New York Mets and Yankees. I had come a long way from the belly-down position looking under a center field gate at Ebbets Field.

Now when I walked into the main entrance of Shea Stadium to write about a Mets' game, all I would do was wave my hand at the security man. He knew me. I would enter the elevator and head for the press room where I would have dinner with the other sportswriters—as a guest of the Mets. In the press box, immediately above home plate, was the transmitter to my paper plus coffee, soft drinks, ice cream, and peanuts for the taking.

I became well acquainted, of course, with the players on the two clubs. And managers, such as Yogi Berra, Joe Torre, Ralph Houk, Billy Martin, and Bill Virdon, would greet me with a smile and a "Hello, Mike" at those times when I entered their offices underneath the stands. Torre loved hard pretzels, and he always had a small barrel of them on his desk available for visitors.

Traveling with the two teams, in the plush style to which they are accustomed, I confess, has spoiled me as a traveling man for life. Moving around with the two clubs was living like the very privileged—like a millionaire.

For example, on the days when the Yankees were playing their final game in a home stand before departing for out-of-town trips, I would drop off my suitcase at Yankee Stadium clubhouse under the grandstand. Then I would go above to write my story when that day's game was finished. I wouldn't see that suitcase again until we arrived at that night's destination. It would be waiting for me in our hotel's lobby. On the registration desk would be a batch of envelopes containing room keys for each of the players and members of the press. A bellhop would deliver the suitcase to my room and presto, I was home safe not having had to lift my bag since leaving it at Yankee Stadium.

Transportation? It was an itinerant's delight. After the last game of a home stand, two charter buses would be waiting right outside Yankee Stadium. It would be a quick ride to Newark Airport. We wouldn't even have to walk through the terminal. Instead, the buses would take us down a side road, away from the terminal building, to the far side of the airport's strips. There, a charter plane, usually a United Airlines jet, would be waiting for us. We'd leave the bus, walk about fifteen to twenty paces to the airplane's stairwell. And after the flight, we'd usually find a charter bus waiting for us again, near the rear of the airport.

"If you keep being treated like that," my wife Cecilia joked after I had returned from my first Yankee trip, "you'll be asking for your own valet, a private barber, and a masseur. What a way to go!" She marveled.

Ceil was one to be really impressed with this high-class living. Having come from a small Vermont village—population about 300—she never had learned much about sports. The nearest motion picture theater to her scenic, tiny community was 13 miles to the south. The only baseball she had ever seen, as a youngster, had been played in a pasture which was next to the village's Creamery Pond. Within forty yards of that "diamond's" home plate, Rutland Railroad passenger trains to and from New York, "The Green Mountain Flier," rattled daily—"one up and one down."

After my first trip—to Milwaukee—with the Yankees, I questioned John Drebinger about the wonders of these great major league baseball trips. Drebbie, a former University of Pennsylvania track star and subsequently an outstanding baseball writer for the *New York Times*, listened to me while I raved over the life of a traveling baseball writer.

"First of all," said Drebbie, who in his day made hundreds of these junkets, "you have to understand that the *New York Times* and not the ball clubs is picking up your expenses for first-class airline travel, restaurants, taxis, and hotel bills. You really mean you never traveled with a ball club before?"

"That's right," I replied. "I've written stories for the paper from three continents and many states—from Maine to the Pacific Coast—but never before have I done an out-of-town baseball."

"You ought to spend a little time with Bruce Henry, the Yankees' road secretary, the next time you get to the Stadium," advised Drebbie, who was well known for his staccato chuckle and sense of humor. "He's the guy who sets up the plane trips and hotel reservations. You want a laugh? Bruce keeps boasting that 'his pilots haven't lost a passenger yet.'

"All you have to do on one of these trips is to bring yourself a portable typewriter and a suitcase filled for what you'll need for a twelve-game tour. Bruce will do the rest.

"Oh yes," he concluded with his chuckle. "Don't forget to bring your dictionary."

CHAPTER 2

Breaking In – Tunney and Dempsey

There was no welcoming committee to greet me as I returned, some thirty years earlier, from my first important news assignment—a baseball game and a fencing tournament, both held at the prestigious New York Athletic Club's summer home on Travers Island in Westchester County.

I arrived at the New York Times building after having made my way across busy Times Square. It was dinnertime, and the only one to notice my appearance was Larry Spiker, the head of the department's sports desk.

"We've been expecting you," he said. "How did you make out? You certainly had good weather. The stories? Are you ready to write?"

"I only have one of them, the important one, the baseball game," I answered not too concerned.

"What about the fencing tournament?" he asked in what I felt was a rather stern voice. "You were assigned to that too. What happened to it?"

"I don't have it," I replied. "When I got to Travers Island, I arranged for the tournament's director to bring the results to me on the other side of the club's field where I was watching the baseball game.

"You know what happened?" I continued, "He never showed up. When the baseball game was over, I went looking for him. Everyone had left. I didn't think the fencing was very important anyhow. Only a few people had been watching it."

"Look here, son," said Spiker with words I never forgot. "In this business, there's only one excuse we accept when a reporter doesn't come through with an assigned story. And that's if your hat and shoes are sent to the office. Then we know you're dead."

8

I wasn't fired—probably because Spiker, kindly but strict newspaperman that he was, took into consideration that I was only seventeen years old. But I never forgot his hat-and-shoe message.

From that time on, I never failed to produce a story to which I'd been assigned. When I was an undergraduate, in my upper freshman year at St. John's College, I worked as many as seven days a week doing rewrite for the *Times'* suburban sports section or reporting, outside the office, on sports events. There were times when I would get to as many as five local boxing programs in as many nights.

"You must like watching fights," Bill Fransworth Jr. of the *Journal American* said to me one night at the Golden City Arena in Canarsie. "I don't get to too many of these, but whenever I do, there you are at ringside eating it all up."

"I hate these things," I answered. "Especially when they're held at these small boxing clubs way out here in no-man's land. But I could be doing worse for the few bucks I make—scrubbing floors or something."

In those early days, when a writer was out in the field, stories almost always were sent back to the paper by telegraph. Western Union or Postal Telegraph operators would arrive with their "bugs"—hand-sized sending units—to dispatch our report directly to the *New York Times* office using the Morse Code dots and dashes.

Oddly enough, it was because of Morse telegraph that I met Gene Tunney, who years earlier had retired as the undefeated heavyweight boxing champion of the world. By that time, I was a freshman in law school and had skipped a class in order to report on a women's trapshooting tournament being held at the Crescent-Huntington Athletic Club on Long Island.

Tunney, an ex US Marine who as a boxer had been identified, of all things, as a Shakespearean scholar, was there to make the tourney's presentation awards. And as he began going through that ceremony, I handed my Western Union operator the opening paragraphs of my story. The retired champion looked over toward us, surprised, as he heard the telegraph instrument start clattering away. He smiled and nodded.

After I finished, I headed for the Crescent's imposing clubhouse. I intended to phone for a taxi to take me to the Long Island Railroad Station in Huntington. I was halfway up the club's driveway, with my portable typewriter in hand, when a long, black limousine stopped alongside me. At the steering wheel was none other than Gene Tunney, the retired champ.

"Where you headed for?" he asked in a pleasant tone.

"For the clubhouse," I replied. "I'm going to phone for a taxi to take me to the railroad station."

"Hop right in," he said. "We're heading that way too. We'll be glad to drop you off."

A distinguished-looking man, also sitting in the front seat, smiled as I opened the car's rear door.

"I saw you typing at the tournament," Tunney said as the car began moving. "Who do you write for?"

"For the *New York Times*" was my answer.

"Kind of young to be writing for a fine paper like that," he replied. "Do you know Jimmy Dawson, the *Times*' boxing writer?

"I sure do," I answered. "I see him in the office all the time."

"Do you do anything besides write for the paper?" he continued.

"Yes, I go to law school. I'm a freshman at St. John's. I have classes in the morning and work for the *Times* afternoons and nights."

"Boy, are we glad we bumped into you," the ex-boxer exclaimed as he elbowed his friend on the front seat. "We were just discussing an important legal question and, of all things, along comes a young lawyer. Perhaps you can help us with an answer."

"Mr. Tunney, you have me all wrong," I answered. "I've barely started my first year in law school. I'm taking courses in Real Property and Contracts, and both, I might say, are still Greek to me."

"Don't sell yourself short, young fellow" was Tunney's reply. "The fact that you're studying to be a lawyer probably means you have a natural leaning for that profession."

Then Tunney posed the legal question which he said that he and his friend had been discussing.

I can't remember what it was and of course, I can't recall my answer. But I do know I gave them my opinion after some urging by my host.

"Please, it's only what I think," I told Tunney. "I really don't have the background to handle that problem with any confidence."

Tunney thanked me, glanced sideways at his companion, and said, "Mike, you were a big help. You gave us a couple of new ideas."

In a few moments we arrived at the railroad station. I opened the car's door to step out and turned and thanked Tunney. We shook hands.

"I just realized," he said as I was about to leave. "I didn't introduce you to my friend here who's with me. Mike, meet Dudley Field Malone."

Dudley Field Malone! I could hardly believe my ears. Malone was considered one of the most talented lawyers in America. I had been had. Nevertheless, I walked into the station happy. After all, a world's heavyweight champion had been my chauffeur and one of the country's most important attorneys had listened to me render an opinion.

What law school freshman could make those kinds of claims?

In the years that followed, of course, I met many prominent professional boxers: Jack Dempsey, Muhammad Ali, Archie Moore, Floyd Patterson, Emile Griffith, Joe Frazier, Barney Ross, Ray Mancini, and Tony Galento, among others.

I was among the writers who interviewed Mohammed Ali, then known as Cassius Clay, when the latter made his first New York appearance at a press conference at Madison Square Garden. Even at that early date, he spouted poetry that rhymed but which didn't make much sense.

Later in his career, as he became "the man" in the boxing world, his verses seemed to improve. Just before his first bout with Sonny Liston for the heavyweight title, he was heard doing what he did best—praising himself—as follows:

> *"This is a story about a man*
> *With iron fists and a beautiful tan*
> *He talks a lot and boasts, indeed*
> *Of a powerful punch and blinding speed."*

As a reporter, through the years, I covered the whole gamut—and I do mean the "whole" gamut—of sports events that included just about everything, from archery to yachting and everything in between.

I enjoyed the variety whether it was baseball, football, basketball, skiing, or horse racing. I even reported on horse shows, all-breed dog shows, and Gaelic football. It was small wonder that in those days, the *Times* sports section was often referred to as "The Bible of Sports."

Back in those early Depression years, I often would be assigned to such New York fight clubs as the Broadway Arena, Ridgewood Grove, Mitchel Field, the Long Beach Arena, Starlight Park, the Queensboro Arena, the Coney Island Velodrome, and the St. Nicholas Arena. On occasion, I would be sent to Madison Square Garden to write about amateur programs such as the Golden Gloves tournament sponsored by the *New York Daily News.*

The boxing personality that intrigued me the most, however, in later years was neither Two Ton Tony Galento nor the colorful, nimble-stepping Ali. It was Sonny Liston, a rugged-looking performer, who, it seemed, could fell a heavy oak with a stroke of his forearm. He was the world heavyweight champion for about two years starting in 1962.

I first met Sonny at his training camp at the Pines Hotel, a large resort in New York's Catskill Mountains. I was introduced to him in 1962 by Phil Ehrlich, the hotel's manager, after the fighter had skipped rope, punched the bag, did innumerable push-ups, and pummeled a sparring partner.

"He looked just great in his workouts," Ehrlich told me. "The only thing that probably can stop him when he tries to take the title away from Floyd Patterson next month in Chicago is an army tank. His major problem is that he may run out of sparring partners. None of them seem able to stand up against him."

I asked Liston, who was still wearing his cushioned head protector, how he felt about his forthcoming try for the championship. His eyes seemed to light up. He began gesticulating first with his right arm and then with his left.

"I can't wait to meet that Patterson," he answered. "I'm already at the point where I have to be careful about being over trained. My reflexes are good. I've been jabbing better than ever, and I've been extremely light on my feet—for me. I know Patterson is supposed to be good. But he just ain't gonna be good enough to beat me."

Ehrlich also said he was eagerly anticipating the contest with Patterson which was to be held on September 25. He revealed that he already had booked a flight to the Windy City to make sure there would be no "snafus." He and Liston had become close friends. And so, he was on hand the night of the championship flight.

"I'm unfamiliar with Chicago," the frustrated Ehrlich explained. "As a result, I was late getting to the arena. I reached my seat moments after it began. I turned my back to the ring to make sure I was in the right place. By the time I turned my head to see what was going on in the ring, there was Patterson down on the canvas—a first round victim. The crowd went wild."

Delighted over the bout's outcome, Ehrlich kept bemoaning the fact that he had traveled all the way to Chicago without having seen Liston launch his knockout punch. And he was not in attendance in Las Vegas the following July when Sonny, defending his crown, again put Patterson away in a single round.

Liston didn't retain his title long. He lost it in February of 1964 in Miami Beach to Cassius Clay who had not yet changed his name to Ali, in seven rounds—a result that was considered a major upset.

As might be expected, Sonny immediately demanded a return bout and succeeded in having his request granted. The rematch was scheduled for the following year, in May, and, of all places, in a small city in Maine—Lewiston.

Because I was doing a story for the *Times'* Travel section on a well-known resort hotel being razed in the nearby community of Naples, I stopped in at Lewiston to look over the territory.

A major championship bout never had been staged there, and for that matter, to the best of my knowledge, nowhere else in Maine. The city seemed like a typical, northern New England, a slow-moving, friendly town. I was surprised just like almost everyone else when it was disclosed that Clay was going to defend his crown there.

There's no doubt that that city came alive on the night of the bout with huge throngs milling around the downtown area. And probably, the proceedings in that fight generated the greatest excitement there since the end of the Civil War.

Clay knocked out Liston, to the amazement of all, in the first round. Few, if any, saw the punch that sent the challenger crashing to the canvas. It was a blow that ringsiders didn't hear make contact but it was one "heard" around the fistic world.

The most seasoned sportswriters from across America attending the program, almost to a man, described the "kayo punch" as a "phantom" one. Many said in jest that perhaps wind, caused by the alleged winning blow, had caused Liston to go down. Ali, however, insisted he had hit his foe with a tremendous right-handed shot.

"He threw a right at me which I took on an elbow," Ali explained later. "He lunged forward with a jab and was coming to me off balance when I let him have it." Few believed him. Typical of the reaction by many was a short story dispatched by one of the wire services from an army base in the south in which soldiers insisted the fight had been "fixed."

Sometime later, I asked the famed Jack Dempsey, the southpaw slugger who had held the heavyweight title for seven years starting with 1919, about the alleged "phantom" punch. I brought up the subject while visiting him at his restaurant "Jack Dempsey's" on Broadway, a few blocks north of Times Square.

Jack was at his personable best. He had emerged from World War II as a full commander in the US Coast Guard and had become a gentle, fun-loving host. He would drop his large hands on the shoulders of even passing acquaintances seated in his establishment. And if he didn't remember their names, he would address them as "doctor" or "pal."

"It's like this, Mike," he told me with a grin. "If a fighter doesn't see a punch coming until it's about to make contact, he's liable to drop from just fright. Some say Ali never connected in that fight. If that's true, it could be that Liston, unnerved because he had not seen the punch coming, decided to remain down after hitting the deck."

The word "deck" brings to mind that when Dempsey was sailing on the *S.S. Wakefield*, a converted troop carrier during World War II, although almost fifty years old at the time, he engaged in an impromptu bout aboard ship. George Burdine II, also a Coast Guard commissioned officer and a former minor league baseball player, confirmed this tale to me recently, which it seems never was revealed to the media.

"There's a sailor on the ship who's supposed to be a terror in the ring," one of Dempsey's aides informed him one afternoon while all hands were on deck on the lookout for prowling U-boats. "They say that this fellow's right hand can do more damage than a wrecker's iron ball whacked against a thin pane of glass."

"So?" was Dempsey's smiling rejoinder. "There are plenty of hard hitters around. In order to do any damage, a fellow like that has to be able to make contact. He may be able to hit. But can he take it? Why tell me about him?"

"Well, there's some men aboard who wondered whether you'd be willing to go a few rounds with him" was the reply. "They say they can rig a boxing ring amidships. There will be no seats for the boys, but they would get a kick out of just standing around and watching."

"I guess it's okay with me," said Dempsey, ever obliging in those days. "But of course I can't make it an official 'yes' until I speak to the ship's CO. If he says yes, I say yes."

Dempsey did take on the highly touted seafaring gladiator two days later on those troubled Atlantic waters.

He knocked him out in the third round for the full count.

"It's a good thing I floored him when I did," grinned the sturdy ex-champion as his handler began toweling him in his corner. "Honestly, I couldn't have lasted another round even if I was told that doing so would save our ship from being torpedoed."

During our restaurant conversation, Dempsey went on to explain that the fight business was loaded with developments often inexplicable to the boxers themselves.

"For example, the hardest punch I ever took was a driving, hard right from Gunboat Smith back in 1918, the year before I became the champion," Dempsey told me. "We were fighting in San Francisco. That shot felt as if a cannonball had hit me.

"When that bout was all over," continued Dempsey, "I returned to my dressing room with my manager. 'Gee, I'm sorry I lost the fight,'" I told him. "That Gunboat sure is one heavy hitter."

"You didn't lose it, you clown. You won it," answered his manager. "You won it with one of your screw-driving lefts. He went down as if he had been struck by lightning."

"Do you know?" Dempsey added as our conversation neared its close. "The record books show that I beat Gunboat in three rounds. It also shows that in the fight prior to that one, I knocked out Carl Morris in one.

"I well remember that Morris Kayo. But for the life of me, I can't recall winning from Gunboat. Maybe it was done with one of those phantom punches that stopped Sonny Liston in the first round in Maine."

CHAPTER 3

Show Me the Way to Go Home – Queens and Italy

It was about 2:00 A.M. The Mets charter jet was approaching LaGuardia Airport. Frank Taveras, the newly acquired New York club's shortstop, sat down beside me. "Home?" The team was just returning from a western trip.

His question surprised me. I barely knew him. There were at least three dozen players and writers on the plane. Some of them must have been better acquainted with him. Why me?

Taveras, reared in the Dominican Republic, had been traded to the Mets by the Pittsburgh Pirates only the day before the New York team had left its home Shea Stadium for a twelve-game road trip. Taveras and I had nodded at each other during our junket but that was about it.

"The players here tell me that you live on Long Island," Taveras said to me. "That's where I live too. But I have no way no way of getting there. The boys here say your wife, that she usually meets you at the airport with your car. I'd really appreciate if you could help me."

"You don't need me," I answered a little baffled. "When we get to LaGuardia all you have to do is pick up your baggage and call a taxi."

"But, Mike, I don't know where I live," replied the twenty-five-year-old Taveras. "*No sabe.* Excuse me for using Spanish," he said. "But I am excited, maybe."

"The Mets," he explained, "found for me and my wife and baby an apartment on Long Island the day we arrived from Pittsburgh after I was traded. By the next night, I was off with the Mets on this trip. All I know is that she's there and our apartment is near a cemetery."

"Near a cemetery?" I asked. "Which cemetery?" The Latin player, looking perplexed, said. "I don't know. All I remember is there's a cemetery across the street from our apartment house. I think it's about five, or maybe ten miles from Shea Stadium."

I looked at him baffled.

"I grew up on Long Island," I told him, "and I know the whole island well—all 120 miles of it. But there must be a least ten cemeteries in the area you're telling me about. I'll be glad to take you to my car.

"Chances are, though," I continued, "that we'll never get you home tonight. You can spend the night in my house in Oceanside and we'll phone the Mets in the morning."

At first, it all had sounded like a big gag to me, Ball players, on occasion, will play jokes on one another, even on writers. But Taveras' story sounded legitimate. He explained that he had expected that the Mets' traveling secretary, Lou Niss, would know where he lived. But Lou Niss didn't.

When we joined my wife in the car, she thought it was some kind of joke.

"Tonight, a cemetery and tomorrow the world," she said in a tone that made it sound as if we were embarking on a hopeless errand. I didn't blame her for feeling that way. It seemed hopeless, particularly in the dark of the night, in the wee hours of the morning.

Once I got behind the wheel, I wasn't sure which way to head. There were cemeteries all over the place—in Woodside, Cypress Hills, Highland Park, Kew Gardens, Flushing, and on Springfield Boulevard near the Belmont Park racetrack. Since most of them were east of LaGuardia and because my house was in that direction too, that's the way we went.

I was driving toward the Van Wyck Expressway when I suddenly remembered that we'd be passing close to a cemetery located on the western rim of the highway, just about three blocks from the Queens County Borough Hall.

"I'm going to give that one a try," I mumbled to my wife. "It's only about five minutes out of the way. It's a long shot. But what have we got to lose, maybe five minutes?"

Soon, we were driving past the cemetery which fronts on Queens Boulevard. Taveras, who had been peering out our rear window as we tooled past the graveyard was silent. I was making a right turn to enter the Van Wyck Expressway and passing the far side of the cemetery when he let out a shout.

"She is it, that's the building," he yelled as he pointed to an apartment house that actually did face the burial grounds. "I never thought I'd recognize it at this hour of the night, but that's it."

It was now past three in the morning. We deposited the player in front of his building and continued home. That incident created a bond between Frank and me. We used to kid about that old tune "Show Me the Way to Go Home."

My reward for this successful exploratory expedition: I picked up a broken baseball bat with Taveras's stenciled signature on it at the Mets' clubhouse at Shea Stadium and had Frank sign it by hand. It's added to my collection that includes autographed bats broken by such players as Dave Winfield and Gary Carter.

Taveras, as a member of the Mets, used to confound opposing infielders because of his ability as a bunter. He kept tapping bunts for singles. His technique was to stroke the ball between the pitcher's box and first base and then streak down the line for the bag.

Repeatedly he'd reach the base with no one covering it, the pitcher and the two men on the left side of the infield having charged in to field the feeble roller. He left the Mets at the end of the 1981 season to play with the Expos in Montreal.

"You're going to another big city," I joked with him the day before he left the Mets. "Make sure you know where you live in Montreal and learn how to say 'cemetery' in French because many of the people up there don't speak English, and certainly not Spanish."

That cemetery safari with Taveras? It was a breeze compared to some of my other experiences in the home sweet home department. One night, after a football game at Syracuse University, the celebrated and friendly sportswriter Tommy Holmes and I became involved in an intensely interesting conversation at the airport.

We were chatting in a small boarding area and sitting immediately right under a sign that read: Mohawk Airlines, departure for New York 7:30 P.M." On the far side of the little room was another sign reading: "Mohawk Airlines, departure for Buffalo 7 P.M." We were headed for New York.

"We have plenty of time, Mike," he said to me as he looked up at the sign. "Wanna get a cup of coffee?"

"I'd rather not," I replied. "It'll keep me up all night."

And then we began talking about those long train trips on sleepers that major league baseball players and writers used to take before they began traveling on planes. And also about how often sportswriters were away from home because of the many out-of-town assignments.

As we gabbed, both of us noticed passengers streaming through the other gate to board a plane that we had heard arrived, just twenty-five or thirty yards away. Tom and I began reminiscing.

At 7:45, fifteen minutes after our plane's scheduled departure, Tommy spotted a Mohawk agent who was passing through the room.

"How late is that plane to New York?" he asked.

"That plane to New York?" the agent replied in somewhat of a startled voice. "Why, it left ten minutes ago. I've seen you sitting here for more than a half hour. Why didn't you board it?"

"For a simple reason," said Holmes. "Because that gate was marked 'Buffalo.' Take a look, right here, right above us, is the gate with 'New York' on it. No one's gone through that. What's going on?"

Now the agent became apologetic. He said that someone had made a mistake, that the signs had mistakenly been switched.

"But we can still get you to New York tonight," he advised. "We can fly you into Albany on a plane that arrives here in about an hour. From Albany, you'll have to change for a New York-bound flight."

What did we do? We did the obvious. We followed his suggestion. But instead of reaching LaGuardia at 8:30 P.M., as we had anticipated, we didn't get there until one o'clock in the morning. It was a rough trip but more so for Tommy than for me. He had only one arm. It became obvious as we were leaving the New York airport that the portable typewriter he was carrying seemed almost too heavy for him to handle.

The most unpredictable homecoming delay, by far, for me, occurred in the 1970s, not in the United States but in Italy. John Fry, the genial editor of *Ski Magazine*, and I had flown overseas to inspect a few of the professional ski racing courses being introduced in that country.

It had been a great visit. John, Canadian born and by far a better skier than me, had led me down the slopes at Courmayeur, in the Italian Alps, near the French border. Then we had traveled up the other end of the long Aosta Valle and skied at Cervenia, which is right next to Switzerland. At Cervenia, we photographed each other at the base of the famed Matterhorn.

Now we were at the new airport near Milano ready to return to the United States via Alitalia Airlines. We had sipped coffee in the secluded boarding area for passengers holding first-class seats. But with only about five minutes remaining before boarding time, John suddenly let out a groan.

I turned and looked at him in astonishment as he slipped to the floor. There he was, clutching his left side, writhing. His face showed extreme pain.

"What's wrong, John?" I asked. "What's happened? Do you need help?" He didn't seem to hear me. I quickly got the attention of an Alitalia attendant at the front of the room. She immediately phoned for the airport's doctor while John continued to be doubled up in pain.

The physician arrived within a few minutes. I was surprised by his quick arrival. He looked at John's ashen face and gave him a cursory examination. Then he gave him a shot. What did he give him? I never found out for an obvious reason. The physician spoke no English.

"He has to go to the hospital," the Alitalia attendant told me. "The doctor thinks your friend has a kidney stone attack. The nearest hospital is at Gallorate, which is a small city north of here. Are you a close friend of this gentleman?"

"Why do you ask?" I replied.

"If you are, you might want to accompany him. Otherwise, he'll be there all alone. Do you want to go? I have to know because your flight for New York is leaving in a few minutes."

"Well," I answered, "I'm going to stay with him. I can't leave him here like this alone. He's a nice guy. Can you please phone my home in America and let my wife know about the delay? She's supposed to meet this flight when it arrives at Kennedy in New York today."

"Of course I will," she replied. "I'll even order a room for you as the airline's guest at a hotel in Gallorate. We'll book you for a flight leaving for America tomorrow afternoon. Is that okay?"

When I nodded my head, she scribbled the name of a hotel on the back of a card and handed it to me. Then came a series of startling developments, at least for me.

Fry was placed on a stretcher and taken to a waiting ambulance. I was escorted to it and was surprised when I was virtually shoved into it to ride with John. Suddenly, I felt as if I was playing a supporting role in an Italian movie.

As the ambulance took off, I pounded on the window that separated us from the driver's seat.

"How long is this ride going to take?" I shouted to the driver.

I might just as well have been speaking Chinese. Neither of the two men up front spoke English.

When we arrived at the hospital, John's stretcher was quickly removed, and I was ushered into the hospital's waiting room.

There were three or four other people waiting there, obviously visitors to see hospitalized patients. None of them spoke English. I found that out after asking them how far it was from the hospital to my hotel.

19

I showed them the card that the Alitalia attendant had handed me. They probably were from out of town because each took turns in shrugging their shoulders. Then they just stared at me as if to say they just weren't getting the message.

In about fifteen minutes, an orderly, dressed in whites, came into the room. He escorted me to the hospital's business office. The person in charge there also couldn't speak English, and the orderly was told to bring in someone who did.

Then came another surprise. I was told that Fry could not be admitted until a cash deposit was paid. John had offered to pay with a credit card but the hospital refused to accept it. Fortunately, I had the necessary cash, in American money, and paid the deposit. While few of them spoke English, they all seemed to know about US currency.

Then I visited Fry in his room. After making sure he had been made comfortable, I headed for my hotel because it was now late in the afternoon and I wanted to get there before it became dark outside.

I was pointed in the right direction by the physician who had come into the room to examine John. He also spoke no English. I remember stopping at least three people on the street and showing them the card with the hotel's name on it. They all nodded to assure me that I was on course.

Upon reaching the hotel—after a twenty-minute walk—the desk clerk who had studied in England, took my reservation and arranged for my dinner. We had no problem communicating. I was awakened early the next morning by a phone call. It was from Fry at the hospital.

"Do you think you can get me out of here?" he asked in a worried voice. "Yesterday's diagnosis of a kidney stone problem seems to have been right. Evidently, I've passed it. I feel as good as ever. But they won't let me leave the hospital."

"That's ridiculous," I said. "Why not?"

"Evidently, there are signs of some kind of an epidemic in this area. The hospital people say I'll have to stay for further examination. They claim that some of my symptoms yesterday were typical of those in the epidemic threat. I know I'm all right. I want to leave."

I told Fry that I would call him back immediately. Then I phoned an important Alitalia Airlines contact that we both had in Rome, which is about 300 miles south of Galloretta.

"I'll see if I can help you," said our airlines friend. "I'll get on this right away. We'll do all we can. After all you both just arrived there. I see no reason why you can't be allowed to leave."

A much-relieved Fry was sprung from the hospital a few hours later. We headed for the airport and made that day's Alitalia plane to the United

States. When I arrived at Kennedy, I told the tale to my wife who listened with raised eyebrows.

I think she really thought my story was a fairy tale; that is, until a few days later. It was then that I received a check from Fry, in the mail, with the small amount I had paid for him at the hospital. I cashed the check. It was a mistake. I should have kept it as a memento for that highly unusual experience.

Getting home? Back in 1978, the New York Mets had just finished a Sunday game with the Phillies in Philadelphia. For longer trips, it was routine, of course, for the team to travel by plane. But since the Quaker City is only 90 miles from New York, the Mets made it a practice to make this journey with buses.

And now, the players and press, seated in two big Interstate buses, were on their way home to Shea Stadium in Flushing Queens. The first one, with traveling secretary Lou Niss in it, took off with a rush.

"Everything okay?" Niss had yelled before entering his own bus. "This guy will get you home," he said as he nodded toward our driver.

Our bus, which had been left behind to wait for the last of the Mets' stragglers emerging from the Phillies' stadium, finally left about fifteen minutes later.

The man chauffeuring us had no difficulty finding the New Jersey Turnpike, the fastest route from Philadelphia City to New York. But as he was passing New Brunswick in New Jersey, which is about forty miles from the Big Apple, our driver took the exit ramp on to Interstate #287.

I wondered. I had used highways in the area often in covering games at nearby Princeton and Rutgers universities. I knew the drive had taken a wrong turn. We were supposed to be going northeast. He was taking us west. The route we were on was a shortcut to northern New Jersey as well as to the Poconos of Pennsylvania.

"Maybe, he's looking for a spot to turn around," I said to myself. "This sure is going to make our trip longer. Route 22 is ahead. Maybe he'll turn off there. If he doesn't use that route then I'm going to speak up because after that, we'd really be going at least forty miles out of our way."

But the driver blithely sped past Route 22 as if there was a sign there marked "Do not enter." It was then that I decided to talk to Skip Lockwood, a Mets ace relief pitcher and the team's player representative.

I did so with some hesitancy. After all, I wasn't in charge of this expedition. I also knew that he probably didn't know the territory. Originally from Massachusetts, he had made the rounds of the major leagues having played with the Kansas City, Seattle, Milwaukee, and California teams before joining the Mets. Interstate #287 probably meant nothing to him. It didn't.

"Are you sure you're right?" Lockwood asked me. "It seems almost impossible. The bus driver knows the road. That's his business."

And so Skip, wondering whether he might be about to embarrass the man at the wheel, asked.

"Are we going in the right direction?"

"I'm not sure" was the reply. "I've never been on this highway before."

Lockwood then suggested that the driver take the next exit ramp and head back in the direction from whence we had come so that we could get back on the New Jersey Turnpike.

Suffice it to say, we reached Shea Stadium more than an hour after the team's lead bus and arrived. Waiting for us was traveling secretary Lou Niss.

"What happened?" he asked. "Did you stop to eat?"

"No," I answered. "But we did do some sightseeing."

CHAPTER 4

The Bird and the Babe

It may be a long wagon train ride from the teeming settlement of Kansas City, sitting as it does on the Missouri River, to Yankee Stadium on New York's Harlem River. But it's that early American pioneer hub out west, Kansas City, that provides the backdrop for one of my two favorite baseball stories.

They involve Charles Dillon Stengel, that often unfathomable linguist better known as "Casey"; and Babe Ruth, the "Sultan of Swat," the famous slugger whose antics off the field, on occasion, received more than passing attention. The Stengel story is an inside one. As for the Babe Ruth tale, it never received any attention from the media, for reasons that will appear obvious.

Just about anyone who was interested in baseball a few decades ago knew that the colorful Casey, often referred to as the "Old Perfessor," had a knack for fracturing the English language.

Asked a simple question that probably required only a one-to-three-word answer or perhaps merely a nod of the head, Stengel would go on and on. He'd keep digressing in a monologue that would include long-winded non sequiturs that often bewildered listeners. By the time he was finished speaking, questioners often forgot what they had asked. Members of the media would come away from Stengel laughing but also perplexed.

"Almost everyone realizes that Case goes into that act on purpose," Elston Howard, the great catcher and outfielder of the Yankees in the 1950s, told me. We were flying between New York and Cleveland. "Stengel is shrewd," he continued. "He realizes that if he keeps giving those long answers, he's going to receive fewer questions."

As loquacious as he was, there was that one afternoon in Kansas City in the late 1950s when Stengel found himself speechless. It was at a surprise birthday party arranged in his honor by his players at the well-known Muhlenbach Hotel. That huge hostelry was the stopping off place for the Yankees when they played in that town.

On the afternoon before the party, Howard and a few of his teammates walked into the hotel manager's office.

"Tomorrow is Stengel's birthday," Howard informed the Muhlenbach head. "Would it be possible to arrange a special party for Case at noon for about thirty-five people?"

"Of course we can," smiled the hotel manager. "We usually receive more notice than this. But for Stengel we can do anything. We'll have a room for it—private and just large enough."

"Come to think of it," one of the Yankees asked. "Could you get us a piano player to provide some of those old tunes that Case likes to hear?"

"I see no reason why we can't arrange that too" was the quiet reply. "We'll have someone up there poking away at the keys."

Came noontime the next day, members of the Yankees began trooping into the room. On hand, as scheduled, was Stengel. Purposely misled as to the purpose of the get-together, Stengel sort of danced into the room because "Happy Birthday" played at a lively tempo that was emanating from the piano up front.

Halfway to his table, Casey, who now was beginning to realize that the luncheon was being held in recognition of his birthday, looked up front where the piano was being played. The "Ole Perfessor" stared, craned his head forward for a better look. Suddenly, he seemed struck-dumb, an unusual state for Stengel.

Once over what seemed a shock, he made a beeline for the piano saying, "My God, I don't believe it. It just can't be."

To the surprise of the entire assemblage, at the keyboard was none other than Harry S. Truman, the former president of the United States. He lived in the nearby community of Independence and was known for his ability to tickle the ivories as well as for his fondness of Stengel.

Truman, with his genial smile, arose from the piano, shook hands with the famous baseball manager and congratulated him on his birthday.

"Boy, am I glad to see you here," Stengel finally blurted.

"Wouldn't have missed this party even if there were a Democratic Convention in town at the same time," was Truman's jovial reply.

Stengel, as baseball fans in his day knew, was somewhat of a joker throughout his baseball career. As an outfielder with the Pittsburgh Pirates, in the final year of World War I, he stepped to the plate at Brooklyn's

Ebbets Field and just like the line in the time-honored baseball poem "Casey at the Bat," he "lightly doffed his cap."

As he raised it, out fluttered a small bird, a sparrow. The players, the umpire, and the crowd roared with laughter. "What kind of gag was this?"

The story became well known through the years. In the seasons that followed, Casey kept explaining "the bird" in his own way. I once heard him relate the yarn when he was managing the hapless Boston Braves during the World War II years.

"In the half inning before I come to bat in that game, there am I standing out in right field wondering whether the sun is in the right place," he reminisced. "Suddenly this little feller, maybe bored with living in a baseball park, drops off the top of the fence that separates Bedford Avenue from the ball field.

"I know it's a young'un and I also know he's too small to do any flying anywhere. What does a man do, even a baseball player, in that case? I don't want it to get stepped on so I shove it under my cap figuring to turn it over to an usher when I return to our team's bench.

"But because I am concentrating on playing right field and not on birds, I forget all about it. I ain't about to miss a fly ball on his account.

"That day is a hot day in Brooklyn which it almost always is when a visiting team comes to that town. So naturally, when I come to bat a few minutes later, I lift my hat to mop by forehead. That's when that peewee bird goes into his act and starts fluttering around."

Sportswriters never let Stengel forget that story. The tale was referred to repeatedly through the years. Because Stengel's reputation as a colorful personality stayed with him and because of his "beat-around-the-bush speaking style," I thought I had what was a brainstorm early in 1965. It was at a time when Casey was managing the then hapless New York Mets.

I recalled that Will Rogers, the famed, witty rope-tossing entertainer, who had starred in the Ziegfield Follie as well as in a few motion pictures, had a daily syndicated column in the early 1930s that appears in hundreds of papers across America.

Appearing under his name would be three- or four-paragraph tidbits, humorous remarks on any number of subjects that might vary from Wall Street to football to Washington politics and to the Barnum and Bailey Circus.

"Why can't we have Stengel become the author of similar syndicated humorous pieces using his unusual speaking style?" I asked Joe Durso, the highly competent baseball writer who was one of my colleagues at the *New York Times*.

"We'd do the ghost writing if we got a press service interested in the idea," I told Joe. "I think hundreds of papers would go for it. Supposing you talk to Stengel. I'll try to get a newspaper syndicate interested. After all, his Mets, as usual, are in last place. This idea might make him a winner at last on paper, with the public."

Within two days, I had contacted an editor at the nationally important Bell-McClure Syndicate. They were immediately sold on the idea and ready to go ahead. Stengel, he felt, would make good copy. After all, he had previously managed the Yankees to ten pennants in twelve seasons.

But Durso came back two weeks later with negative news. He said that it wouldn't pay us to get involved.

"Stengel and his wife Edna want too big a percentage of the potential income," he told me.

In the meantime, I had submitted five or six samples to the chief of Bell-McClure the United Syndicate. One of them read as follows. Picture it. This supposedly is Stengel talking while at the Mets' spring training camp in Florida:

"I see by the papers where some writers are finally picking my Mets to finish out of the cellar which is all right with me. Remember them writers have been wrong before. And, how do I know that they've seen our club down here in all this sunshine long enough to know whether them other clubs in the league aren't going to be madder and hungrier this season than they were last?

"I remember one year in spring camp when I am playing with those Dodgers of Brooklyn. We were having a heck of a season even if the finishing wasn't good and we did have lots of rain. The writers began saying that we wuz so good that them other teams in our league would be afraid to show up to play us.

"So what happens? When the regular season opens, our pitchers can't find the plate and our batters don't see the pitches. In two weeks, we're nudging last place as if it wuz heaven. And that kind of heaven, the Mets have become used to, if you know what I mean.

"See me next June and we'll know whether my Mets are heading for those pearly gates or for the IRT subway."

That was a Stengel sample. In retrospect, the Mets never did get anywhere near heaven that season. They again finished last in the National League's standings, the fourth time in a row that they found that cellar "heaven."

And so I gave up on the entire ghost writing idea and decided to wait until another Stengel came along. One never did.

The real Stengel, the one who could bewilder his listeners with answers that amounted to "yes and then again no," did not really surface as an attention-getting personality until he became a manager. This occurred for the first time in Brooklyn in 1934.

In previous years, the fun-loving, home run-hitting Babe Ruth had been baseball's top conversation piece. In bringing his talents from the Boston Red Sox to the Yankees in 1920, the home-run slugger found that he was now under orders of a New York manager—the diminutive Miller Huggins—who was less than half his size.

The solidly built Bambino, in keeping with his love thy neighbor attitude, had respect for his new manager even if the latter did have the physique of a jockey.

"The only thing I find wrong with the Babe," Huggins who was quoted as saying one day, "is that he refuses to take offense even when I fine him. He laughs. But I know Ruth's no angel. He keeps breaking rules."

Yes, the Babe was sort of a clown—overeating, drinking, and womanizing. Fans, however, seemed to romanticize about Ruth's bad habits. They chuckled over the fact that their baseball idol was known to have eaten as many as a dozen hotdogs in one sitting while guzzling sizable quantities of beer. But they also knew that he loved baseball and he liked people.

Frequently, just before the spring training season began in Florida, Ruth would head for Hot Springs, Arkansas, and they stay for a few weeks to "boil out" and trim down at that resort's hot baths. Marshall Hunt, the knowledgeable baseball writer for the *New York Daily News*, sometimes would accompany him.

Ruth also was a golfing enthusiast but far from a pro in that sport. He would get out on the links regularly during these visits to the "baths." When he tired of the food at his hotel, it was not unusual for the Babe and Marshall to hire a car and head for the country looking for a "farmhouse combination."

"What Babe really wanted," Hunt wrote some years ago, "was a good chicken dinner and the farmer's daughter. That was his combination. And it seemed to work out more than you'd think."

Stories about his escapades, harmless ones, liberally dotted his career with the Yankees. In contrast, it was acknowledged by all of the writers that he had a big heart when it came to considering those less privileged than he was. He made many trips to hospitals and homes to visit people—men, women, and children—who were bedded down and couldn't come to the ball park to see him.

There was one day, however, in the early 1930s that Babe demonstrated that maybe he was entitled to a SPECIAL ticket to heaven. It was on an afternoon in which he and his Yankee, the slugging Lou Gehrig plus some minor leaguers picked up in the local area, were to play against the semi-pro Bushwicks.

The game was scheduled at the latter's Dexter Park, located on the Brooklyn–Queens boundary line. What happed with the Babe on that day is a compassionate story that shows a heartwarming facet of his character. I sat in on it. It's a tale that's never been publicized because I never wrote it.

In those earlier years, major league stars regularly participated in post-season barnstorming trips. Ruth would join "Larrupin Lou" Gehrig in playing at local semi-pro parks throughout the east. His aggregation, with tongue in cheek, would be referred to as "The Major League All-Stars."

It was all sort of a fraud. Because the only major league starts in lineup usually would be Ruth and Gehrig. The remaining players on these pickup teams would be men who might have played in the major leagues in previous years or who were in the minor leagues at that time.

A main requisite was that these players live in the cities where these games were being played. Why? Because there was no budget for their traveling expenses.

On the morning of that game at Dexter Park, the Bambino arrived at the ball field at about eleven o'clock. It was Sunday in the early fall, and it was raining heavily. The downpour showed no signs of letting up. Ruth's arrival that early for this barnstorming fame, which was scheduled to begin at 2:00 P.M., was puzzling to Max Rosner, the owner of the Bushwicks. But he quickly learned the reason. The Babe, decked out in a tan camel's hair coat, after shaking the raindrops off it and placing it across a nearby chair, got down to business immediately.

"I came early for a good reason," he told Rosner. "I'd like to make a deal on the game with you. Are you interested?"

"You have a proposition?" asked the Bushwicks' owner who knew Ruth well because of similar past season games at Dexter Park games. "We expect a big crowd. I'm hoping the weather improves."

"Don't think it will?" Ruth replied. "It's raining so hard out there you could almost swim in it. We may not be able to play. Wanna take a gamble?"

"What've you have in mind?" answered the Bushwicks' owner.

"Well, you know," said the famed player, "the share Gehrig and I were supposed to get was at least 60 percent of the day's gate receipts. Supposing you give us $1,500 right now and we'll call it square. If we do not get to play, you'll keep all the receipts. If we don't play, it will cost you the $1,500."

Rosner thought, but only for a few moments. He knew well that Dexter Park could seat about 8,000 in its grandstand, bleachers, and box seats. General admission at that time was priced at $1. The box seats were more expensive. With luck, he realized, he could make a lot of money.

"I'll tell you what," Rosner announced, "I'll do it."

They shook hands on the deal. The handshaking sequence, as it developed, occurred only about thirty minutes before the sun began peeking through the clouds.

Within an hour, at about noon time, there was little else but blue skies appearing over the right field section. By that time, Rosner's crew of groundskeepers were well on their way of mopping up the infield.

They dumped loads of sand around home plate and the three bases in order to get the playing field in reasonably good shape. Their job was made much easier by the fact that Dexter Park was on high ground and that water drained from it easily.

By 12:30 noon, crowds began appearing at the ticket windows in droves. They came from all directions—from the Eldert Lane rapid transit elevated station that overlooked Dexter Park, from the Jamaica Avenue trolleys that stopped in front of the ball park's entrance, and by automobiles which were parked on the field's picnic grounds and adjoining streets.

Game time, in keeping with New York State's Sabbath Law, started promptly at 2:00 P.M. And in the park at that time was an estimated overflow crowd of more than 16,000. The outer rim of the outfield swarmed with standing fans.

"This is the biggest crowd in our history," Rosner told us reporters from the *New York Sun*, the *New York Times*, the *New York American*, the *Brooklyn Eagle*, and the Standard Union among others.

We were all seated in the screen-protected press box section behind home plate, almost at field level. The quick change in the weather was unbelievable. I thought it was a miracle. I lived only about three miles from Dexter Park and had delayed getting to the game because I never dreamed that morning that it would be played because of the weather.

Babe Ruth? He seemed to take the overflow crowd and his costly losing gamble right in stride. It was estimated that the share for the Babe and Gehrig would have come to about $10,000 under the original contract. Nevertheless, Ruth kept smiling at the crowd as though he was enjoying the weather. For spectators, even for those standing in the outfield for nine innings, it was all an afternoon to remember.

It was in that game's second inning that the Babe demonstrated that he really had heart. After the Bushwicks had been retired to end that inning, the Bambino was seen trotting toward the "All-Stars" dugout which was on the third base side.

Suddenly he stopped. He made a ninety-degree turn and headed for the box seats behind first base. Some fans in the stands, upon seeing the Babe changed direction, thought someone in the crowd had made a snide remark and that Ruth was bent on answering it.

29

But they were wrong. The baseball slugger stopped in front of a box, chatted for a few seconds, reached out, and was seen taking a baseball from it.

Ruth, thereupon, jogged up to us in the small press box and said to Rosner who was in his usual seat with us, right behind home plate.

"Max, some fan behind first base just handed me a ball to autograph. It's for his son who is crippled and watching the game from a wheelchair.

"I don't want to sign this ball," continued Ruth, "because it's only a 'kiffee'—a cheapie that probably costs only a dime. There's only sawdust inside it. How about getting me a better ball, a game ball, so I can sign it for the kid. I know it would make him happier."

Rosner lost little time in motioning to the nearby Bushwicks' bat boy. He asked him for one of the game's balls. Max promptly gave it to Ruth who signed it and then trotted back to the first base area where he handed the ball to the incapacitated youngster. If that ball is still around, it's worth a lot of money particularly with the story that goes with it.

None of the fans present, of course, knew about the financial licking that the famous slugger had taken that morning in his rainout deal with Rosner. Had they known, their cheers, as the Bambino came to the plate for the first time that day, would have awakened the dead in the nearby cemeteries behind the home plate area. It indeed showed that Ruth had greatness in his soul.

It was while covering my first Bushwicks' fame earlier that season at Dexter Park that I ran into the problem known as "payola." It was customary for the Bushwicks' owner to give each reporter on hand during the regular Sunday double headers, a small envelope in which there was a $10 bill. It was called a "good will offering."

New to the sportswriting game as I was, I didn't know if I should take it. But I did. The next afternoon, I showed the envelope with its contents to Joe Gephart, the editor of the Brooklyn–Queens section who had hired me.

"No, we don't make money around here that way," he told me. "You get that $10 bill back to the Bushwicks as soon as you can. It's definitely against our rules."

I was back at Dexter Park the next morning. I realized that I didn't plan to make money that easily either.

Rosner sure was surprised when I handed the envelope back to him with a brief explanation.

"I understand entirely" was his reply.

CHAPTER 5

Clowning Around – Emmett Kelly

You're supposed to brighten up a place
And Laugh Clown, Laugh,
Paint a lot of smiles around your face
And Laugh Clown, Don't Frown. –
(From an old song)

The first time I met Emmett Kelly, the famous clown, who performed across America for the Barnum and Bailey Circus and who had kept hundreds of thousands of spectators across the United States chuckling, was at the Newark Airport in New Jersey. It was in August of 1957.

Kelly, when made up for a performance, would be dressed like a hobo, wear a battered derby hat, appear with reddened cheeks and a wide swath of white paint around his mouth, and carry a kitchen broom in his hand.

I had recognized Kelly instantly although he was out of character. He was wearing a rumpled brown suit and an old brown felt hat. I walked over and greeted him. In a way, I felt that I knew him rather well for the simple reason that he, at that time, was performing for Brooklyn Dodger crowds at Ebbets Field and keeping them amused with his antics. We had spoken to each other several times at that ball field.

"What are you doing here at the airport?" I asked the popular clown. "Aren't the Dodgers playing today?"

Kelly, with the same pathetic look that was very much his trademark when he entertained, nodded his head.

"Yes, they're playing," he answered. "But Branch Rickey, our boss, asked me to go up to Williamsport in Pennsylvania where the Little

League Series is being played. He wants me to go through my act for the kids and the crowds up there. He thought it would be a nice gesture on the part of baseball."

Rickey, the Dodgers' major domo, who in 1947 had been the first baseball executive to bring a black player into major league baseball in the person of Jackie Robinson, had dipped back in his memory to hire Kelly. In earlier years, clowning in the field by nonplaying fun-making specialists provided lots of extracurricular entertainment for fans.

Major performers in this department were the hilarious team of Nick Altrock and Al Schacht. Both had been major league pitchers. When their talent in hurling fast strikes over the plate began ebbing, they became a comedy team. They would appear thirty minutes or so before a game's start and go through their routines.

Their act included having Altrock pitch specially made baseballs that contained nothing but sawdust and having Schacht hit it with a huge bat that was about five times the size of regulation Louisville Sluggers—the bats players actually used in games.

The sawdust ball, when hit, would emit a cloud of spraying grains. Schacht would dash for first base, fall flat on his face en route, and then rise and slide into the bag. He could have run around all the bases because the ball, shattered as it was, could not have been used to tag him out.

This comedy team went through its act for well over a decade; Schacht finally retiring from the diamond and opening a restaurant in New York's midtown Manhattan. For years, there seemed to be no one to replace them until Kelly came along with his unique routine.

These early comics were unlike the fun-themed mascots that now appear at big-league ball parks. The modern-day ones. They, in most cases, wear exaggerated bird or animal-like outfits, and their job is to perk up the crowd with their hi-jinks. They are popular. Even some minor league clubs now have them.

King clown Kelly? He did a superb job at Ebbets Field in keeping fans regaled. But when I met him at Newark Airport, it was on a Thursday, he didn't seem happy over the prospect of flying of Williamsport. As it developed, he wasn't.

About thirty minutes before we were scheduled to take off, the announcement came over the public address system that the Allegheny flight to Williamsport had been canceled. No other trip to that destination was scheduled for that day. It was particularly bad news for me because I had driven all the way from Long Island—about forty-five miles—to get to Newark.

As usual, in cases such as this, I looked for an alternative, a train, a bus, or perhaps a small plane that could be chartered.

"Do you know what?" I said to Kelly with whom I'd been chatting. "I wonder if it's possible to hire a private airplane to fly me up there. It can't be more than 175 air miles away. I never tried to get one here in Newark before. Are you interested in joining me if I'm successful?"

"Yes. I'll go along," he answered in his characteristic mournful manner. "How much will it cost? I'll split the fare."

And so off I went to the different airline desks to make inquiries. Within fifteen minutes, I was in contact with the pilot of a charter service who said he'd be happy to fly us to Williamsport. He instructed me to meet him at a closed doorway at the far end of the airport's large waiting room.

I returned to Kelly to tell him the good news. He nodded and picked up the bag in which he was carrying his costume. We headed to the proper door. I knocked on it and was greeted by the pilot. Right outside the doorway was his small Piper Cub plane, a four-seater.

As I walked through, I noticed that Kelly wasn't following me through the doorway. Where was he? He was standing at the entrance staring at the airplane. I saw him shift to his right foot to gaze at it and then shift to his left foot for another look. He shook his head.

"I'm not going," he told me. "Not in that tiny thing. If you really want to know the truth, I'm really afraid to fly in the big ones let alone one that size."

"Well," I said to him. "Then how are you going to get to Williamsport?"

"I'm gonna go home," he replied. "I'll fly up the regular way tomorrow." And he did. He arrived late Friday morning in plenty of time to entertain for the championship final on Saturday.

I was amazed by Emmett's attitude about small planes. I always had felt that this was one clown who would be ready to cope with any challenge when it came to open space. I had seen him perform at Madison Square Garden several times and had come away convinced that here was one fellow who had no fear of height.

Those familiar with his act know that part of his circus routine was to climb a dangling rope ladder while acrobats soared nearby through the air on flying trapeses. I'd seen him fearlessly clamber up one of those swinging rope contraptions halfway to Madison Square Garden's ceiling while balancing his long-handled broom in one hand and his black battered derby in the other.

As he would descend down the rope ladder, he would deliberately make a sloppy job of it, as one foot and then another, was allowed to slip into the air. When he returned to the circus floor with the spotlight on him, he would take his broom and try to sweep away the circular spot on the floor.

The technician, of course, would give Kelly a hard time by continuously shifting the spotlight providing elusive target for the clown. Nevertheless, on occasion, Kelly would remove his hat and scratch his head perplexed.

The crowd would howl.

All this was done by Emmett with what seemed to me remarkable aplomb. He appeared as comfortable up on the frisky rope ladder as he did on the ground. Yet here was a fellow who said he didn't like to fly in planes. I found it unbelievable.

But there he was, the next day, at the Little League ballfield early that next Friday afternoon attired in his hobo getup. He already had amused the spectators in some pre-game routines when I arrived. Upon seeing me, he motioned for me to come over to him and he shook my hand.

"Glad to see you made it," he said with a grin.

Pat Burns, the *New York Times'* veteran photographer, was nearby. When he saw me with Emmett, he dropped a baseball glove in front of me. As I bent to pick it up, Emmett waved his broom over my head as if to strike me. Pat got the picture. It was a great shot and subsequently appeared in the *Times'* in-house newspaper. Emmet and I in a "sweeping photo."

The final game in that series on Saturday, incidentally, was one of the classics in the history of Little League. Angel Macias, who pitched for the Monterrey team of Mexico, turned in a perfect no-hit, no-run game. Watching him, sitting adjacent to the press box, was Ted Williams, the Boston Red Sox's great slugger.

"That kid sure has control," said Williams who always displayed a keen interest in the achievements of youngsters and who founded his well-known Jimmy's Fund. "That boy certainly knows how to throw strikes."

I've always remembered that weekend because of my contact with Kelly and also because of the unusual sidelights that developed.

Following my arrival in Williamsport on Thursday, I did a feature story on the Mexican team from Monterrey, which was a land-locked city and a terribly hot one on many of its summer days. In Macias, Monterrey had an unusual pitcher who could throw equally well with either arm. He was no problem to the coaches.

The team's star catcher, a youngster who had been dubbed "blimp" by his coaches and "Campanella" by the sports reporters there, had eaten himself off the starting lineup.

"It all began this way," Bob Stirrat, an official at Little League headquarters, told me when I arrived. "This kid Campy, a fine young catcher, discovered bacon and eggs as his team kept working its way up from Mexico through Texas. He ate so much that it looks as if he'd wind up as the team's third base coach."

Further investigation disclosed that what apparently had amazed the young Monterrey players the most as they traveled north was the abundance of water that they had seen in the Gulf of Mexico. And when they were taken to a private estate in Texas and saw gallons of fresh water in the huge swimming pool there, although it was mid-summer, they had really become incredulous.

"The water," one of the coaches explained to me at Williamsport. "That's the thing that really made our 'hijos' (boys) marvel. Back home, in the summertime, there often is almost no water. This season as well as some other summers, water is brought into Monterrey on freight trains."

I wrote about such sidelights in the story that I had telegraphed for our Friday morning's paper. That afternoon, I received a person-to-person call from a woman editor at *Life Magazine*.

"We saw your story in today's paper," she said, "and it sure has some fascinating aspects. Do you think we'd be allowed to have a couple of reporters and a photographer from our magazine go up there on such short notice and do a picture story on the Mexican youngsters?"

"I can't see where you'd have a problem," I answered. "Everyone up here has been very cooperative."

Sure enough, three members of the magazine's staff appeared that Saturday morning. They took plenty of photographs and thanked me for making the story surface. Their article and picture display appeared in *Life Magazine*'s United States and foreign language issues around the world.

As for the victorious team's members, they rounded out their invasion of the United States in true all-star style. They were taken to Washington to meet President Eisenhower. Then they moved on to Yankee Stadium to watch such New York baseball stars as Mickey Mantle, Yogi Berra, Elston Howard, Edward Charles (Whitey Ford), and Bob Turley, among others, in action.

Probably their greatest thrill came when they were taken to Coney Island. They were treated to everything there including hot dogs and the amusement rides. But again, the sight that evoked the most surprise was the view of New York Bay from the famous community's boardwalk—"all that water out there . . . and in the summertime," no less.

Having been captivated by this young Mexican team, I kept watching the developments in the Little League World Series final games in the years that followed. Monterrey retained its championship the following season. A team from foreign shores, however, wasn't destined to win that small-fry classic again until 1967. For the first time, a Japanese nine captured the title that year and came through with a repeat victory in the season that followed.

In 1960, Jimmy Roach, our sports editor at that time, suggested that I revisit Williamsport for another go with the youngsters.

"You have your choice," I told him, "Oscar Godbout told me he was taking a vacation. If you want me to fill in for him, as you have in the past writing his Wood, Field and Stream column, then we'll have to put the Little League World Series on the back burner for this year."

Roach decided that because it was August and many fishermen either were on vacation or contemplating one, that I do Godbout's column for a few weeks. And so I had to forget all about the Little League in order to begin my fishing safaris in Massachusetts, on Cape Cod.

There I had an unexpected experience in angling for brook trout in one of that resort area's twenty-six reclaimed lakes. But despite some successes I had with the fresh water trout, on that next day I wrote a story on the remarkable successes sportsmen were having with striped bass in the salt waters near Buzzards Bay. They were pulling in whoppers—thirty-five and forty pounders.

But to get back to the Little League Baseball, the two triumphs by the Japanese teams in 1967 and 1968 started a new trend in which players from the Orient began enjoying sensational triumphs at Williamsport. It made me feel that the United States was being beaten over the head with its own weapons. After all, baseball was supposedly American's national pastime.

The real shock wave began surfacing in 1969 when a collection of young gangbusters from Taiwan brought their nation its first championship. And when the Taiwanese stormed back to capture the title in 1971 and then kept monopolizing it, I became intensely interested and curious about the secret of their successes.

By the end of 1978, Taiwan's youngsters had ruled the Little League roost with eight titles in ten years. It was small wonder that many of those interested in this junior baseball competition began expressing doubts as to the legitimacy of the attested ages of the Chinese teams. Some insisted that the Republic of China was playing ineligible boys, age-wise.

"Some of these Chinese lads just have to be older than the legal Little League ten- to twelve-year-old range," I heard someone remark in one of visits to the international baseball jamboree in Williamsport. Their youngsters look awfully big."

"No wonder they keep winning," I heard another suspicious spectator say. "The birth certificate situation in Taiwan must be one big job and fraud."

"The devil with returning to Williamsport next year," I said to myself after that visit to Pennsylvania. "I'm going to see what's going on for myself, firsthand, in Taiwan." So off I went, with the blessing of a magazine editor interested in the story. I was eager to determine whether in kids' baseball, "Nothing could be finer than to be in Taiwan, China."

One of the first officials I met in Taiwan, at a sports banquet, was a balding, bowing, benevolent Yi-Ton Chow. He, at that time, was an official of the Republic of China's Amateur Baseball Association.

"We have no secrets," he told me. "At first hand, it should be remembered that we Chinese believe in that old saying that 'practice makes perfect.' Our young men start playing baseball at our grammar schools when they are six years old. And they keep playing the year-round because of our favorable climate. The only time they don't play is when it rains."

Mr. Chow asked me to visit him in his office the following afternoon. It was there, in that nation's spacious amateur baseball offices, that I received proof positive that no hanky-panky was going on with the ages of Taiwan's players.

"Naturally, we've heard that our boys' ages have been suspect in the United States," said my genial host who spoke with the aid of an interpreter. "Maybe it shouldn't surprise us. But we here in Taiwan abide to the letter of the law so far as Little League eligibility is concerned.

"I must say," he continued as a grin crossed his face, "I've read that Confucius once said that 'Here in Taiwan, we do nothing by memory when it comes to birth certificates.'

"The officials in Williamsport are presented with the exact ages of our players," he continued. We dare not have it otherwise. We have military conscription at the age of eighteen in our country.

"To lie about a birth certificate is the equivalent of committing a crime. The age of a child at birth is placed immediately on the family's birth record. This is a document on which also appear the names of parents and grandparents and when THEY were born."

Then Chow went into detail about the importance that Taiwan places on its physical education program.

"In our grammar schools, students starting from the day they matriculate, spend one-quarter of their time at school playing games and toning up muscles. We hear that it's been said that some of our boys are bigger than the opponents they face in America. Not necessarily true," he concluded. "Some of the American boys they have played against have been as big or bigger."

Before I left the island—it was my first of two visits—I sat in on two national tournament games that were played by adults at the city of Taipei's huge baseball stadium. The umpires, four of them, all wore freshly laundered white gloves. Each time a batter approached the plate umpire, he smiled and saluted him.

Having seen scores of major league games all over the United States, I really was impressed by the deportment of Taiwan's players there. Never was there a hint of an argument. On one occasion, a batter lined a ball down the left field foul line which the plate umpire promptly called "fair." The manager of the team in the field approached the umpire.

He gently took off his cap to show his respect and in a low, courteous tone, questioned the call. The umpire pointed down the line and held one hand parallel with the other to show how close the ball had been to the fair side of the foul line. The manager bowed, thanked the umpire, and slowly backed away toward his dugout.

"My Lord," I said to myself at the time, "fiery Billy Martin or kick-the-dust King Earl Weaver should be here to see how managers conduct themselves." That kind of behavior in the United States probably would revolutionize America's national pastime.

CHAPTER 6

Throw the Ball, Not the Game

For when the One Great Scorer
Comes to mark against your name,
He writes—not that you won or lost—
But HOW you played the Game.
—Grantland Rice

When I walked into the sports department of the *New York Times* in 1929 for the first time, this familiar bit of verse was the first thing I spotted. It was in a rectangular walnut frame and hung high on a wall just to the right of columnist John Kieran's desk.

It was in a fitting spot. Because if ever a sportswriter impressed me it was the erudite, graying Kieran. He wrote, I thought, great prose for his daily column "Sports of the Times." And he had a delightful touch in the light verse he frequently used to introduce his essays on sports.

Kieran, however, probably gained his greatest fame, not as a writer, but as the mainstay of radio's popular "Information Please" program which was aired nationwide for many years. He knew answers that ranged from the field of ornithology to Shakespeare and could quote lines from the classics that kept audiences in awe.

Grantland Rice's four lines come to mind because of an unforgettable City College basketball game I witnessed on December 9, 1950. In a contest against the University of Missouri, the heavily favored City College of New York (CCNY) quintet lost. HOW that game was played became a cause celebre in the months that followed.

The game was fixed. I sensed it as it was being played. Immediately after its completion, I told everyone around me at the press table about my suspicions, but no one concurred. I remained convinced. And in the story I began writing moments later, I intimated that the contest was highly suspect.

Nine weeks later, it was indeed disclosed that several of the players on the CCNY team had thrown the game. Taken into custody were the team's co-captains, Ed Roman and Ed Warner plus Al Roth. Confronted with incriminating testimony, they shamefacedly acknowledged payoffs from gamblers.

District Attorney Frank B. Hogan, at that time, said "they have admitted receiving sums up to $1,500 each for 'fixing' three Madison Square Garden games during that season." Arrested with them was Tarto Sollazzo, a forty-five-year-old gambler and jewelry manufacturer, and Eddie Gard, a former Long Island University player who had been the intermediary in making the contacts with CCNY's players.

Professional gamblers, who knew in advance about the fix on the Missouri game, of course reaped a harvest from this betting scheme; many of the wagers undoubtedly being made with out-of-town bookies.

When the story about this basketball scandal finally broke on February 20, 1951, it was deemed so important by the editors of the *New York Times* that it was placed on top of the front page. Alongside it was a four-column wide picture showing the accused in custody.

I had watched this CCNY–Missouri game from an excellent vantage point: while sitting in the front row, at courtside, with the other sportswriters. An astonished, sell-out crowd of 18,000 had seen CCNY, a 14-point favorite, lose the contest, 54–27.

Convinced that the New York team had deliberately lost, I included a paragraph, written immediately after the game's conclusion, pointing out that the City College team's play was highly suspect.

Having met with nothing but disbelief around the press table about my suspicions, I repeated them, an hour or so later, at Leone's Restaurant on West Forty-eighth Street. There members of the media always gathered for a "Basketball Steak" after Garden programs.

"You're too suspicious," one of the other writers said. "City College just had an off night." The rest of the reporters there agreed.

The next day, I talked to Peter Brandwein, our sport editor's secretary, who had phoned to question me about my report of the game.

"We noticed," he said, "that in the eighth paragraph of your story, you wrote: 'There is little question that City College did much to damage its own cause.' The boss wants to know why? You made it sound as if the losers weren't trying to win."

"As far as I'm concerned, they weren't," I replied. "I watched that game very carefully. City has outstanding players. As you know it had the same starting lineup out there that had won the National Invitational and NCAA championships earlier this year, remember? They called it 'The Cinderella Team.' But last night, they were the fairy godfathers for Missouri.

"I would have liked to have written about my convictions higher up in my story," I continued. "But I learned in law school that you should have proof before making allegations. I had no proof, and so had to temper my remarks. However, I just couldn't let this one get away. I had to include my gut feeling about it."

This was not the first time that I had witnessed games that I thought were open to suspicion. And I've seen others since that I've suspected. Indeed, I believe, because of the point spread wagering on games, that fixed contests in basketball as well as in basketball have increased.

I also believe, with no proof mind you, that players who are principals in these wagering schemes are told that winning a game within the point spread is primary. But in trying to attain that key objective, games may sometimes have to be lost.

In that outrageous, fixed CCNY–Missouri encounter, it was all so clear to me. City College's outstanding players performed as if they couldn't throw the ball into the ocean. It had entered the game as a fourteen-point favorite. There were many, before game time, who felt it should have been favored by at least twenty points.

Sure enough, other skullduggery involving college basketball surfaced about a week later. Three Long Island University players, Sherman White, Adolph Bigos, and Le Roy Smith, admitted they had taken $18,500 in bribes to "fix" seven games, four that season, and three a year earlier.

Gamblers Sollazzo and Gard were also involved in this scandal. By that time, it already had been revealed that players at NYU and Manhattan College had been approached by the same people. These exposures created a sensation among basketball fans causing large numbers of them not to attend subsequent Garden games.

The conspiracies became the subject of criminal actions. Fans—and there were many of them—who had bet with professional bookmakers on those fixed contests, felt duped.

When the CCNY scandal finally broke in early 1951, I was out of town. Brandwein reached me by phone. He asked whether I had any inside information about that game which Missouri had won so easily.

My answer, of course, was in the negative.

"Then how did you spot the fix?" Brandwein asked me. I gave him the same answers that I had offered two months earlier at a time when no one would listen to me.

"It was purely by accident," I explained. "I happened to see Ed Roman, the team's star center, pass the ball directly into the hands of an opposing player in the game's opening minutes.

"Even a grammar school scrub could have done better." Roman was nervous, very nervous, for an experienced player particularly since he matched against a rival team that should have been an easy touch.

"I saw him do something equally as odd a minute or so later," I told Brandwein. "Then he took two shots that bounced off the backboard like cannon balls. I began watching only him rather than watching the ball. He was no Gregory Peck, no professional actor. In trying to help rig the game, he subsequently kept making other stupid mistakes."

Roman scored a paltry three field goals in seventeen attempts during the encounter—a ridiculously inept performance for a man of his ability. Two of his goals were made in the game's late stages when possible victory by City College was out of reach.

His teammates who also had been in the fix? Had I spotted them doing equally foolish things? Brandwein asked.

"Absolutely not," I replied. It was for good reason because I had simply concentrated on watching Roman for the entire game. I hadn't watched the movement of the ball nor had I watched Warner or Roth.

Roman, the City College center, finally fouled out before the finish because of the maximum five infractions he had committed. Also removed before the game's end were Roth and another teammate, for an equal number of committed fouls. Ridiculous?

The CCNY team had made an easy opponent look superior. Roth, who always had been a City mainstay, connected for only one field goal in nine tries while the usually high-scoring Ed Warner hit for only three in ten attempts.

My story on the CCNY–Missouri fiasco was reprinted in the 1950 edition of the *New York Times*' Best Sports Stories of the Year. Brandwein, one of the editors of the book, said, "We felt we had to include your story Mike because you called that thrown game. It took courage to go out on a limb like that with a story written immediately after the game's finish."

I concluded, then and there, that the only way an average observer can detect a possible fixed contest is if he sees a player pulling a boner or two early in a game. In that case, just watching that player alone—and NEVER the ball—might reveal that he's giving himself away.

After all, ball players are not professional actors. During games, in football as well as in basketball, spectators concentrate mostly on the movement of the ball and justly so. But that may well be the reason questionable performances do not surface more often.

There have been occasions when a team involved in playing within a point spread in order to win bets, was demonstrated in a game. For example, Long Island University (LIU) "doctored" in an effort against Bowling Green early in 1951.

District Attorney Hogan explained the difficulties that sometimes arise in game rigging. He did this one day just after having emerged from an examination of the three accused LIU players. "So inept was the opposition provided by Bowling Green in that contest," District Attorney Hogan said, "that the players in on this 'fix' told me that had acute problems. They confessed that it had been difficult to keep down their winning margin so as not to beat the point spread as planned by the gamblers back them.

"It was after that game that the LIU trio became panicky and decided 'to quit while the quitting was good.' They also told," the District Attorney continued, "that they had been informed a letter had been written to the school complaining of their play. They told me that then and there, they had agreed among themselves that it was becoming too risky to continue the deception."

I repeat, that there's no doubt in my mind that games are still being controlled by players for betting reasons. There have been uncovered betting scandals since the siege of fixes by New York and teams in other states. Why, I question would those who are unscrupulous players on a team suddenly stop agreeing to take bribes?

An unwitting accomplice to fixed games, when they occur, I feel are many of our newspapers across America. Why? Because point spread for the different games appear in these publications well in advance of contests. Such a practice provides free advertisements for professional gamblers, thereby providing fans with the necessary advance information to deal with the bookmakers.

The point spread format, of course, provides professional gamblers with an easier setup to rig games. With such a betting system in effect, they are able to approach players and salve their consciences by telling them that there is no need for them to lose any given game—that they can win while keeping the margin less than that set forth in the newspapers.

What ever happened to the days when wagers were made on just who won or lost—like in the elections?

Has the integrity of games improved since the early 1950s era when scandals involved New York City's basketball teams and the University of Kentucky among others? I'm convinced it's gotten worse not only for basketball but for some of the other major sports as well.

Any doubt that I might have harbored about the integrity of basketball, for instance, was completely dissipated as the year 1981 was moving in to 1982. I was assigned at that time by the sports department to cover the lengthy jury trial of five defendants accused of conspiring to manipulate the scores of six games played by Boston College's varsity.

"Go down to the court. See if you can talk to any of the defense attorneys," the sports editor told me. "You went to law school. You can handle this. We'll want daily stories on the progress of the trial."

I attended almost all the hearings. Held in Brooklyn's Federal Supreme Court Building, the trial lasted for about seven weeks.

After listening to trial testimony day after day with relatively few observers in the audience, the jurors were finally sequestered to make their deliberations.

All five men charged were convicted of a point-shaving scheme. Included was the tall, personable twenty-six-year-old Rick Kuhn, who had served as a substitute player with the BC team during the 1978–79 season. He was accused of being the contact in accepting and paying bribes to his teammates. Some of the latter also subsequently were put on trial. Kuhn was sentenced to ten years in prison by Judge Henry Bramwell.

Tom Davis, the coach of the Boston College team was among the trial's witnesses. And he, just as Nat Homan of CNNY and Clair Bee of LIU, had testified more than two decades earlier, said he had been unable to detect any "intentional" errors by anyone on the team during the 1978–79 season.

"I couldn't even tell by hindsight after reviewing on videotape several of the six games in question," Davis said. "There was nothing I saw that I consider a subject of suspicion."

At the time of the City College and LIU snafus, of course, Nat Holman and Clair Bee, coaches respectively of those two teams, also had been asked whether they had seen anything of a suspicious nature during the games that were proven to have been fixed.

Holman, a star member of the famed member of the professional Original Celtics of an earlier era, and one of the most respected members in college athletics, said he had seen nothing wrong in his team's efforts. The highly competent Clair, an author of several books on how the game should be played, insisted, in watching the questionable games, he also had been in the dark about his players' shady actions.

I was present, a few days after the CCNY scandal broke, at the regular Monday luncheon of the Basketball Writers held at Leone's Restaurant. The usual program called for basketball coaches from each of the metropolitan New York college teams to speak. And now came Bee's turn.

"I thank the good Lord," he said, "that I have a bunch of boys on my team that are honest and apparently unapproachable. It's indeed a blessing."

That very night, word came through that LIU's team had become involved in a scandal involving four games. Included in the scam by its players were contests in which the Long Island team beat Kansas State by a single point and Denver by two. The betting line had favored LIU to win both of those encounters by wide margins.

For many fans in the early 1980s, who believed in the cage sport's complete integrity, the reputation of the four men accused of collaborating with Kuhn must have served to weaken their faith.

One of the defendants, from the Queens borough of New York City, was a convicted extortionist and reputed organized crime figure. He suffered the heaviest punishment of all: twenty years in jail and a $30,000 fine.

Henry Hill, a government informant, had testified that he had first met Kuhn and another team member, Jim Sweeney, in a hotel at Boston's Logan Airport in November 1978.

"I assured the players," he continued, "that our deal didn't mean they had to lose games, that the main thing was winning them, but by less than the point spread. Before they left, I gave Kuhn $500 or $600 of goodwill money while the man that accompanied me gave him a quarter of an ounce of cocaine." Sweeney, also implicated, like Hill, cooperated with the government and had not been indicted.

In passing sentence on the five men, the quiet-mannered Judge Bramwell read a list of ten questions, all rhetorical. Among them were:

"Does anyone care if college basketball players took money and agreed to engage in illegal sports activity? Does the court have the responsibility to protect the integrity of sports? Will acts of racketeering and sports bribery have a negative effect on recruitment, voluntary support of an institution, and the success of athletic programs?"

When the jurist had finished, a toss of his head made it apparent that he felt the questions answered themselves.

Kuhn, in his testimony, recalled telling the FBI a few months before the trial:

"Two men originally approached me in Swissvale, Pennsylvania. I talked to them in a car across the street from my home. I told them that

I had been advised by my gambling contacts that the procedure would be for them to tell me a few days in advance of a game by how many points my team would be asked to win. It all seemed so harmless."

By coincidence, on the same day that Judge Bramwell imposed his sentences, a trial in Providence was concluded with the sentencing of a Robert Martin to eighteen months and a fine of $10,000. Martin, who said he helped set up the sports betting lines in Nevada, had been convicted a year earlier for transmitting betting information by telephone over state lines.

Indicted by a Providence federal grand jury at that time were sixteen other defendants. They were charged with being involved in the betting of thousands of dollars on horse racing and college and professional football and baseball games between November and December of 1977.

Professional gamblers were indeed busy in those days and undoubtedly are busier now. It's been estimated that billions of dollars are wagered each year by followers of the different major sports. And unknown to those fans, I feel, in some cases, they're watching contests tainted by bribery and betting conspiracies.

A Chicago writer, in a book published in 1989, maintained that many pro football games through the years—as many as seventy—had been fixed. He reiterated this statement in an interview on national television on the probing "Night Line" program.

The head of the National Football League's Security Division, at that time, as might be expected, refuted these allegations. He also denied the stand taken by the Chicago author that many fans attending games were doing so because they wagered on the contests.

"Our fans come out because they like to see our teams in action," he averred. "Even if they didn't bet, they'd come anyhow, to enjoy the game."

Evidently forgotten was the fact that there were sell-out crowds, in the 17,000 range, at Madison Square Garden, prior to the basketball scandals of 1951. But once news about the game fixing by CCNY and the others surfaced, attendance plummeted.

Many regular fans who had been betting on games played at the Garden just stopped coming. And for several years, thereafter, it was a rare evening, indeed, to find as many as 6,000 paying spectators there.

A fortnight or so after the CCNY scandal had unfolded, a crowd of only 7,400 turned out to see the City College team meet Lafayette College at the Garden. The size of this modest turnout, however, was misleading.

Some 3,291 spectators in attendance were City College students—the largest such delegation ever to witness a Garden game. They had turned out to demonstrate their loyalty to their college. Without them present, there would have been a crowd of only about 4,000.

And when NYU met Notre Dame at Madison Square Garden about a week after the illicit goings-on by the three CCNY team members surfaced, there were only 6,022 spectators on hand. Ordinarily, these two teams, in previous encounters, had played to packed houses of more than 18,000. How easy is it to fix an athletic contest? It's easy. It's been done often through the years.

Way back in post-Civil War days, shortly after General Grant had accepted Lee's surrender at Appomattox, professional gamblers evidently had no problem having players cooperate in throwing baseball contests. Harvey Frommer, in his highly interesting publication "Primitive Baseball," wrote:

"The practice of players consorting with gamblers to fix scores of games became the vogue in that early era. At some ball parks, gamblers were out in the open quoting odds, taking bets, and collecting money. The Troy (NY) Haymakers team was reported as being under the total control of gamblers.

"'So common has betting become,' noted *Harper's Weekly* in the 1870s, 'that the most respectable ball clubs in the country indulge in it to a highly culpable degree.'"

In more modern times, the fixing of athletic contests came into greater focus after the World War I era. Professional wrestling became what might be called an entertaining exhibition rather than a sport. And, little if any big gambling was done on that form of combat because many spectators began realizing that the winners of matches were predetermined.

Early in the twentieth century, when such grapplers as Frank Gotch, Freddy Beall, and George Hackenschmidt, the Russian Lion, were in their prime, the sport was considered to be more or less "up-and-up." But that was an era when fans often saw a wrestler obtain a full-nelson on his rival and hold it for an hour or more. The two men would lie on the mat while spectators yawned.

Well aware that there's nothing as damaging as "boredom on the part of an audience," promoters jazzed up the act. Soon such action-oriented techniques as the airplane spin, the body slam, and the flying mare, were introduced by contestants. Now the programs became livelier as performers turned to acting-showboating.

Wrestlers soon were adding other new gimmicks, some with a touch of melodrama. A familiar one was to have one of the contestants assume the role of "the villain." He would dominate the act by going through such illicit maneuvers as twisting his opponent's ears or elbowing him in the stomach.

In the end, however, just when it seemed that "the hero" was struggling for breath and ready to be pinned, he would suddenly become revitalized and win the encounter. In many cases, such performances had been rehearsed by the two combatants in a gym.

Their act would be repeated in the same fashion in another city before the week was out. Wrestlers began performing as many times as six nights per week while living out of a suitcase.

Many of them do such a good job of grunting and groaning as they are being thrown about the ring, that it appears as if they actually are in pain. They compete so frequently that soon they have their acts perfected. Taken in by it all are newcomers to the sport.

My own mother, at age seventy, who watched some of these matches on television, kept saying to me, "But Mike, this sport must be honest. They keep hurting each other. No one could suffer that much punishment and not be hurt."

"Mother," I would say, "it's fixed. A good rule of thumb is to pick the man who is getting hurt the most as the winner. If you do that, you'll be surprised how expert a picker you'll become."

Another example of how easy it is to control a contest is demonstrated by the ever-popular Harlem Globetrotters. They win all the games they play each year. But even when pitted against a vastly inferior team, such as their regular foes—the Washington Generals—they usually deliberately managed to keep the issue in doubt until the final minutes.

Spectators who turn out for this great basketball attraction come to be entertained. After all, the Globetrotters are a fun-themed combination that intermittently engages in hi-jinks to keep fans laughing. But still, they try to make the game seem highly competitive. Why? Because they have become pros in acting. Roman, in his debacle against Missouri, was no pro actor.

In the post-World War II years, I managed and coached a semiprofessional women's basketball team, the Arthur Murray Girls. Sponsored by the well-known dance impresario who had studios across America, the team, in a seven-year span, played games, usually on weekends, in sixteen states.

Was there anything unusual about that? There was, because the women played only against men, usually at a benefit program. This was a team that also was seen in preliminary games at Madison Square Garden, the Philadelphia Arena, and the Atlanta and Richmond (Va.) Armory.

Since men's basketball rules were then a novelty for women, crowds came not necessarily to see the ladies win but to determine how well they could play under rules originally conceived for men. Naturally, there were no professional gamblers involved.

Ever since the turn of the century, girls at high schools and colleges had been indoctrinated in the use of their own easy-does-it rules that provided for a slow-moving game. There were six on a side, and the court was divided into three zones. Only the two forwards on each team were allowed to be scorers and a girl could make only two dribbles (bounces) before being required to pass the ball.

Because as a sportswriter, I had seen athletic women perform extremely well in such sports as softball, track and field, golf, tennis, and field hockey, I felt that the basketball rules for girls were not allowing many of them to live up to their potential. There were some, not many, who felt the same way.

And so, by the time the Arthur Murray Girls started playing against men, there also were such other teams as the All-American Red Heads and Texas Cow Girls touring America with only men providing the opposition. Such games, which might well be considered one of the sparks that ignited the Equal Rights movement for women, attracted large and appreciative crowds.

Until the advent of such teams, the women's physical education programs in all of the states in America used these old women's rules.

With such teams as the Red Heads, the Murray Girls, and the Cowgirls in action, this picture slowly changed. For years though, Iowa, as the only state to do so, continued to cling to the six-girls-on-a-team zoning format.

I saw the Murray Girls play at least sixty games, and I can safely say that the women were outmatched by the men. Because of their physical differences in build, the girls could not jump as high for rebounds or run as fast as their opponents.

However, the girls demonstrated that when it came to accurate shooting, they could excel. The Murray Girls, for example, had a team— Dot Whalen, an ex-Marine—who could sink long shots with remarkable consistency.

One night, while on such a scoring spree, she caused the all-male Elmira team of the American League to nearly miss a train connection. Because of her remarkable shooting, she caused the game to go into two overtimes.

However, such a development was unusual. The Elmira quintet had, in the game's earliest stages, allowed the girls to keep pace with them by not trying to block shots that they could have stopped with ease.

Other male teams opposing this girls' combination used a much slower tempo than usually was their own in order to keep games interesting. They found it difficult to perform as though they were doing their utmost on the court. But just like Ed Roman, they weren't professional actors either.

CHAPTER 7

When is the End the End? – Yogi Berra

Although your goal seems out of reach
And you're a doleful doubter
There's always time to win a game
Don't be a down and outer.
Remember there are fields of clover
And nothing's over 'til it's over.

Colorful Yogi Berra, who probably has acquired more recognition for his "it's not over," observation than Captain James Lawrence did for his famed "Don't Give Up the Ship" directive during the War of 1812, proved many times during his baseball career that he really knew what he was talking about.

As a catcher, for seventeen full seasons, of the high-flying New York Yankees, his dogged slugging enabled his team, time and again, to come from behind and win games. But what often is overlooked in the Berra saga is that he also piloted the Yankees and the NY Mets—once each—into World Series classics.

Apart from his achievements on the diamond, Yogi was one of the boys, whether he was a player or a manager. Everyone, it seemed, liked him, including myself. He really won my heart one day while we were sitting side by side at a baseball writers' luncheon at the Mets' Shea Stadium in NYC. He was then a Mets coach.

"Mike," he said to me with a smile, "have you any plans after you retire from the *Times*?"

"None, so far," I answered. "But because I've always loved baseball, I would like to buy a small minor league club. Only the other day, I was talking to one of the Mets' officials about the possibility of becoming the owner of the NYC–Penn League's Little Falls franchise in upstate NYC."

"I'll tell you what," the baseball famous Berra said to me with his familiar grin. "You buy a minor league team for yourself, and I'll manage it for you."

Berra, who in his day has made his share of advantageous business decisions, often has delighted listeners with his down-to-earth comments. While he was no silver-tongued William Jennings Bryan, many of the more "inspired" remarks, of the inane variety, attributed to him, I feel, were contrived by others. Berra was just a good guy who sometimes went along with that kind of nonsense.

Yogi knew how to get a meaningful message across and usually with the use of just a few sentences. There was that evening in Montreal when the Mets and the Expos had an off day.

The Mets, staying at the plush downtown Queen Elizabeth Hotel, announced that a party was to be held for the coaches and press that evening. Berra, as manager, was the host. He handled that chore as capably as a Washington politician; he arose and spoke briefly—to the point.

"Fellows," he said. "We, of the Mets, are delighted that you all came tonight. Enjoy yourselves. Nothing else that I could say right now could make this evening better."

Simple and to the point, right? Some of the fabricated tales about Yogi's rhetoric certainly were laughers. There was the tale that surfaced during a televised roast held for the spunky baseball manager Billy Martin. Somehow, Berra, who was among those present, came in for some of the roasting.

"Did you ever hear the story about Yogi Berra and pizza?" one of the jokesters arose and said. "How about that afternoon when Yogi went into a restaurant and ordered a big pizza pie?"

"How would you like it?" Yogi was questioned by the counterman. "Would you like it cut in eight slices or twelve?"

"I'll take it in eight," Yogi was reputed to have said, "I never could eat twelve."

I'm willing to bet that Berra never made that remark although I do know that he liked pizza.

Yogi's achievements spoke for themselves. As a member of the Yankees, he was a key to his club's successes in winning fourteen American League pennants. He was voted the American League's "Most Valuable Player" three times, rounding it all out with a host of World Series records. Finally, in 1972, he was voted into baseball's Hall of Fame.

I covered a pre-game ceremony that honored this famed player on a "Yogi Berra Day" at Yankee Stadium toward the end of his playing career. He was the recipient of everything from a new car to a multicolored beach chair. The car was a beauty.

But what did Yogi do? He passed right by the sleek automobile, opened up the beach chair in front of the thousands of fans who had appeared to help him celebrate, and perhaps in a show of his characteristic humility, promptly proceeded to recline in the lounge while closing his eyes to get into the fun-oriented spirit of the occasion.

"He's the first player I've ever seen," joked baseball writer Jimmy Dawson, who was standing close by, "who was willing to show he can fall asleep on a ball field. I've seen outfielders do just that before chasing after fly balls."

But to get back to Berra's oft-repeated "it's not over 'til it's over." What's really so funny about it? Many make such self-evident statements often, in a situation that has built-in excitement. The story goes that Berra came up with this gem one day when the Yankees, trailing badly in a World Series game, suddenly rallied. Berra, in the heat of the moment, came forth, voiced this remark which has been repeated so many times by others.

Berra's career was filled with incidents that warranted statements of such a nature. There was the great comeback, for example, staged by the NYC Met's that he managed in 1973.

His team, beset by a series of injuries to some of its key players, meekly wallowed in the National League East's cellar for two months. But it finished with a roar, as the injured came back into action. His Mets went on to win twenty of their last twenty-eight games and the divisional championship.

In the ensuing playoffs for the NL pennant, Berra led his team to victory in that best three-of-five series against Cincinnati, winning the last game by a comfortable 7-to-1 score, the Mets producing thirteen hits.

Indeed, the NYC team might have made it a sweep to the pennant in four games had not the Reds' Pete Rose hit a home run in the twelfth inning to provide Cincinnati with a 2-to-1 victory in that fourth contest.

And in the ensuing World Series, with the Oakland Athletics, the Mets extended their rivals to the limit before bowing, 5–2, in the seventh and last game. During this series, Berra did everything short of pinch-hitting himself. In the second game of the series when eleven pitchers were used by the two teams, Yogi really showed his acumen with his changes from the bullpen to manage the Mets to a 10-to-7 triumph in eleven innings.

About a quarter of a century earlier, in 1947, Berra, as a fledgling big-league player, had participated in one of the most unusual World Series games in the classic's history. That one could well have over-dosed him with wonderment about when a game is really over.

I wondered too as I watched that contest from a press box seat in the back of home plate at Ebbets Field. I hadn't planned to be there, but a night earlier, Larry Spiker, then the head of the *Times'* sports desk—the slotman—came over and said, "Mike, how would you like to go to tomorrow's World Series game? I've got a ticket and can't use it. You want it?"

"I sure do!" I answered. "I'd be glad to go."

The contestants were the Brooklyn Dodgers and the Yankees. The NYC team had won the first two games and then lost the third, 9–8, despite a pinch-hit home run by Berra—the first pinch-hit round tripper in World Series history. And now came the fourth game played at the Dodgers' Ebbets Field.

In that one, the Yankees boasted a 2–0 lead after five innings. The Dodgers narrowed their deficit in the sixth to a single run, at 2–1, without the benefit of a hit. And, when the score remained the same after eight innings, the usual exodus of at least part of the crowd in trying to beat traffic away from the ball park failed to take place.

There was good reason: Bill Bevens, the big Yankee right-handed, by way of Hubbard, Oregon, was throwing a no-hitter. No one since the World Series had begun in 1905 had ever pitched a no-hitter in the baseball classic—not Christy Mathewson, Iron Man Joe McGinnity, Warren Spahn, Carl Hubbard, or lefty Grove. No one!

And now eight innings had been completed and the score remained the same. I remember saying to the famed veteran baseball writer John Drebinger, who as usual, was writing the lead story on the game for our paper, "This is the first WS game I've ever seen," I told Drebbie. "Just think, and it's probably going to be a no-hitter."

"Maybe you will or maybe you won't," answered John with a reply I never forgot. "Bevens keeps giving up too many bases on balls. If he's trying to pitch a no-hitter, he's certainly doing it the hard way. If he keeps walking batters, the roof is apt to cave in on him."

No roof fell on him but the Dodgers did, as "Drebbie" had suggested, because of walks. For in the ninth inning with the no-hitter still within reach and the score still 2–1, Bevens, with one out, walked Carl Furillo. The Yankee pitcher got Spider Jorgensen for our No. 2 on a popped foul.

Now, only one batter stood between Bevens and a history-making no-hit game.

Brooklyn's manager Burt Shotton sent rookie Al Gionfriddo into the game to run for Furillo and had Pete Reiser pinch-hit for pitcher Hugh Casey. On a count of one strike and two balls on Reiser and with the rookie Berra catching, Gionfriddo stole second, putting the tying run on that base in the event of a long single.

Manager Bucky Harris of the Yankees then used some strategy of his own. Fearful of the batting ability of Reiser, even though the latter had been sidelined because of a swollen ankle, the NYC skipper ordered Bevens to walk Reiser on purpose thereby putting a Brooklyn runner on first as well as on second. Eddie Miksis thereupon was sent in to first to run for the ailing Reiser.

Up to the plate came the veteran Cookie Lavagetto to pinch-hit for second baseman Eddie Stanky. Cookie, thirty-five years old at the time, was, as it turned out, in his last season as a big leaguer. That year, he only had been used sparingly by the Dodgers.

Bevens delivered his first pitch to Lavagetto who swung lustily and missed. But on the Yankee tosser's second offering, the Brooklyn pinch-hitter clouted a mighty drive that went caroming off the right field wall.

The smash was a double. It enabled Gionfriddo to score with the tying rule and Miksis to rush home with the winning on for a 3–2 Dodger victory. Bevens had lost not only his no-hit try but also the game. The WS was now tied at 2–all.

The Yankees, however, had too many guns in their lineup to be dominated. Manned by such power hitters as Joe DiMaggio, Tommy Henrich, and Johnny Lindell, among others, they proceeded to win the WS championship. But it took them the full seven games to do it.

Two interesting WS records immediately surfaced after Lavagetto's winning blow in that classic's fourth game. It marked the first time that a team—the Dodgers in this case—had won a WS game after making only one hit.

And since Bevens had walked ten batters in that contest, his performance eclipsed the sorry record of Jack Coombs. Back in 1970, that star Philadelphia Athletics pitcher Jack Coombs had yielded nine bases in a nine-inning winning effort against the Chicago Cubs.

Wrote Arthur Daley, the NYT's top columnist, after Bevens's unusual losing effort: "The more you think of it, the more dubious you get. Maybe it was all just an optical illusion. This one-hit defeat can't be believed until the official scorers file their formal report. Bevens, for one, must be waiting for a recount."

That game may have been the one that spawned the thought in Yogi's brain about chicks not being counted until they had started breaking eggshells. That Berra, an impressionable young player—he was only twenty-two at that time—was the catcher on whom Gionfriddo had stolen that all-important base in the ninth inning led Daley to a humorous observation: "The suspicion is growing that Berra will have to take out burglary insurance."

Berra didn't have to. He improved tremendously in all departments in the years that followed to become a great star. Even more dramatic for surprise endings, perhaps, than that fourth game of the 1947 WS, was the deciding National League playoff contest I saw in October of 1951 between the NYC Giants and the Dodgers.

It had such an unexpected finish that all—and I mean ALL—of the sportswriters in the press box were seen yanking early lead paragraphs out of their typewriters. They had been convinced the pennant-decisive game was over when it wasn't.

The scene was the Polo Grounds, the Bronx, home of the Giants. The NYC and Brooklyn clubs had split the first two contests of the series. Now they were clashing in the tie-breaker to decide the NL pennant. Interest among local fans was intense because the two teams were archrivals.

As the contest moved into the top of the ninth inning, many fans in the crowd of 34,320 were seen departing for the exits. Why not? The Dodgers had moved to a comfortable 4–1 lead an inning earlier. Spectators were out to beat the rush for the IRT elevated train platforms that bordered on the ball park's center field gates.

The game's outcome, it seemed certain, had been determined minutes earlier. The Dodgers had scored three runs in the top of the eighth inning to gain their three-run advantage. The Giants, managed by the fiery Leo (The Lip) Durocher, had been retired in order in their half of that frame and now had only three outs left for their turn to bat in the ninth.

Big Don Newcombe, the Dodgers' husky pitcher, having yielded only four hits, had had no difficulty in keeping NYC's batter under control. "It sure is a wrap," Drebinger, our NYT writer joked to his WU operator in the press box as he continued to write his story about how the Dodgers, on that afternoon, had won the right to oppose the Yankees in the WS. "The only thing that can stop the Dodgers now is a kamikaze attack."

Drebbie proved wrong. Because the Giants stopped the Brooklyn team with a battling attack—staging an incredible finish that remained a key conversation piece for years wherever baseball fans gathered. I have added reason to remember that game well because Ralph Branca, the victim of that remarkable last-ditch triumph by the NYC team, visits Palm Beach every winter.

I had seen Branca pitch at least a half-dozen times when he was a student at NYC University in the Bronx, and I was reporting on those games for the NYT. He comes to Palm Beach every winter for a prestigious seniors' golf tournament at the plush Breakers Hotel.

I, then the sports editor of the modest-sized *Palm Beach Daily News*, spoke to him each time. Quote a coincidence after all these years.

But I never discussed that critical afternoon in NYC when he, as a star pitcher for the Dodgers, suffered the worst setback of his notable career.

"Why don't you talk to him about it anyhow?" a colleague at our Palm Beach paper asked me one day. "It's all old news. He can't mind discussing it now after all these years."

"I just can't do it," I answered. "He's here to enjoy himself. Why bring back bad and probably sad memories?

"He's a popular guy," I continued. "Everybody loves him. So why should I take a chance and have him hate me?"

And so a few years ago, when he became the winner of the Palm Beach golf tournament, played under the tricky Stableford rules, we just talked about birdies and pars.

But let's get back to the ball game, which incidentally, was watched with considerable interest by Berra. After all, he was to be a Yankees' catcher when WS play commenced at the Yankee Stadium the following afternoon.

The Dodgers, having scored their three runs against the Giants in the eighth inning for their 4–1 lead, went down in order when they came to bat in the ninth. Not even the most rabid Brooklyn rooters showed concern. A Dodger triumph, with only three Giants outs to go, seemed as sure a thing as netting goldfish in a bowl.

Even when Alvin Dark, the Giants' shortstop, opened the bottom of that last inning with a sharp single off Gil Hodges' glove at first base, there was barely a murmur from the NYC team's cohorts. Don Mueller followed with a single to right, Dark stopping at second.

Even then, the home team's fans only let out a dispirited cheer. Lou Effrat, another of our writers—he was a self-confessed Dodgers' enthusiast, having been raised in Brooklyn, about two miles from Ebbets Field—let me know that he was unimpressed by this sudden thunder from the Polo Grounders' bats.

"All these Giants are getting now is a consolation present," he remarked. "Newcombe may be weakening but the Dodgers have a strong bullpen."

When Monte Irvin popped up for the first out, a Dodger fan sitting below us was seen shaking his fist in the air triumphantly while a discernable moan was heard from NYC supporters. Now only two outs remained before the Dodgers' victory would be finalized.

If that success was to be finalized, Whitey Lockman, the Giants' outfielder, proceeded to show that he was in favor of a delay. He rifled a double to left field, to score Dark and to reduce the Giants' deficit to two runs.

Chuck Dressen, the Dodgers' manager, did what he thought was wise. Convinced that Newcombe was fatigued, he decided to take him out of the game. To replace him from the bullpen came Branca, a tall right-hander with plenty of top credentials.

"Newcombe's arm had good reason to be weary," Dressen said later. "He had performed for us like, not one, but three firemen, at a three-alarm fire. Remember, just a few days ago, he pitched fifteen innings over a two-day span. And he had tossed a great game that very afternoon."

The first man at the plate to face Branca was Bobby Thomson. The new pitcher promptly fearlessly fired the first pitch past the batter for a strike. But that offering proved the high-water mark of Branca's extremely brief effort. Because on the next pitch, Thomson connected solidly to send the ball sailing into the left field stands for a three-run homer and a spectacular 5-to-4 Giants' victory.

Pandemonium broke loose. Giant fans in the stands went wild. Torn paper, hats, and empty boxes of popcorn and cracker jacks flew all over the place. Security officers had all they could do to suppress the crowd which fortunately had not been a sell-out one because of a threat of bad weather.

Possibly the most surprised player on the field as the home-run clout cleared the wall by a narrow margin was none other than Thomson.

"Imagine being able to win a ball game that way," he said after some of the ensuing excitement in the Giants' clubhouse had subsided. "Actually, that home-run pitch wasn't the kind that I like to hit best. It was high and inside, the kind they've been getting me out on all season."

John Drebinger's lead paragraph in next morning's story in the NYT's front page paid a fitting tribute to the totally unexpected conclusion. It read: "In an electrifying finish to what will long be remembered as the most thrilling pennant campaign in history, Leo Durocher and his astounding never-say-die Giants wrenched victory from the jaws of defeat at the Polo Grounds yesterday, vanquishing the Dodgers 5-4, with a four-run splurge in the last half of the ninth."

Forgotten, for the most part, whenever the story of the NL pennant down-to-the-wire race surfaces, is that the Giants staged a mighty uphill surge late in the regular season even to gain the right to meet the Dodgers in that memorable playoff game. A little more than seven weeks earlier, they had trailed the first-place Brooklyn Dodgers in the NL's standings by a big 13 1-to-2–game margin.

The NYC team, however, proceeded to overtake Brooklyn, which earlier had been hailed the "wonder team of the modern age." The Giants launched a sixteen-game winning streak on August 12. From there, they rolled on to gain their first-place tie with the Dodgers as the regular leagues' schedules came to an end. The three-game playoff ensued.

Thomson's home-run clout to end that series ensured that there would be no joy in Brooklyn, for days to come, among the long-faced Dodgers' rooters. The fact that the "hated" Giants were eventually beaten by the Yankees in the WS, four games–to-2, provided them with no solace.

In Brooklyn, the gloom among Dodgers fans following this surprising upset at the hands of the Giants was described by a NYT headline as being "a wake."

The headline certainly was a fit one for the occasion considering how rabid the Dodgers' fans were in those days.

Surprising endings?

The football game I never forgot was not one played by such pro teams as the Giants, the Jets, nor the Green Bay Packers. It was a relatively inconspicuous, nonconference contest waged between the Red Raiders of Colgate University and Dartmouth College. It was staged at the former's little stadium in the quiet upstate community of Hamilton, New York.

It produced one of the most dramatic finishes I ever saw. After three-quarters of the game had been completed, Dartmouth's Big Green, under its brand-new coach Bob Blackman, led, 20–0. I was delighted by its one-sided nature. Why? I had been able to start writing my accounts early—during the half-time break.

Finishing my story as soon as possible that afternoon was important, My itinerary that weekend called for tight traveling connections—for me to rush for a plane immediately after the completion of that game because I had another assignment farther west on the following day.

It seemed obvious to everyone, as that final period began, that Dartmouth would be the winner. I was sure. And so, I began typing my lead paragraphs after the end of two periods in which I hailed a final Dartmouth victory.

"I'm starting to write my final story – about how one-sided this game is," I mentioned to my friend, the famed old-time coach, who was sitting beside me in the press box. "I was worried about getting to the Utica airport on time. But thanks to this easy win by Dartmouth, I can write this piece early. I should have it finished by the final whistle."

"You're being premature, Mike," said Kerr, who had retired as Colgate's head football coach after an 18-year stint with the Red Raiders, "our players may have looked bad out there up to now, but they're bound to improve. I've watched them practice. They're going to do better."

"Better!" I exclaimed. "Colgate hasn't shown a thing. What is it waiting for?"

And so I continued to write my story. In it, I gave high praise to Blackman, who, I said, in this his first game as Dartmouth's coach, had done a fantastic job in preparing his Big Green Eleven for its meeting with favored Colgate.

I probably should have known better after hearing Kerr speak. After all, Kerr was a gridiron pundit, an old hand at football. Many years earlier, he had introduced the "hipper dipper" style of flashy play to football. He was held in such high esteem that he annually was still coaching the All-Star college team in the annual big charity game played in Chicago.

I was well into my story when Colgate scored its first touchdown, after less than two minutes had been played in that final session. The Raiders, paced by a suddenly more accurate-throwing Guy Martin, tallied after only four plays in a march that produced seventy-four yards. Martin booted the extra point from placement and the home team now trailed 20–7. I shrugged.

"So what?" I recall saying to myself. "Dartmouth's still way ahead." I resumed my typing. But minutes later, when the Red Raiders started on the move again with another impressive display, I looked up at Kerr and said,

"How come your Colgate boys didn't do better up until now? How can you explain it?"

"Isn't much of a mystery," the veteran coach answered. "They were just fast asleep. Now, they're finally showing signs of waking up. Our quarterback and our receivers weren't living up to their potentials. Martin finally has gotten his offense out of its mud hole."

And now to my dismay, the Red Raiders scored again, for the second time in the period. With only four minutes left in the game, it had advanced sixty yards on only five plays. Martin kicked the extra point and his team's deficit was narrowed to 20–14.

Realizing I could no longer write about a one-sided Dartmouth victory, I ripped my story out of the typewriter. Now I began relating a different type of tale, relating how The Big Green had managed to outlast a late-closing Colgate team in gaining its triumph.

I should have spared myself the effort. Because only one minute and eleven seconds before that final whistle, much to my amazement, the home team accounted for its third touchdown, this time on a twenty-nine-yard pass. Martin proceeded to boot the extra point to give his team a 21–20 victory.

It was all so inexplicable. It seemed perhaps that Martin had been helped from outer space—perhaps radar. In the game's first three quarters, he only had been able to complete three forward passes in ten tries. Suddenly, he had connected with eight of nine in the final period. Jack Call, an 185-pounder, had come on to tally all three of the victor's touchdowns.

Last but not the least was Colgate's defense. After yielding a Dartmouth touchdown, in the second period and two more in the third, it suddenly had set up a stone wall. In that last quarter, Dartmouth was unable to mount even a threat; its quarterback, Bill Beagle, suffering sacks and near-sacks almost every time he tried to pass.

Kerr? He seemed to take the surprise ending in stride. When he got up to leave the press box, he spoke to me as I kept furiously typing away to rewrite my rewritten story about the Colgate's inspired come-from-behind triumph. "Mike," said Kerr, "that new Dartmouth coach now knows how it feels to have his pocket picked."

"I feel I'm in the same pickle," I answered. "I am now starting to write this story for the third time, and in it I have to change the tune of my first two efforts. That makes it extra difficult. It looks as if I'm never going to make my plane in time."

But I did. It arrived late because of the weather. And I had learned a lesson I've never forgotten, that is, never take anything for granted.

And then there's that fishing story involving a two-day expedition to Cape Cod in Massachusetts that brought joy to my spirit which had been filled with gloom.

I was in Buzzards Bay in the month of August to do some Wood, Field and Stream columns for the *Times* when I learned that big-striped bass had swarmed into Cape Cod's waters in innumerable numbers.

The report was substantiated when an angler named Stan Gibbs, who did his fishing from only an eighteen-foot runabout, began using the scale of the local Red Top sportsmen shop to weigh his day's catch.

"That Gibbs fellow," Bunny De Pietro, who managed the shop, told me that same night, "bagged fifteen stripers weighing a total of 400 pounds.

The largest was a fifty-pounder. How do I know? He weighed his fish on our shop's scales right outside our doors. The pickings out there seem easy. You ought to try it."

So off I went the next day with De Pietro and a small group of other anglers, to get in on the action. In contrast to the small boat from which Gibbs had latched on to his prizes, we did our fishing from a plush thirty-seven-foot craft. This boat, if necessary, could be used to cope with a 600-pound giant tuna or swordfish with ease.

What did we get after five hours of hunting? Only four bass, the largest being an eight-pounder—a sardine in contrast to the trophies Gibbs had caught only a day earlier. As frequently happens, the local picture for stripers had changed drastically. The finny creatures were doing their shopping elsewhere.

Disheartened because I had arrived on the scene one day late, I was all set to return to NYC. But I was collared by Cliff Davis, an octogenarian who was working with one of the local chambers of commerce to publicize the area.

"Want to go fishing?" asked the old-timer who drew the line on telling his exact age but who admitted to having been born during Chester A. Arthur's administration.

"I already have," I told him. "And I was practically skunked. As far as I'm concerned, this visit to Cape Cod is done. The bass are no longer around."

"But that's saltwater fish," Davis said. "We have thirty sizable freshwater ponds on Cape Cod. There's plenty of brook trout in them."

"You're kidding," I replied. "The Cape is famous for its saltwater fishing. Are you trying to tell me that I can have some fun here on ponds?

"I certainly am," he answered, nodding his head without blinking an eye.

"Not interested," I said. "Even if you were on the level, it wouldn't work out. I couldn't possibly get together with you tomorrow until noon. The forecast called for clear skies and temperatures that will be in the mid-eighties. Even you must know that a fisherman isn't going to latch on to a brookie with the weather that hot and the sun immediately overhead."

"Just come out with me and I'll prove it can be done," he replied. "We'll have a man go with us who knows our ponds the way Eisenhower knows his generals."

Unimpressed but curious, I agreed to go. And on the following afternoon, Davis and I, accompanied by Stu Hudson, the manager of the local state hatchery, met in the fish nursery's office.

To give the outing the equivalent of a blindfold test, Hudson allowed me to pick from all of Cape Cod's reclaimed ponds. He showed me the list. I picked Little Cliff Lake, only because Davis' first name was Cliff.

"There are ponds a lot closer to here than that one," said Hudson, obviously unhappy that I had picked a pond about fifteen miles away. "But the trout in all of our lakes are about the same, so off we'll go."

Hudson, who, it soon developed, had a good sense of humor, attached an aluminum skiff to his pickup truck, dug out some fishing lines and other light tackle, and off we went toward mid-Cape. En route, he explained that he expected to find trout that had been stocked as fingerlings a year earlier.

When we reached Little Cliff, as expected, it was hot. The bright sun was immediately overhead to round out just about the worst possible conditions for a brook trout safari. An outboard motor attached to the skiff soon had us stopping near the lake's center.

"At this time of day and in this kind of weather," Hudson explained, "it's best to make up your mind where you want to fish and to stay put. So I'll be dropping two anchors. We must not move around as if we're trying to elude a bill collector. You have to give trout a chance to get interested.

"In view of the conditions," Hudson went on to explain, "this is no time to try casting and fishing with flies. Our fish are way down deep where the water is coolest and so we'll have to use garden tackle: worms."

Hudson then puttered his boat about slowing while probing the bottom of the pond with a drop line. He finally reached a point where the water was twenty-four-feet deep.

"We've arrived," he finally said confidently. "Now, just drop your line so that your hook hovers only a few inches from the bottom."

All three of us did. Nothing happened. After a few minutes, we pulled up our lines, checked our bait, and let them down again. Still nothing.

Suddenly I saw Hudson reach back toward the stern of the boat. He pulled out a can of cooked corn and dropped some of the kernels overboard. Within a minute, we all had action. The trout responded as if they had been on a hunger strike. We each pulled up a brookie immediately—fish that were ten- and eleven-inchers.

After rebaiting our hooks and dropping our lines, Hudson again threw some cooked corn overboard. Again the brookies responded immediately. My two companions both stopped fishing and asked me to keep trying.

There was nothing to it. Thanks to the same procedures by Hudson, I pulled up four more trout within seven or eight minutes. It was too easy. And so, I finally quit too.

"I'm glad you're going to write about our trout," Davis said to me. "Otherwise I'd be telling people for the next hundred years about our freshwater fish and they just wouldn't believe it. I might just as well be talking to the fish. When anglers come here, they only think saltwater."

My wife believed it. After the skiff had been beached, Davis insisted on having my picture taken. He set out the eight trout, side by side on the sand and snapped the photo, in color. He insisted that I show it to my wife.

No! I didn't bring any of those trout home with me. It was too darned hot to be toting fish 200 miles by automobile.

LITERARY FRUSTRATION BY A DOLT

I ain't much of a poet as you will cleerly see
But not being one of dem has allus trubbled me.
I guess I'll be a pugilist instead of riting rhyme
'Cause writing poems I find, is just a waste of time.
But all the saim I'm wonderin' Mr. Edgar Allen Poe
Is fer a guy to sell a poem, who does he gotta know?

I've ritten poems on histry of Dempsey's last great fite
I've even writ on science, 'bout Shakespeare and his kite.
My poems about the classics are gems me friends admit
'Specially the one on Tarzan in the lion's pit.
Editers must be prejudiced, they sure do treat me low
I only get rejection slips. Say who DO you gotta know?

The poem I reed in magazeens, I gotta say are bad
I read 'bout Napoleon and trubble he once had
It mentioned about Moscow and the ice and cold and sleet
I guess that stupid poet never heard about steam heat.
So I'm givin' up on ritin', you can bet it's quite a blow
'Cause I'll allus be a wonderin.' Who do you gotta know?

CHAPTER 8

Beating the Deadline -
Ivy League Crew

You write, you edit,
You're watching the time.
If you make the edition
That moment's sublime.

The first time I ran across the word "deadline" was when I was a high school freshman. It was then that I first read about the horrors of the ill-famed Andersonville Prison during the Civil War.

The squalor and pestilence in that Confederate States' compound in Georgia was capped by the existence of a "deadline." It formed the perimeter of the virtually fenceless prison. Any Union prisoner stepping past the line, no matter for what reason, it was mandated, was to be automatically shot.

Once I began working at the NYT, the word "deadline" suddenly came into focus as used in newspaper parlance. It's the hour and minute when an edition must go to press.

Joe Gephart, the kindly suburban sports editor who picked me out for summer work in 1929, was the one who introduced me to the term.

"If you really want to make a hit on this job," he mentioned one evening, "get your stories in early. Remember, we must read them and put headings on them. And, we're usually in a rush."

I've never forgotten those words. Even in my later days as the sports editor of the *Palm Beach Daily News*, I never forgot that time was of the essence in getting my story to the copyreaders on the desk—on time.

Beating the deadline often presented a difficult challenge particularly in the days before computers. A breakdown in communications in those earlier times could occur particularly if the event was taking place in the boondocks, nowhere near a telephone. Even if there was a Western Union operator available to send your story by Morse Code, problems could arise.

One Saturday afternoon in Fair Hill, Maryland, Willie Dupont—of the Delaware Duponts—was playing host to his annual one-day hunt meeting in his huge, rolling estate. Ray Kelly, our sports editor, had assigned me to cover that steeplechase racing story.

"You'll never be able to get your story in on time for the first edition," he said. "That meet is being held deep in the woods and the feature race, the one we're interested in, doesn't start until 5:25. We go to press at six. Think in terms of making the nine o'clock edition."

I knew Kelly, a former Fordham prep teacher, always made a big issue about edition times. In fact, I often felt, he didn't care so much about how stories were written. His chief concern was to be sure all available space would be filled, with as much live news as possible, in his sports section.

But as I traveled by train to the Wilmington (Delaware) station that morning, I began thinking of how I could get my story into the first edition.

"There must be a way," I thought. "I can send some copy on the early races and the crowd by 3:00 P.M. And then, when the feature race is finished, I can write three paragraphs about that race to top the early stuff that I've already sent."

But when I reached the Dupont race course, particularly famous because of one of its jumps—the high Chinese Wall—I found to my surprise that there were five other writers in the open-air press box—from Baltimore, Wilmington, and Washington. And there was only one Western Union telegrapher—and no nearby telephone.

"This Western Union man isn't going to do me any good," I said to myself. "If I wait for my turn to have him send my story, my article might be the fifth or sixth to go. At that rate, it may not even make that nine o'clock second edition."

Having previously filed notes of stories by telegraph for one-day events such as this one at Fair Hill, I knew that a telephone lineman possibly was still on the grounds.

The procedure, in those days, was for the Western Union to rent a line from the telephone company. A lineman would arrive, in such cases, in the morning of the event and connect a wire from the nearest telephone pole to the press box.

When the telegrapher arrived, he would connect the wire with his "sender," an instrument that clicked and clacked dots and dashes to the different newspapers. When he was finished tapping out the stories, the telephone company's lineman would then detach the wire.

Fortunately for me, Bryan Field, who formerly had been the horse-racing writer for the NYT, was handling the public address for the program. I knew him well.

"Bryan," I asked as he sat with his microphone near the finish line. "Do you know whether the telephone lineman is still on the grounds?"

"I'll find out right away," he answers. "I'll page him."

In a few minutes, much to my surprise, the lineman appeared.

"I have a problem," I explained to him. "There's only one Western Union telegrapher up in the press box, and five other newsmen. At that rate, I'm never going to make my edition at the *Times*. Can you help me?"

"I certainly can try," he joked. "But I don't know the Morse Code and don't want to know it. As far as I'm concerned, all those telegraph boxes do is make noise."

"Could you climb the telephone pole at about 5:15 and attach an extra wire to an overhead one and bring it down to the ground? If you can do that for me, I'll be able to call my office with three paragraphs describing the feature race."

"I sure can," he replied. "It's no big deal. The only thing I have to know is whether you can make your phone call to the NYT—collect. I would have no way of billing them."

"That's fine," I replied. "All of our calls to the paper are made collect. And incidentally, I'm giving you a ten spot for this favor."

After that, it was easy. I spent the early part of the afternoon writing paragraph after paragraph about the crowd, the weather, and the developments in the program's first three races. By 4:00 P.M., I had written about 600 words. The Western Union telegrapher sent them to the *Times* for me with no trouble because the other reporters were waiting for the running of the feature race to turn in their stories.

As soon as the main race was finished, and I knew the official results, I ran to the base of the nearby telephone pole where the lineman was waiting for me with his handset telephone. I dictated three paragraphs off the top of my head about the feature race, in which I included the margin of victory and the time of the contest.

At the office, the hastily dictated three paragraphs were placed on top of the many paragraphs I had written and telegraphed earlier. Once finished, I gave the wireman the promised $10 bill.

Then I returned to the press box where I did the usual. I rewrote the entire story—a more polished version—in time to make the second edition. I now had the full cooperation of the telegrapher, who by that time had finished servicing the other writers.

Ray Kelly sure was surprised. He laughed when I saw him on my return to the office the following Monday.

"You not only made the second edition, you beat the first," he said. "And I know you didn't do it using a carrier pigeon."

Yes, making the deadline when one was on land sometimes was difficult, but getting your story into the office on time when on water—for an aquatic sport—could present much greater problems.

For me, the greatest of all occurred in June of 1958 when I was asked to cover, for the third time, the historic Harvard–Yale rowing regatta on the Thames River in New London, Connecticut. The first crew race between the two colleges dated back to 1852.

In reporting on almost all crew races in the past, I had found myself, on occasion, delayed in a press boat on a river when I wanted to be near a telephone or at least a telegrapher.

The latter, if telegraph was being used, would then tap out the messages, on a hand-sized instrument, known as a "bug," often working right from the boathouse. Almost all of these races would be completed in plenty of time to make the first edition of Sunday's papers.

But Yale–Harvard regattas provided extra problems for newsmen if only because they weren't completed until late afternoon. The late finishes? They couldn't be helped.

"We just keep waiting until the tide on this river is favorable," Jim Rathenschmidt, the Yale coach, has explained to me a few years earlier, just before my first regatta in New London. "The oarsmen race with the tide. On this 'drink' the tide isn't at its fullest, until at least, mid-afternoon."

The Thames flanked the city of New London. On it, on regatta day, would be a freshman two-mile race to open the program. It would be followed by a three-mile pull for the Harvard and Yale jayvees and a four-mile haul for the varsities.

"This event is a big deal for us," Burke, the sports editors' assistant had said to me the first time he sent me out to cover it. "And so, you just have to make the first edition with your early story. It's the only edition that goes up that way. You're going to find it very colorful."

When I reached New London for my first regatta, I found that Burke had not exaggerated. The city was bedecked with flags and with dark blue banners for Yale and crimson ones for Harvard. The old Hotel Mohican on the main street was loaded with Yale and Harvard alumni, many of them "old oars" who had pulled shells there "for alma mater" in earlier years.

Just before stepping onto the press launch, for my first regatta there, with other members of the media, I saw passengers boarding the special "Race Train" that was to run on tracks paralleling the course.

And as we started to chug our way up the river to the race's starting point, I saw a few thousand spectators lining the banks. And lining the course was a huge spectator fleet—scores upon scores of craft, ranging from large luxurious yachts to rowboats with tired-sounding outboard motors.

"Why, there are almost as many people here for the race as there would be for a football game up at Harvard Stadium," I said to Hank Johnson, the *Crimson's* sports publicity director.

"What you see here is nothing," replied Johnson. "In the old days, back in the years that followed the first World War, at least five times this number would turn out for these races here. And as for the spectator fleet, it would be immense."

Once the oarsmen in the two freshmen shells—in that days' first race—would start rowing, a diesel-drawn race train would keep pace along the shore with the oarsmen. When that contest—the two-miler—was finished, the engineer would back the train down to the starting point for the three-mile junior varsity event.

It all made for an exciting scene. When a race was finished, skippers in the spectator fleet would toot their whistles and raucous horns. Passengers and people on shore would wave their pennants. And, on the train, passengers would keep up an incessant chatter, enjoying libations as they cheered.

I learned upon reaching New London on the eve of that 1958 edition of the famous regatta that there were going to be "impossible" problems in getting my story to the paper on time for our early Sunday edition.

In earlier years, my practice had been to scribble a description in longhand on the press boat while the first race was in progress. Then, as the launch reached the finish line, I would hand it to a WU messenger who would be waiting in a small boat to "grab" it as well as some of the early copy written by other newsmen.

He would then putter down the short distance to his office which backed onto the river to deliver it. Then he'd return near the finish line and wait until the second race, the jayvee event, was finished and pick up the copy detailing the happenings in that contest and then again return with his boat to the WU office.

Once the varsity race was over, however, it would be every reporter for himself. Newsmen from perhaps a dozen papers would scramble out of the press launch at the New London dock and rush for the telegraph office which was near the dock—less than 100 yards away.

Once there, I would quickly type a few paragraphs to be placed on top of the earlier copy I had sent describing the freshmen and junior varsity races and which by now already was in type in the *Times'* composing room.

As a result, my early story always had made the early six o'clock edition. Once I had completed my take for that edition, I would redo the entire piece in a much more polished form, I hoped. In the new presentation, the focus would be only on the varsity race, token treatment being given to the two events that had preceded it.

But then came that day in June of 1958. I arrived a day before the regatta to learn that the admiral, who was at the head of the Coast Guard Academy, had been named the chief official of the race for the first time. And it was obvious that he wasn't taking his job lightly. He had immediately issues an order, to wit:

"No stray boats are to be allowed on the course or near the finish line until the entire regatta is finished."

What did this mean to the media? The WU messenger could no longer pick up copy near the finish line as had been the custom in previous years. And it seemed, there was going to be no way of getting early copy from the river to the WU office. It was evident that I was going to be a confined passenger on the press launch for the duration of the regatta.

"This is ridiculous," I told Jimmy Carfield, the friendly reporter from the *Boston Herald*. "This Admiral probably knows something about ships and boats but he knows nothing about press deadlines.

"I'm sure if someone pointed out that millions of readers who get only the early editions of the different newspapers here were not going to see anything about this regatta Sunday morning, that he might change his ruling."

The night before the regatta, I thought about it in bed. Then I came up with a crazy plan that I hoped would work.

The next morning, I hustled over to the coffee shop located opposite New London's ancient, red-bricked railroad station.

"Do you have any containers of milk?" I asked the white-aproned counterman at the small establishment. "I'm looking for containers that have tops that can be pinched together? Cardboard ones?"

"We do," he replied, giving me somewhat of an odd look.

"Could I buy three of them?" I queried.

"You know, we're not a grocery store," he answered. "You can probably get them there for about 35 cents. I'll have to charge you a dollar apiece."

"That's okay," I replied, happy that at least the first step in my plan was working. "Please empty the milk from them. You can keep the milk. All I need are the containers."

The man rolled his eyes a little and sort of leaned over the counter, I thought, to look at me more closely. I felt he was probably wondering whether I was sane. Then he shrugged and went to his cooler to get the milk. When he returned with it, it was obvious to me judging from his manner, that he wasn't about to empty any container until I paid him.

"You're not being hazed for a fraternity or something?" he asked, "What are you going to do with these?"

"I'm a newspaperman," I told him after I had placed three one-dollar bills on the counter.

"I need them for a special story I am doing."

Fortified with the containers, I headed for the small dock area on the river side of the railroad station. Now, I was looking for someone with a small motorboat interested in earning a few dollars. I spotted a man with his young sub-teenage son nibbling sandwiches in the stern of a small motorized dory.

I greeted them and said, "What I'm about to tell you is no joke. I'm a sportswriter for the NYT. I'm here to report on today's races. But I have a problem. Unlike past years, the order from the regatta committee is that no spectator boat is to be permitted on the course at any time.

"They've never had such a ruling before," I explained. "To cope with it, I need the help of someone with a small boat. I will pay you $15 for the afternoon if, after each of those first two races are over, you have your boat idling about thirty yards past the finish line."

"What for?" understandably asked the surprised parent. "Why?"

"As the first race is being conducted, I plan to write a description of it in longhand on the press boat. When that race is finished, I'll put that report into one of these milk containers, pinch its top tightly, and throw it into the river.

"As you know, the tide will be ebbing. The container will float down to you. Do you think that you can pick it up for me and take it down to the WU office on the river, just about 100 yards from this dock? A telegrapher will be expecting you.

"I won't be able to get to the WU myself at that point because as soon as that race is concluded, our press boat will be making a wide turn and then heading back up the river to the starting point for the junior varsity race."

71

The man seemed intrigued with my plan. "I think we can do that," he said as he looked at his son to see his reaction.

"Then," I continued, "I'd like to have you come back with your boat to a point, again, just below the finish line and pick up my second container which will have a description of the jayvee race. That also must be brought by you to the telegraph office. After that, I'll take care of the last race—the varsity race—myself."

It was apparent that I had found two takers.

"Sure sounds interesting," the man said. "We've been to several of these regattas in the past. But this is different. Are you certain WU knows about this deal?"

"I'll take care of that," I replied. "I'm going over to that office right now to let them know what to expect."

The plan worked perfectly. My hurried handwritten description of the first two races arrived in the telegraph office within 10 minutes of the completion of each of those contests. When the varsity event was finished, our press boat, which had about fifteen reporters aboard, covered the four miles through the spectator fleet back to the starting line as quickly as possible.

It pulled into the small dock at the railroad station. I trotted the 100 yards or so to the Western Union office with five more paragraphs about the feature race which I had already written. There I found my courier with his son waiting for me.

"Here's the $15 and I can't thank you enough. You made my day."

Then I turned my five paragraphs in to the hands of a Morse telegrapher there and beat the deadline for the first edition with my entire account with about twenty minutes to spare.

As usual, as was the case with such rush jobs, I rewrote the entire story for the second edition and had the telegrapher send that. My colleagues at the *Times* enjoyed a big laugh a few days later when I told them that I had turned in an expense voucher—with an explanation—that had included an exorbitant price for three quarts of milk and "rental services of $15 for a small boat and its crew."

No questions were asked. Our auditing department was well aware of some of the unusual tactics I had devised in the past to make an edition.

"Why did you buy three milk containers instead of two," asked Harry Ferguson, a member of our sports staff, who subsequently wrote a full account of this episode for the NYT in-house paper.

"That's easy," I told him. "I decided to take along a spare one for insurance—just in case something happened to one of them."

The Harvard–Yale crew race always was one of my favorite sports events. It usually provided a relaxing weekend. On the eve of the regatta, the publicity departments of both colleges would play host to the press. We would dine at the Lighthouse Inn which overlooks Long Island Sound and then engage in a tournament of miniature golf at nearby Ocean Beach. John Ahearn of the *Boston Globe*, as I remember it, always won.

But on occasion, as in 1958, this regatta provided a stiff challenge for beating the deadline. As the train returned to its starting point at the end of each of the first two contests, a WU messenger would be on hand, alongside the track. He would take the account of each of the early races back, one at a time, to his downtown office.

That was an easy-does-it year compared to a subsequent Harvard–Yale regatta I covered one June when the races were to be held on a Friday instead of the usual Saturday. To boot, the crews were going to race upstream to take advantage of a flood tide, instead of downstream.

"Of course that's going to make this regatta altogether different," Johnson had told me a few days earlier. "The races, instead of ending at the railroad bridge in New London, are going to finish about four miles away from New London at Gales Ferry, near the Yale boathouse.

"How are we going to get our stories into the paper on time?" I asked him. "That finish line is four miles from New London."

"You're probably going to have to miss your weekday nine o'clock first edition," he replied, "because it's going to take the press launch an hour to return to the city. After all, our boat will have to take it slowly getting back there because all the spectator fleet also will be heading down the river."

This was one regatta that was going to be started a few hours before dusk so that the oarsmen could derive the full benefit of a following tide. Making that first edition loomed as an impossible task.

I decided there was only one course of action. Somehow, I had to find a way to write and file my story up river, just opposite the finish line, in the woods if necessary. That would eliminate the hour-long launch ride back to the WU. I went up there a day in advance to check the terrain.

When I returned to New London, I headed for its Western Union office and spoke to Bill Delany, that company's district supervisor.

"Mr. Delany," I said. "I'd like to file my story after tomorrow night's races—in the woods—just opposite the regatta's finish line. I'd never make my edition if I had to wait on that press boat while it was chugging its way back through the huge spectator fleet that will be on the river."

He laughed. "How are you going to do this, with mirrors?" he joked. "Where would we possibly find a wire out in the woods to connect with our office?"

"I've looked into that," I answered. "There are telephone poles right alongside the railroad's nearby trackage. Isn't it possible to connect into them and then attach about a 100-foot-long wire that would run right into a little clearing I've discovered near the river bank?

"If you could do that," I continued, "I would bring a bridge table and a couple of light chairs out there. Once I came off the press launch, I could write my story on my portable typewriter."

His eyes seemed to light up. After reflecting for a few moments, he said, "That would require a relay from there into our office here in New London," he finally replied. "We've never done anything like this before. But let's see if it'll work out. If it does, your story can be relayed automatically right into your office in New York."

He contacted me at my hotel within an hour to let me know that he was going to comply with my request. He also told me not to bother about the small table and chairs. He'd have the telegrapher who was going to send my story from the woods bring those items with him. He added, "I'm keeping my fingers crossed."

One other detail of this offbeat approach for my coverage remained. How was I going to get from mid-river at the finish line to a landing spot near where my WU telegrapher would be waiting?

To cope with that problem, I phoned one of the most enthusiastic members of the regatta's race committee. He was an old oar and a Yale alumnus. I told him about that problem.

"There's no reason why we can't accommodate you," he said. "As soon as the variety race is over, I'll have the team's managers who will be close by, aboard the Yale launch 'Meteor,' pick you up. They'll be happy to ferry you that short distance to land. And they'll have no trouble finding you because your press boat will be well-marked."

But when the next days' big race was completed—it was about an hour before dusk—that promised cooperation by the Yale managers never materialized. Their varsity crew beat Harvard in what was considered a major upset.

It was evident as Yale's supporters went wild with joy at the finish line, that the managers, in no way, were going to worry about picking up a newspaperman. They probably had rushed to the Yale boathouse to join the celebration. I never saw them.

Meanwhile, there were at least a dozen newsmen on our press boat, including Carfield, Ahearn, and Lou Black of the Associated Press. All of them were anxious to have the launch return over the four-mile route so that they could write their stories in New London.

As for myself, I was anxiously hoping I could spot a passing boat that could ferry me to the nearby river bank and deposit me near where my telegrapher was waiting in the woods.

The point was being reached where the other impatient newspapermen were beginning to demand that publicity manager Hank Johnson order the press boat to start on its return trip.

Fortunately, at this time, two twelve- or thirteen-year-old youngsters, at best, appeared nearby in a peeling, red-painted rowboat powered by a little squawking-sounding outboard motor.

I waved for them to approach. When they did, after a little hesitation on their part, I told them I would pay them to take me the thirty or forty yards to land. They nodded and said, "Sure, hop in," as they pulled the boat alongside.

I hurriedly stepped into the boat and found that I was up to my ankles in water, and as the lad at the tiller swung the craft around in a sharp turn for land, I almost fell out of the boat. The newspapermen, watching this from the press boat, kept chuckling.

The last thing I heard one of them say was, "That Mike would even get himself killed just to make an edition." Do you know? I think he was telling the truth.

They watched as the boat reached the bank. With my wet shoes, I slipped as I stepped on a sizable rock before jumping onto land. I gave the youngsters a $5 bill for their trouble. They were delighted.

Oh, yes. In a subsequent issue of a Harvard football game magazine, Johnson, the publicity director, wrote that the rock on which I had stepped would henceforth be known as "Strauss Rock." I'm told it's still there.

The telegrapher was puffing his pipe in the nearby woods when I arrived. With him was a telephone company lineman assigned to "rip" out the wire attached to the railroad's poles when we were finished with it.

Immediately, I thrust four sheets of paper into the hands of the telegrapher on which were handwritten the description of the days' first two races—reports that I had scrawled while on the press boat as those events were in progress.

"Send these right away," I said to the Morse man. "I'm going to sit down and type a few paragraphs on the feature race to top what I've just handed you."

And so, while his telegraph instrument clicked the dots and dashes pertaining to that day's early races, I wrote the necessary lead paragraphs about the varsity race. I made that first edition with ease.

But as I was redoing the entire story for my "wrap-up" for the subsequent editions, I ran into an unforeseen development. For, as I was pounding out the last few paragraphs, darkness began setting in. It became so dark that I could barely see what I was doing. And I had about six or seven minutes of writing left to do.

I asked the telephone company lineman whether he had a flashlight. He answered in the negative, saying that it was with his gear in his car on the highway about 600 yards away. Then I noticed that the telegrapher was sitting on a copy of the NYT which he had been reading when I reached him.

"Better still," I said to the lineman. "Suppose you keep lighting a page of this newspaper, one at a time, with matches, while I keep typing. That ought to do the trick."

It did.

When the telegrapher finished transmitting my story a few minutes later, he asked for the unusual good night ("gn" is the Morse Code abbreviation) from his wire chief in the New London office.

"Do you know?" he told me, as he detached his "bug," his sending instrument, from the wire leading to the telephone pole. "Those other newspapermen who were on the press boat with you have just reached the Western Union office in town. It did take them an hour to get there."

The story behind this story has a bit of a sequel. About five years later, I was among the guest speakers at a journalism seminar held at the NYT for college and prep school students. The late, always pleasant-mannered Orvil Dreyfoos, then the publisher of the *Times*, was the host.

My topic at the seminar dealt with my favorite subject, "Beating the Deadline." And so I related my woodsy climax to that Harvard–Yale boat race. I finished it off with the details of the newspaper-burning incident. After I finished, Mr. Dreyfoos, well known for his graciousness, moved to the podium and, with a big smile, turned to me and said, "That certainly is an interesting ending to an interesting story. In my day, I've heard of the NYT being used for many purposes but this is the first time I ever heard of it being used to provide light for a story."

As difficult as it was sometimes in earlier years to transmit stories or to get accompanying photographs into the paper from points inside the US, accomplishing the same from European or South American points, as might be expected, provided added problems.

If it had not been for my discovery of Yvette, a charming young French woman, who spoke virtually no English but who was fluent in French and Spanish, I would have had considerable trouble in transmitting my stories by telephone during the 1968 Winter Olympics held in Grenoble, France.

There were plenty of telephones around but the language barrier in trying to place calls with the French outside-operators often caused significant delays. Yvette, a local telephone operator, was a life saver.

I know only a smattering of French and Spanish, but I knew enough of each tongue to speak to her in sentences that had bits of each language in them.

Yvette usually understood me. As a result, she placed my calls and expedited them for the fifteen days that the Games were in progress. If she hadn't been available, it would have meant as much as a forty-five-minute delay at the phones until an English-speaking outside-operator was available.

When I left her in Grenoble, I gave her a small bottle of perfume and told her what a great help she had been. Her answer was typical of a girl who had generously given me every cooperation, even on her own time.

"I want you to know I didn't do this for a *cadeau* (gift)," she said graciously. "I enjoyed every minute of it. You see, I've always wanted to be a journalist. Now I feel I have been one."

A European episode that lingers in my memory involved a ski jumping tournament that started on a cloudless Sunday morning in St. Moritz, Switzerland. When I arrived there and was told about the event, I wondered to myself whether it would be possible to get a picture of a skier in flight into the following day's sports section in NYC.

If there had been wirephoto facilities available at that popular Alpine resort, there would have been no problem. But St. Moritz, I was told, hadn't had such transmission equipment available since 1948 when it had been the host of the 1948 Winter Olympics.

What's new? It presented a challenge. Wouldn't it be a great accomplishment to get a picture of one of those tournament jumpers into the following morning's NYT? I spoke to Fritz Kasper, the director of the St. Moritz national tourist office. He went for the picture idea like a seal might go for a herring.

We concocted a complex plan based on the six-hour difference in time between St. Moritz and NYC. After all, when it's noon in St. M, it's only six in the morning on Times Square. That gave us lots of extra time to make this project work.

We had Kasper's photographer arrive at the ski jump at about 9:30 A.M. He photographed a jumper coming off the chute on the morning's first practice flight. Then he rushed to his darkroom. He had the film developed and the picture printed within an hour—plenty of time to get it on the 11:30 A.M. train leaving St. M for the Swiss city of Chur.

"I will have my niece on that train with this picture," Kasper told me upon receiving the photograph. "She will take it to Chur and turn it over to the head conductor of the train leaving there for Zurich."

"That conductor is a good friend of mine," Kasper added in his German-accented English. "He'll be very cooperative. We'll enclose instructions on what he's to do with the photograph and give him a little gratuity for a schnapps."

The conductor cooperated to the fullest degree. When he arrived in Zurich, in keeping with his instructions, he rushed to the city's nearby main post office. By use of the wire facilities there, the photograph was transmitted to the NYT's Paris bureau.

Both the photo and the story—I dictated the story by phone to our London bureau—were relayed to NYC in time to make our first edition the following morning.

It was only recently that Martin Banberg, a veteran NYT copyreader and editor with whom I had worked for many years, reminded me recently of this St. M incident. It was at the annual "30 Year Club" ball that the *Times* hosts at the Marriot Marquis Hotel on Times Square. Marty came over to me and said: "Do you remember the time you sent that ski jumping picture out of St. M? I was in charge of the Paris bureau when it arrived and had it forwarded to NYC. I was surprised. You know, it was the first photo out of St. M that ever got into our paper the very next day. I've never forgotten it."

Yacht racing on Long Island Sound attracted large fleets for its weekend regattas, sometimes hundreds of them that included such one-design sailboats as Internationals, Atlantic, S Boats, and Thistles to name a few. One Saturday, I was assigned to go out on a committee boat to report on that day's races.

The skies were clear and the wind had been brisk, blowing at about twelve knots from the southwest. The regatta—held under the aegis of the Yacht Racing Association of Long Island Sound—was over earlier than usual, and the finishers of the different classes were concluded without a single protest by the skippers. A Saturday regatta never—and I mean never—made the first edition because of the Sunday paper's early deadline.

A chief reason was that the chartered boat, which accommodated regatta members as well as press, was a creaky, slow-moving old tub that its captain, on weekdays, used for party fishing outings.

To add to the problem of making a first edition on that particular day was that it was being hosted by the Bayside Yacht Club, located at the western end of the Sound. That entailed about an hour's cruise—the longest of all—from that club's headquarters to the event's starting point in mid-Sound.

Now the regatta was being finished. The last two sloops in the race had crossed the finish line. The regatta's committee was getting ready to return to the Bayside. Suddenly we all noticed a speedboat buzzing toward us at a tremendous rate. It was immediately identified as a hydrofoil, a craft that in those days was an uncommon sight on the Sound.

As the boat drew alongside, the man at the wheel, who it developed was a hydrofoil boat salesman, leaned over the rail and yelled, "I'm about to return to the Bayside Yacht Club. Anyone interested in getting there quickly?"

Since I had already assembled all the facts for my story, I was a ready candidate. I volunteered. "I'm interested," I said. "If I go back with you, I'll be able to get my story into the paper faster."

Just one other person on the committee boat joined me. Then the craft took off with a rush. Once underway, with its hull raised above the water, the boat began humming along at about forty knots per hour. On the outward trip, in the old fishing boat, we had averaged about seven knots.

We reached the Bayside Yacht Club in less than fifteen minutes. It was a breeze! I wrote my story quickly and handed it to Ranhoffer, the telegrapher who had been waiting for me in the clubhouse. He sent it directly from here to our sports department. It was said to be the earliest Yacht Racing Association story ever received by our paper.

"How did you do it?" the puzzled assignment editor, a yachting aficionado, asked me a few days later. "How did you get the story in so quickly?"

"It wasn't with mirrors," I joked. "It was with a hydrofoil."

A deadline story that always tickled me had to do with the NYC Yankees baseball team as it was leaving its Florida training camp at Fort Lauderdale on April 5, 1977.

"There's nothing new to report," Gabe Paul, then the president of the Yankees, had told me about an hour before the team departed for the north. I had kept in close touch with Paul at that point because I was remaining in Florida to start a vacation. I wanted to make sure no news would break at the last minute.

But news did break—just as the charter bus that was to take the Yankees and the newspapermen back to the Fort Lauderdale airport was being boarded. With all the passengers already in their seats, and the driver about to start the engine, Paul came rushing out of his nearby office.

"We just signed Bucky Dent of the White Sox to play shortstop for us," he yelled at me as he entered the bus. Right behind him was George Steinbrenner, the Yankee's principle stockholder.

"Yes, we got him," Steinbrenner confirmed. "But we couldn't be sure until a few minutes ago. We've been on the telephone."

Then the doors of the bus closed, and it rolled off toward the airport. In the bus, undoubtedly, were an unhappy bunch of writers eager to get this late-breaking news to the papers. They were unable to do so at that point. They were now "prisoners" in the airport-bound bus.

Even those who did contact their papers during the short wait at the airport couldn't do justice to the Dent purchase because the team's charter plane awaited them. What did I do? I drove to my nearby hotel and leisurely wrote a detailed story of this new acquisition which had been made to help the Yankees plug a hole at the shortstop position with a highly competent player.

How important was the acquisition of Dent considered? To get him, the Yankees had parted with three players: Oscar Gamble, LaMarr Hoyt, and minor league pitcher Bob Polinsky. In addition, the Yankees paid $200,000 to the White Sox.

For me, making my early edition on this important trade was a breeze. I realized then that fate and time could play a strange hand on sportswriters and their deadlines.

As for Dent, he moved on to the Texas Rangers in the middle of the 1982 season only to return to the Yankees as their manager as the 1989 campaign was nearing its end. Even I, with the good luck I usually enjoyed in making editions, couldn't have envisioned that!

CHAPTER 9

Drink 'Til They Nod and Wink

New line at the punch-bowl's brink
Let the thirsty think
What they say in Japan:
First the man takes a drink
Then the drink takes a drink
Then the drink takes the man!
Edward R. Sill, 1841–1887

A familiar joke in the 1930s dealt with a youngster looking for his father who habitually patronized saloons.

The story goes that the lad finally pushed open one of the swinging doors of a bar and called out.

"Is my father in here?"

"There's only one bum here" was the answer from the bartender.

"Well," answered the lad after a pause, "that's my father."

I was attending college mornings and working nights and on some afternoons when, as a seventeen-year-old, I began reporting on some minor sporting events for the suburban section of the *New York Times*. I soon became aware that drink played an important part in the lives of some newspapermen.

At least one of the reasons for the drinking seemed obvious. It stemmed from the nature of the business. Free liquor, all you could drink, for example, flowed freely before and after sports luncheons. Noontime repasts were held frequently at popular midtown restaurants, such as the 21 Club, Toots Shor's and Sardi's, by promoters desirous of putting the focus on their events. They felt that for being such hosts, they would get some "ink"—free press—for whatever they were fostering.

Availability of the free "juice" continued throughout my career but to a lesser extent in my latter years. Still, at the time I stopped reporting on the baseball games at Shea Stadium and at the New York Yankee's ballpark, among others, there was an open bar at the free dinners enjoyed by the media. After games the bar was opened again.

"Back in the good old days—in the twenties and early thirties—there really was no such thing as 'prohibition,'" Jim McCully, one of the *New York Daily News*' most colorful sportswriters, told me while we were in Aqueduct race track's press box. "At many sports events, booze for the press would be flowing all over the place. Bootleggers coolly flaunted the law as if they were dealing in lemonade rather than alcohol.

"Humorous incidents about sportswriters who overdrank abounded in those days," he said. "The one that still makes me laugh occurred just before the world heavyweight championship bout between Max Schmeling and Young Stribling. That bout was fought in Cleveland back in 1931.

"Schmeling was training at Conneaut Park Lake in Pennsylvania, a small resort community near the Ohio state line," he continued. "Since he was going to be defending his title, many sports writers, probably twenty or thirty of them, made a nearby hotel their headquarters."

McCullough continued, "In keeping with their usual modus operandi, bootleggers had descended on that small town like a swarm of locusts on a cornfield. They came loaded with their 'refreshments' because training camp sessions before a big fight often lasted for weeks. They knew that there were sportswriters who were dyed-in-the-wool boozers.

"Soon after they arrived, the hooch men, having already stashed their booze in their hotel rooms, got wind that federal agents were going to stage a raid that very evening," said McCulloch. "The bootleggers were frantic. What were they going to do? They didn't want to lose their liquor to the 'revenooers' in what would have amounted to a legal hi-jacking as well as finding themselves all being arrested.

"'Let's hide the liquor,' suggested one of them.

"It so happened that a mortician's convention was being held at the hotel at the same time," continued McCully, as a smile started to crease his lips. "So the bootleggers, ever on the alert, hid their liquor bottles in the coffins on display in the hotel's big ballroom. Then they sat back and hoped for the best.

"The revenue agents never found the hooch and left," concluded McCully. "But were those bootleggers in for a big surprise. Because when, after making sure the coast was clear, and they went into the ballroom to retrieve their liquor, the coffins were empty. Because earlier, as soon as they knew the Feds had left, the sportswriters descended on the coffins and removed the spoils."

As for the Schmeling–Stribling fight, held to decide the world heavyweight title that had been vacated by Gene Tunney, that also proved somewhat weird. Schmeling won with a knockout with only fourteen seconds remaining in the fifteen-round bout, referee George Blake maintaining he had stopped the fight "to keep Stribling from suffering further punishment."

Of course, there have always been some writers more interested in liquor than others. For them such popular brands as Canadian Club, Three Star Hennessey, and Gordon's Gin remained well-known preferences. In many cases they like out-of-town assignments because, as one of them put it to me, "there was little to do after writing his story and then having to wait when the time came for him to do another story on the following day."

"Let's face it, many of us did seem to live in a world of our own," a retired baseball writer told me one night between innings of a game at the Yankee Stadium. "Baseball trips in earlier days were made by train. You could be on one of those rattlers for about twenty-five hours on a trip, say from New York to St Louis.

"We would read the papers, play cards, and drink to while away the time," he added.

At press luncheons in midtown New York that were hosted by promoters, sports reporters were made to feel like important guests of honor. All meals usually were topped off by having a box of top-grade cigars passed among the diners. It was a fool's world at best.

During prohibition, John Barleycorn, a name jokingly used as a synonym for intoxicating beverages, was as well-known as were Coolidge, Hoover, and even Volstead, who fathered the Prohibition law.

It was an era in which some newspapermen, whether they worked downtown at the *New York Sun*, the *Journal*, the *American*, or the *Telegram* or uptown at the *Tribune* or the *Times*, would make it a habit upon leaving the office to stop at nearby speakeasies before heading home.

News reporters, sportswriters, and even prominent editors had their favorite hangouts. It was just like in the movies. Almost all of the "speaks" had outlandish names. Some had slits in their front doors—at eye level—so that a visitor on the outside could be viewed from the inside.

"There was the 'Green Door' in Manhattan's mid-40s alongside the Hotel Markwell," Joe Nichols, the fun-loving *New York Times* hockey, boxing, and racing writer, once reminisced with me.

"I remember that one well," he said. "It had a slogan. A sign outside its door read 'Where guests rest well.' No one could argue with that type of 'come on,'" he concluded. "Many a fellow who had had one too many often would be found sleeping it off on one of the Green Door's tables."

Nearby was Mack and Willie's, a popular hangout for thirsty *New York Times* employees. *Tribune* people were partial to Jack Bleek's, which, in some cases, had a hypnotic advantage over some of the other newspapermen's drinking spots. This one did business right next door to the *Tribune*'s entrance on West Fortieth Street.

And in a downtown alley, by the New York Journal building which fronted on the East River, was the Rain House. The joke around that popular "spa" was "At this oasis, liquor didn't rain, it poured."

Who was Barleycorn? It was a name that was used freely in early days as a joking substitute for spirits. "John" had a "personality" brought into focus by the Scotch poet Robert Burns in the eighteenth century. It was Burns's well-known poem, "A Red, Red Rose," that contained the line:

> *"inspiring John Barleycorn*
> *What dangers thou canst make us scorn."*

These two lines, we may rest assured, were not written with sportswriters in mind, but they certainly could have been. For liquor certainly made some consumers in our ranks brave and yes, foolhardy. Believe it or not, it also caused some, it seemed, to turn in their best writing efforts.

"That fellow sitting right behind the winner's corner does his best job when he's loaded," Vernon Van Ness of our paper once told me back in the thirties during a boxing match at Madison Square Garden.

"Put a match to him right now and he's apt to go up in smoke. He's that saturated in alcohol. But when he gets through with his fight story tonight, I can guarantee it'll be almost good enough to rate a Pulitzer Prize. He just thrives on the smell of the cork."

Sense of responsibility? For those who over indulged, there often was none. I recall an episode earlier in my career when a sportswriter Bill Cavanaugh[2] really went berserk. Bill was a highly competent writer and copy reader, but he was looked upon in the trade as a "drifter." Not because, he was a hobo riding the rods, mind you, but because he couldn't keep a newspaper job.

Bill would toil for a few months at one Fourth Estate establishment and then get fired for hitting the bottle on the job. That wouldn't stop

[2]   Name altered

him. He would just apply at another newspaper office and get hired there. He was employed, at one time or other, at least a half a dozen papers throughout the east.

Finally, he moved from sportswriting to doing a little publicity at the end of the regular 1932 season for the Newark Bears baseball team of the International League. The Bears had won their first league championship and he was hired by George Weiss, the top man in that club's front office, to help with the New Jersey team's publicity for the Junior World Series playoffs.

This colorful competition annually pitted the International League champions against the American Association titleholders, both of which were Triple-A circuits. The Minneapolis Millers, who had won the western loops championship, were scheduled to play the first three games of the series in Newark.

"And that's the number of games for which he was hired," related Hy Goldberg, the crack baseball writer for the *Newark News*. "After those three games were finished, however, Bill, loaded to the gills, appeared at the Newark railroad station as the Bears were taking off 'on a sleeper' to play the fourth game of the series in Minneapolis.

"He had been told that there was no longer any need for his services because he had been hired only for Newark's home games," continued Goldberg. "But Bill insisted on going. He sneaked on the train. He was discovered shortly after the 'Special,' which was transporting both teams, began heading west."

"It was decided then and there that he, in his inebriated condition, was going to cause nothing but trouble. And so, he was deposited 'for safe keeping' in the baggage car which was then locked. The plan was to remove him from the train once it reached the Philadelphia station, about eighty miles distant."

In those days, sleeping cars on trains were a "must" for teams in the higher echelon baseball leagues. Travel by airplane for players and press at that time was still just a dream. A trip from Newark to Minneapolis by rail could take twenty-five hours. Bill clearly had wanted to make the trip if only for its "socializing" opportunities.

What did the writers do on such long junkets? They would compose "an en route story" about the teams and drop it off at an approaching railroad station to be telegraphed to their papers. But after that, they might read newspapers or books, play poker with some of their fellow reporters and team coaches, or spend time in the club car drinking.

Many years later, when a few members of the Yankees and I visited President Nixon in the White House's Rose Garden, he asked me what sportswriters did during our long baseball trips. By that time, of course, baseball teams were traveling by airplane.

"Do you writers spend that time playing cards?" the president said with a smile.

I took the question right in stride.

"Sometimes we do, and I always win," I joked.

"How come?" the president asked in a curious voice.

"Because I always play with my own cards."

The president laughed.

But to get back to the Newark Bears, there they were traveling with Bill, locked in the base baggage car. Bill may well have thought he was flying; he was that oiled. Even as the train pulled out of Newark, he barely could stand let alone walk.

Enraged over his incarceration and the knowledge that he was going to be deposited in Philadelphia, Billy Boy was boiling. Immediately, he began wondering how he could get revenge. He looked out of the train's windows as it whizzed through the New Jersey countryside. Suddenly, a contemplative grin broke out from his bleary-eyed countenance.

"A great idea," he slurred to himself. "A great idea. This will teach 'em."

Without further ado, he turned about and spotted the Bears' equipment—bats, balls, and uniforms—in trunks and carefully wrapped huge bundles. Then he swung open the baggage car's big door. He felt the cool New Jersey September air rush past his ears.

With dedicated diligence, he shoved and hurled all of it, piece by piece, through the wide-open door into space. Once finished, he gave the matter no further thought. He merely sat back to await his release from his temporary "jail."

This bit of villainy was discovered immediately. It was for good reason because as the steam locomotive pulled its baseball passengers toward Philadelphia, players suddenly began seeing trunks and huge bundles go whizzing past their windows. The incident provided one of the season's hilarious baseball conversation pieces.

Bill, as scheduled, was dropped off on the Philadelphia platform and no charges were lodged against him. Why not? Because the Bears' management realized that in his stiff condition, he didn't really know what he was doing.

Did he have any regrets? Not in the least. During a subsequent drinking spree with some of his saloon cronies a few weeks later, he was quoted as saying,

"Those bastards who run that club deserve to see their team play in underwear."

Mention of sloppy wearing apparel brings to mind a New York sportswriter who had a habit of over-indulging with the bottle and then falling asleep with a lighted cigarette dangling from the lips. Its ashes would get all over his clothing while he slumbered.

While such a habit presented no major problems while baseball teams were doing their traveling by train, it worried players and writers, no end, once all hands began making their trips by plane.

"I remember that guy well," said Stan Lomax, who formerly had been with the *New York Journal* and later was one of the city's top sports radio broadcasters. "Once we started flying, the writers in our group placed a round-the-clock vigil on this guy."

"The stewardesses and one or two of us would take turns watching him as soon as we became airborne. After all, a lighted cigarette on a plane floor in a pressurized cabin, we felt, might trigger a disaster.

"As regularly as day follows night, this guy would drink himself stiff," continued Lomax. "And that was easy to do. Those familiar little liquor bottles on our charter planes were served to the press by the stewardesses free of charge. Each of them only held one-tenth of a pint.

"But after having five or six of them, this man would light a cigarette and go into slumberland. We kept cautioning him about the danger. We might just as well have been telling him our plane had no wings. He just wasn't interested in listening. Lighted cigarettes kept dropping from his lips once he dozed off. At first, we kept picking them up and putting them out.

"Finally," concluded Lomax, "we warned him that if he didn't cut it out, that we'd have him grounded. We threatened to make him return to train travel—alone.

"Couldn't do that" was his answer. "If I miss my train, I'll miss my deadlines."

"'But if you keep flying with us, we'll miss more than deadlines,' I told him.

"Our friend was much more careful thereafter. He explained he had never had liked trains."

CHAPTER 10

More Drinking Stories

Lomax also told me about a writer who worked for a New York City tabloid newspaper before and during the early years of the Great Depression who would go on such binges that he couldn't even write the start of a story.

"This guy would take off on periodic benders," Lomax said. "But he was a good egg, and we tried to help him keep his job. Remember, this was an era in which a sportswriter would think nothing of filling in for another who had become incapacitated because of a drinking spree.

"There was that spring training session in St. Petersburg, where the Yankees did their spring training, that this fellow went on a week-long tear," reminisced Stan. "Although the Florida sun was hot and those afternoons mighty uncomfortable—remember the only air conditioning then came from electric fans—he became high as the skies to make himself even hotter.

"What did we do? After a short conference among ourselves, we took turns writing his stories for him, signing his name on them and then sending them on to New York by telegraph. On one occasion, we ghost-wrote five columns in five days.

"The big laugh," continued Lomax, "was that our drinking friend benefited from our efforts beyond even our wildest dreams. The following Monday, he received a telegram from the big shot editor at his paper complimenting him on his superb work. The editor focused his praise on the fact that our tipsy colleague had demonstrated tremendous variety of style, that none of the stories sent resembled another and that they were all 'so good.'

"Our friend was shocked, but also delighted, particularly when he received a special bonus check the following Tuesday. Such commendation came as no surprise to me," concluded Lomax, "because he had had some of the best baseball writing talent in America pinch-hitting for him—Will Wedge of the *New York Sun*, Bill Slocum of the *New York American*, and Harry Cross of the *Tribune*, among others."

While there was considerable camaraderie among sportswriters in my early days as a writer—much more than there is now—many of them were not above pulling a harmless prank on a new member of their writing fraternity. It was done usually just for laughs.

Easygoing Joe Nichols, with whom I worked at the *Times* for more than forty years, used to tell the story of the sleepy-looking Bill Chessnut[3] who regularly would get "stoned" at the open bar provided for sportswriters at the Six-Day Bicycle Races held at Madison Square Garden.

"One night Lou Burton of the American and I glanced at his typewriter in the press room," said Nichols. "We noticed that on his machine, Bill had inserted a page on which only his byline—'By Bill Chessnut'—was written. He had gone off to the free bar to have a few snorts."

"With no malice and strictly for laughs," continued Nichols, "we took turns tapping out paragraphs on his typewriter that were loaded with off-color language. Just after we finished, Bill, much the worse for wear, staggered into the room.

"Bill looked at his machine, noticed the byline on the sheet of paper and saw that it was followed by a story—two pages of typewritten copy. He looked at it closer and evidently began wondering when he had written it. He was so far gone that he concluded he actually must have written it earlier. Suddenly a smile appeared on the guy's face."

"Gee," he mumbled, "that's great."

"And without really trying to read it, assuming he could have in his condition, he handed it to the Western Union operator. Actually no one could have written anything that early in the evening. That night's bike races had barely begun.

"Get this right off," he told the telegrapher. "My desk will sure be glad to get my story this early. If there are any questions, call me. I'll be out at the bar talking."

The telegrapher, according to Nichols, began sending the story but then, when he came to the obscene language, he suddenly stopped tapping on his instrument as if someone had suddenly pointed a loaded gun at him.

---

[3]   Name altered by editors

"It was then that we let the whole thing out of the bag," concluded Nichols. "Lew and I started bursting with laughter and for that matter so did the telegrapher who now realized it had all been a put-up job.

"Lew and I eventually rewrote a proper story, put Bill's name on it and sent it on the wire to his paper. We wondered the next night at the bike races whether he had read it in his paper and wondered. But we didn't ask him. We didn't want to get THAT involved."

A bit that really did follow the tenets of our commandment "Help Thy Fellow Worker," occurred right in front of me during a college football game. George Ca., a *Cap Journal* writer, had drunk himself into a state where he knew he couldn't write his story. Someone in the press room, Joe Basso, volunteered to write it for him.

George, a little worried that Basso might not do him justice, kept peering over the volunteer's shoulder while the story was being typed. After three paragraphs were on paper, George's blurry eyes started gleaming with pleasure.

"That's great stuff," enthused George, stumbling over each of his words. "That's great. That's just the kind of crap my paper wants."

Another New York writer, on the *Herald Tribune* staff, whom I'll call Sam Richmond, always seemed either to be on a binge or on the way to one. On occasion, when he appeared on an assignment—right into the 1970s—he would have a flask with him. In cold weather, the liquor would be placed in his left inside pocket of his overcoat.

I never got up the courage, even though I knew him well because of the many stories we covered together, to ask him why he kept drinking so heavily. Another reporter on this now-defunct paper explained it all to me one day.

"Sam was in World War II as the pilot of a fighter plane," I was told. "Evidently his nerves went from bad to worse as his tour of duty continued. When the war was over, he was shot, perhaps even worse than if he had been hit with a bullet."

Richmond was a handsome man, seemingly in top physical condition. He was trim and bright-looking—when he wasn't on the bottle—and probably the neatest dresser in our ranks. If he got to a press party though, he soon would allow himself to get under the weather.

I've often said that I could write a book just about him. He almost always seemed to be under the influence of the bottle whether it was in a racetrack's press box, at the ski jumping tournaments at New York's Bear Mountain, or even at a simple boarding school football game.

Repeatedly, he would say to me, "Mike, honestly, I got to start laying off this stuff. It keeps giving me the Willies."

He never did. Once, only three days after I had heard him give himself one of his pledges to "lay off the booze," he was up to his old tricks. How did I know? Because we found ourselves together in the Duke University press box in Durham, N.C. We had arrived there separately to cover the Duke–Army football game. In keeping with the college's policy of seating reporters from the same cities together, I found Sam seated to my immediate right. Nattily dressed, as usual, but bleary-eyed, he soon became his old familiar self. He never even acknowledged my presence in the press box. For him, the day had already been too long.

As the game progressed, Sam kept digging into that inside coat pocket and taking short naps from his flask. After the contest's first half had been concluded, he wrote a description of the first two periods for his paper and handed it into his telegrapher. So did I.

"I'm going to need all the cooperation I can get from you," I remember telling my telegrapher as I gave my early copy to him. "We're going to have a rough time making our first edition. As you know, we lose an hour because Durham is on Standard Time and New York is on Savings Time."

"Don't worry," answered the Western Union operator, who was sitting a row behind me, about five feet away. "I'm in touch with your paper right now on a direct wire. Just hand me those opening paragraphs when the game is over and we'll have no trouble."

But we did have trouble. Because as the game's final play was completed, Richmond let out a gasp. He slumped limply against my shoulder, his head finally landing on my lap and my portable typewriter dropping to the floor. Sam was out cold.

"Don't move!" Duke's worried sports information director yelled at me as he rushed to our side. "He may be having a heart attack. Don't move!"

Within a few seconds, my telegraph operator reached over and handed me a terse message. It was from our sports department. It read:

"Rush score and opening paragraphs of your lead immediately. We are post scripting the edition for your story. Hurry!"

I showed the message to the publicity director.

"I have to start writing at once," I told him in what I guess was a frantic tone. "I just have to—"

"Better not move," he warned. "Your friend is liable to be dying. Looks like a heart attack."

Aware of the concern that was going on at my office about not having my opening paragraphs, I felt like dropping over myself.

I followed instructions. I didn't move. But instead of writing those four or five paragraphs, with Sam's head still on my lap, I dictated them orally, yelling the sentences to my telegrapher above the noise in the press box.

The Western Union man, tapped out my sentences by Morse Code and off they went to my office.

With that done, I had at least an hour to write the usual "sub" (substitute) story about the game. And so I, along with other people in the press box, awaited the arrival of a physician. He appeared within ten minutes.

He smelled Richmond's breath, opened his mouth and stuck his fingers into it. Within two minutes, Sam began to stir. Soon he was breathing normally—that is, normally for him.

"What gives?" I ask the doctor.

"Nothing much," he replied. "This man has been drinking. He lost control of himself and swallowed his tongue. That can happen to a person who's had a few too many."

Did Richmond write his story? We both did, but not until I had finished my own. And he never remembered passing out. The episode marked one of at least half a dozen times that I had become his ally in getting his story to his paper which, like the *New York Times*, was a morning publication.

Newspaper people, just like men and women in other walks of life, seem to have ready reasons for lingering over the bar too long. For Richmond, it was the nerve-wracking experiences he had suffered in the war. For John Keller, one of my favorite people who worked with me at the *Times* during the World War II era, it was pressure. He lived in Staten Island and work nights in our sports department. In the daytime, he taught mathematics in a parochial school near his home. The reason for his double schedule was that he was supporting his two elderly parents.

Judging by his clothing, John was usually short of money. He seemed to do most of his drinking at night, after his working hours at the *Times*.

As our first edition went to press and midnight approached, he would head for Kiernan and Dineen's, also known in our office by those who drank as "K&D's." For those who didn't frequent the place, it was jokingly referred to as "The Cesspool A. C." This beckoning spa was on Eighth Avenue, only about three blocks from our West Forty-Third Street office.

K&D's was not a disreputable-looking establishment as saloons go. This palace of drink had a sawdust floor, a long mahogany bar, and the familiar small round tables with lightweight wooden chairs. At times when some of us had had our fill of the menus offered in the *Times* cafeteria, we would eat our dinners there. The food wasn't bad.

As for Keller, he would stop in at K&D's after work, several times a week. Once there, he would order a beer and down it slowly while seated on one of the chairs. When he finished, he would put his head on the table and go to sleep. Almost always red-eyed, even in afternoons, sleep was what he needed most.

He would awaken from time to time, walk to the bar where there would usually be several *New York Times* employees in attendance and order another drink—not always beer. He often remained in the saloon until its closing time of 4:00 A.M. He considered me a good friend.

"I have to have a shot every now and then," he told me one evening in our office after I had suggested that he was working too hard and maybe drinking too much.

"Do you know, John," I told him more than once. "You ought to consider going straight home after work. You're getting to look like a wreck."

"Need to relax," he answered. "And I never worry about liquor because I can handle it. Never had any trouble with it."

John often bragged that he could outdrink anyone, and he meant "anyone." He accepted such challenges, and to the best of my knowledge, never lost a bout. But once the early hours of the morning arrived, and he had been drinking, he became a very tired fellow. By 3:00 A.M., he often was a very inebriated one.

From time to time, someone would call our sports department from the saloon to inform us that Keller was loaded, that he needed help getting to the subway.

"Somebody better come and get him," we were told one night. "He could fall down the subway steps and kill himself. He needs someone to lean on."

"We'll take care of it right away," one of us would say.

On such occasions, someone in our sports department would leave our office to give John the necessary assistance. Held by one arm, both would stagger the four blocks to the nearest IRT subway station at Seventh Avenue and Broadway.

Often, because he was so helpless, one of us would accompany him on the train ride to the Bowling Green station. Once there, John would be assisted on to the Staten Island ferryboat for the five-cent, twenty-five-minute trip across the bay.

I was among those who, from time to time, came to his rescue, even though these calls came as late as 3:45 A.M. Usually some of us were still in the office, for an obvious reason. A poker game would be in progress in our department almost nightly, after the last edition had gone to press.

I rode the subway with John to Bowling Green at least five times, and I ushered him right onto the ferry. I'd accompany him because he didn't even seem capable of sitting in the subway train without falling to the floor.

"Please help him off the other side when the boat docks," I would ask a deckhand. "This guy's had one too many and needs help. He's a good fellow."

"Don't worry about it," I recall having a deckhand once reply. "I know how he feels. I go on a bender myself every once in a while."

But the deckhands, having other duties, on occasion, would forget about good old Keller. Maybe it was because they couldn't find him. John had a habit of plopping himself down in a remote corner of the huge ferryboat, letting himself down on a bench and going to sleep.

"I remember this guy," one of the boat's crew told me one night when I arrived with John. "He came aboard and must have had three or four round-trips without being disturbed. I didn't know anything about him and so when I saw him, I just let him sleep it off. I reckon there were other nights when he slept through several round-trips." Keller, on such occasions, would be awakened by the hustle and the noise of the morning rush-hour crowd. His next step? He would walk over to the concession stand in the Staten Island ferry-house and treat himself to a quick coffee and a helping of Danish pastry. Then he would head for school and shave, he still had the time, in the faculty room. Those of us who knew him best could tell when he had overstayed his cruise on the ferryboat. Unable to get home to change his clothing in these instances, he would appear at our office at four that afternoon to shovel, his clothes badly rumpled.

How did he keep his job? He always seemed to be able to survive the effects of the night. He had a pleasant personality. Just about everyone liked him.

I lost track of him shortly after he had married. His wife left him and returned to her parents' home in Oklahoma. To be near her, he enlisted in the Army and managed to get himself stationed nearby, at Fort Sill. The word we got was that he died shortly thereafter at age, we guessed, of about forty.

CHAPTER 11

That Ol' Devil Rum

Spirits may be helpful
My physician's often said
To keep your spirits buoyant
But not to keep your head.

For some reason, liquor, even wine or beer, has always turned me off. I just don't like the taste. My favorite beverage has always been milk. I keep telling people, but in my opinion, milk—cold milk—is the greatest drink ever invented. So any drinking I've done through the years has been minimal. I probably have had as many as two drinks in one evening only four or five or six times. One Manhattan, or perhaps a screwdriver, generally has been my limit. I usually just pass when drinks are offered.

However, I must confess that I've been loaded from drink—exactly two and a half times. The halftime? That memorable occasion occurred in Princeton, New Jersey, after I had reported on the Ivy League's Heptagonal Track and Field championships. It was held at that university's Palmer Stadium.

It had been a bitter cold day considering that it was spring, and the wind was whipping up dust as it blew across the stadium's playing area. I was so numb I decided that I was not going to write it in the open-air press box. It would be smarter, I concluded, to work within the warmer confines of the Western Union office in town.

"I got to warm up," I remember telling Don Coyle, the university's sports publicity director as I left the stadium. "I'm numb. Is there a good place in town to get a quick drink before I start writing?"

He suggested a bar and there I went. That one whiskey sour raised havoc with my empty stomach. I became tipsy. An hour after I had written my story and turned it in at the Western Union office, I couldn't remember having written it. When I got off the train in New York, I called the office to ascertain if my copy had been received and was it okay? The reply was affirmative.

That episode, I feel, qualifies the one halftime in my lifetime in which I thought I'd had too much.

With the details of that minor "escapade" out of the way, I now move onto my first major one—in 1956 at age forty-four—about a quarter of a century after I received my first paycheck from the *New York Times*.

On a Saturday, in the summer of 1957, I was assigned to report on the $135,000 Atlantic City handicap held at that New Jersey seaside resort. It was featuring the highly regarded Dedicate as the early line favorite, ridden by the great Eddie Arcaro.

For Dedicate, that day's race seemed routine—an easy test. There didn't seem to be any horse in the field capable of upsetting him.

As often is the case at racetracks on Saturdays when the sports section goes to press three hours earlier than on weekdays, a matter of ten or fifteen minutes could make the difference in whether or not I was going to get the story to the office in time to make the first edition. The feature race was scheduled to finish at about 5:30 P.M. I had no more than twenty minutes to spare if I were to get at least a brief account of the big race to our paper on time.

As I left my Long Island home and headed for New Jersey, I picked up a copy of *Marjorie Morningstar*, a best-selling novel written by Herman Wouk. I wanted something to read during the two-and-a-half-hour ride on the special race train from New York's Penn Station to the track's railroad siding in New Jersey.

"Please don't take it," my wife said as she saw me pick up the book. "I borrowed it from Grace, and I promised I would return it to her tomorrow. You'll probably leave it somewhere."

"Not a chance," I told her. "I'm not even carrying a portable typewriter. There will be plenty of them in the press box. Besides I want to read this. Don't worry, you'll have it back tonight."

And so off I went. I succeeded in immersing myself in the book during the trip. When I reach the press box, I immediately became busy. I wrote what is known as "early copy." I did paragraphs about the crowd, the climate, the skies, and the proceedings of the early races.

By the time the feature event was ready to start, my telegrapher had sent at least a dozen paragraphs with his dots and dashes. By then, I had read about fifteen additional pages of the book.

All I needed now was to await the outcome of the future race. I planned to write about five paragraphs about this Atlantic City handicap as soon as it had been run. These would be used to top the details about earlier races and the crowd that I had sent earlier. It all seemed to be going well.

Just before the big race began, I carefully sit down *Marjorie Morningstar* next to me on my desk and watched the contest through my binoculars.

There they finally were, the horses charging down the stretch and to the surprise of a few, Dedicate crossed the finish line in front. I lost a little time and starting my lead, typing words that went somewhat as follows:

"Dedicate, ably ridden by Eddie Arcaro, came streaking through the stretch this afternoon to capture the second running of the $135,000 Atlantic City handicap impressively. In second place at the finish was Royal Beacon."

I kept writing. I had three paragraphs written by 5:40 and was just about to have the telegrapher send them when the "objection" sign was flashed on the infield odds board. The track's stewards were questioning whether Arcaro, on Dedicate, had interfered with Royal Beacon in the rush through the stretch.

"That's all I need," I said to Walter Haight, the well-known race writer for the *Washington Post*, who was sitting near me. "Here I am on a tight deadline, and I can't send the story to my office until the stewards have that 'objection' sign taken down."

Holding back my few lead paragraphs, I wrote two more. I was convinced Dedicate would be named the official winner. I felt that the stewards would be reluctant to disqualify a horse in a stakes race that rich. Besides, Arcaro, strong jockey that he was, was not apt to allow his mount to impede a rival horse.

The editor in New York? He repeatedly kept urging me to expedite my copy.

"I can't," I responded by telegraph. "The stewards are still checking the race's films to determine whether there was a foul."

It took the officials about twelve minutes to come to a decision. To my other dismay, Dedicate was disqualified. My deadline time had just about run out.

I couldn't use the few paragraphs I'd written for the first edition. I immediately rushed three other early lead paragraphs to the office relating that Royal Beacon had been named the winner because of interference by Dedicate in the stretch.

Now I had to change my entire thinking for my wrap-up—the second edition—story. It was rough. In my earlier treatment of the race, in the paragraphs I had held back, I had described Dedicate as a great horse with a winning spirit and Arcaro as a jockey who had again demonstrated he was a top rider.

Instead, I now wrote that Arcaro had been careless and pointed out that he had allowed his mount to zig when he should have zagged. I also noted that Dedicate had shown that perhaps he wasn't so great. Those close to the sport know that when a horse bears outward—fails to keep on the straight line in the stretch run—it often means that he's run out of stamina.

To add to the tension, my office rushed another message telling me that I should write my new account as quickly as possible; that it was planning a postscript on my wrap-up story. "Speed is essential!" I was advised in that brief telegraph message to the press box.

My new redone and complete description of the Handicap was going to be placed on the first page of Sunday morning's sports section. A postscript meant that when my new story arrived at the office, the presses would be stopped for a few moments to get it into what remained of the first edition run.

Tension started building up within me. By the time I had finished typing another sixteen or seventeen paragraphs to replace my entire earlier effort, my stomach was in knots.

"Boy, am I glad that's over," I said to Haight who was still writing his own story for the *Washington Post*. "But my stomach," I added. "It's tight. It's shot. I never felt like this before."

"Wait till I finish my piece," he replied. "It'll take me about ten more minutes. Then we'll see if we can fix you up."

I wondered what he meant. I should have known. Haight, always a kind soul, was a fellow who liked to drink. And it was well known that he could hold his liquor extremely well. After finishing his story line, he looked up at me and said with a smile.

"Now let's see what we can do for you. Let's go down and see John Kelly. He ought to be able to help us out."

Of course, I knew who John Kelly was. He was the president of the Atlantic City racetrack and also the father of Grace Kelly, the actress who became Princess Grace of Monaco. What John didn't know was that I wasn't much of a drinker.

"John," the helpful Haight said to Kelly when we entered the trustee's office below the clubhouse section of the track, "Mike, here, has had a tough time up there rewriting his story because of the disqualification. His stomach is all tensed up. I told him that you could help him out."

"Of course, we can," Mr. Kelly said blandly. "Mike, you've come to the right place."

Mr. Kelly made a phone call. Within a few minutes, a waiter appeared with martinis—in champagne glasses. We each helped ourselves. It sure was a large helping for a martini. I remember carefully putting *Marjorie Morningstar* down on a couch as I picked up the drink.

"Swig it right down," said Haight. "You'll find it's just what the doctor ordered. It'll do the trick."

I sipped it slowly. I barely had placed my empty glass on the coffee table in front of me when the waiter appeared with another martini, again in a stemmed, wide champagne glass. I drank that one too. Somehow, I vaguely remember putting away a third drink. I remembered nothing thereafter.

All of a sudden, I felt somebody shaking me. It was Haight. I had apparently fallen asleep on the couch right in the Trustees' room.

"We gotta get started if you're going to get home tonight," Haight said to me in a paternal way. "Mr. Kelly has asked a chauffeur to drive us to Penn Station in Philadelphia."

"Philadelphia, hell," I said in a sleepy voice. "All I have to do to get home is to take that special race train here at the track back to New York."

"You can't do that," replied Haight. "You really must have been in dreamland. It's already 8:30. That race train left the track two hours ago."

Haight helped me put on my jacket and off we went to a waiting station wagon. Within fifteen minutes, however, Haight had the chauffeur stop the car on the Black Horse Pike, a main highway to Philadelphia.

"You know what?" he told the driver. "I'm thirsty again. No sense rushing. Let's all get into that bar up ahead on the Pike for a quick drink."

I had little to say about the decision. I wasn't fully alert. So in we went. I headed for the telephone booth. As had been the case in Princeton, I wanted to call my office to find out whether my story had come through in good shape.

While I was in the booth, Haight thrust a regular-sized martini at me. I thought he chuckled as he said, "We wouldn't want you to think we forgot you."

I drank it. And as we were leaving the bar, Walter motioned the bartender toward him and said, "I think we better take some insurance along. Do you have an empty pint bottle that you could fill with a little bourbon?"

The bartender did happen to have a small empty bottle. And as we continued writing toward Philadelphia, all three of us took turns at taking a slug. I must have fallen asleep in the rear seat. Somehow, I vaguely recall being in a railroad terminal.

But when I finally came to my senses, I was on an airplane. A stewardess was bending over me with a tray loaded with assorted finger sandwiches. She had shaken me lightly to awaken me. I opened my eyes slowly. I looked at the tray.

"These are all my favorites—egg salad, tuna fish," I mumbled as I began stirring. "I'll have one of each."

With my eyes blinking, I soon noticed I was in the front seat. And as I looked around, I realized I was the only passenger on the plane—a big DC-7B with about 150 empty seats behind me. Up above on the front bulkhead was a TWA logo. And as I looked out of the window, I realized we were airborne.

Suddenly, a horrible thought crossed my mind. Many times, up until then, I had chartered small planes whenever I thought it necessary to reach an assignment, almost always at the expense of the *New York Times*, of course.

In previous years and in the ones that followed, I have flown from points all over the United States—from Twin Falls, Idaho to Sun Valley; from Providence Airport in Rhode Island across Narragansett Bay to Newport; from California's south end of Lake Tahoe to Reno; from Duluth to Cable, Wis.; from Rutland, Vermont, to Lake Placid and, so on.

'Gee," I blurted at one of the stewardesses. "I didn't happen to charter this DC-7B. How did I get here? What am I doing on a plane? I'm supposed to be on a train heading for Penn Station in New York."

"You ARE headed for New York," she replied. "We don't know why or how you were allowed to board this plane. We flew into Philadelphia from San Francisco with a load of passengers. We are now flying deadhead into Kennedy. All any of us know is that we were to pick up a Mr. Strauss before taking off for New York. We should be landing at Kennedy in about thirty minutes."

"Can't you tell me something more?" I pleaded. "You have to know something." Incidentally, I plucked up the courage to ask, "How much do you think it would cost to charter a plane of this size for a flight to Kennedy?"

I recall holding my breath while awaiting an answer.

Neither the young lady nor the pilot, when she asked him, could provide me with even an educated guess as to the cost.

In this state of confusion, I saw the lights in New York City approaching. I conjectured the price for such a charter might be around $6,000 to $8,000. Whatever, it probably was a lot of money for a sportswriter.

I couldn't wait until the plane landed at Kennedy. I was eager to get to a telephone to find out how I had happened to be the lone passenger on this flight. But I shouldn't have been so eager. Because when we reach New York, it was 1:30 A.M. Sunday, much too late to phone anyone.

Besides, I was worried about how I was going to get home. The stewardess took me by the arm, walked right through the terminal and put me in a taxicab.

Somehow, I reached my house, but I don't remember that part of the trip. I don't even remember paying the taxi driver. My younger brother Seymour, in later years, told me that the taxi dropped me off at his home which was near mine, and that he had paid him.

My wife? She wasn't around. She had gone off to spend the night at her mother's in Brooklyn. What I do know is that when I awakened the next morning, I was home, in my own bed.

It was 9:00 A.M. I was anxious to phone Atlantic City to find out whether anyone knew anything about my plane trip. I waited an hour before making a call. It was a Sunday and I didn't want to phone too early.

Then I called Muggins Feldman, the genial soul who did publicity for the Atlantic City track. I told him the story and let him know I was worried about having chartered a big plane out of Philadelphia. Could he shed some light on the subject?

"I don't know a thing," Muggins told me. "Are you sure you were the only passenger on the plane? I'll call around myself. I'll even phone Mr. Kelly. I'll get back to you if I find anything out."

I went back to bed but not to sleep. An hour later, my phone rang. It was Muggins. He had the answers.

"Is that you, Mike?" he asked.

"Yes, all of me," I answered. "What did you find out?"

"You're home safe. It didn't cost you a cent," he said, as I sighed with relief. "You're lucky you know Mr. Kelly. I just spoke to him and he chuckled when I told him about your worry. You didn't charter that plane, you knucklehead. No one did.

"When you and Haight got to Philadelphia last night with the chauffeur," he explained, "both of you had missed your trains by minutes, Walter's to DC, and yours to New York. What did you guys do after you left the racetrack last night, start looking for women?" Muggins joked.

"Anyhow," Feldman explained, "once the chauffeur realized that neither one of you were going to get anywhere on a train, he phoned Mr. Kelly from the Philadelphia railroad terminal. He told the boss that he was making the phone call while holding Haight up against the wall with one hand and you against it with his other shoulder. The chauffeur was told to stand by the phone.

"The boss called back in about twenty minutes," Muggins told me.

"'Take them both to the Philadelphia Airport,' Mr. Kelly told the driver.

"He said that he had learned that American Airlines had a scheduled flight leaving for Washington in an hour. He added that he was still working on a flight for you for New York. There just didn't seem to be one that late on a Saturday night."

Following the instructions he had received, the chauffeur had Haight deposited on that Washington plane. Then he phoned Mr. Kelly again.

"I've contacted a TWA executive who's a friend of mine and he's helping us out," Mr. Kelly told the chauffeur. "There's a TWA plane arriving from the Pacific Coast with a load of passengers. After they get off, the plane is scheduled to return to New York empty.

"My friend at TWA has arranged to have Mike taken aboard for that flight to Kennedy," said Mr. Kelly, according to Muggins.

Muggins said that he knew nothing more, and I never tried to find out anything more. After all, the flight I took may have been in violation of regulations because I never even had purchased a ticket. The next time I saw Mr. Kelly I thanked him. He nearly grinned and said, "Anytime. Forget it."

Did I profit from that experience? You bet I did. It made me determined never to have more than one drink at a time—anywhere at any time.

Oh yes, that book *Marjorie Morningstar*? I never brought it back home. I must have left it behind on that couch in the track's Trustees' office. Maybe I left it on the plane.

I eventually did see the movie *Marjorie Morningstar*, starring Gene Kelly and Natalie Wood. I thoroughly enjoyed it as well as its theme song. But I would have liked to have read the book.

The DC-7B story, it should be noted, accounts for only one and a half times that I hit the bottle too heavily. An assignment, about a decade later—in 1961—rounds out my series of drinking bouts with good old John Barleycorn. And once again, it occurred after I had reported on thoroughbred horse racing, this time at Delaware Park.

Willie Dupont, who always seemed to be wearing a battered felt hat, was the principal stockholder of that well-appointed track. I didn't know him well. But I was well acquainted with his track's general manager, Bryan Field. Bryan had been the *New York Times* race reporter for years, but I hadn't seen him for some time.

Well known for his Oxford English accent, Field, while still working for the *Times*, began broadcasting football games over the radio. Subsequently, while still writing thoroughbred racing for the paper, he had become the announcer at New York State's tracks—Belmont Park, Aqueduct, and Saratoga.

He became so talented at describing thoroughbred races that track operators across America asked for his services for their important races. As a result, Field regularly appeared before the microphone, for television as well as for radio, whenever the Triple Crown races—the Kentucky Derby, the Preakness, and the Belmont—were held.

I was very pleased when I was assigned to the stakes race at Delaware Park because I knew it would give me a chance to see Bryan again. There were no problems in reaching the track, which is in Stanton, just south of Wilmington. But I was to have more than a little trouble leaving it.

After I wrote my story that afternoon, on Field's invitation, I went down to his office to visit him. I was in no hurry. I was checked in at the DuPont Hotel in Wilmington, and the dinner hour was still a few hours away. Sitting with Field in his office, when I arrived, was the track's publicity director and two newspapermen.

On Field's desk were two bottles—fifths of rye and scotch. When I came in, Bryan was speaking on the phone. Everyone in the room had a glass in his hand. And when I entered someone said:

"Help yourself to a shot, Mike. Take your choice. You're way behind us. I've had my second one already."

I poured myself a little "snifter" and joined in the conversation. Field, who was a pretty good drinker when he wanted to be, poured himself a sizable shot when he finished his phone conversation. Noticing that I had finished mine, he favored me with a little more scotch. That was my second drink.

"This will be all I'm having," I told Bryan. "But I don't want to spoil the party."

Party? Within a short time, I was in the office with Field—alone. All three of the other men had departed and as Bryan and I discussed the experiences in which we had both been involved, I kept drinking.

I can remember him finally "closing the bar" and saying, "Mike, suppose we go into the hotel and have some supper? I'm driving that way anyhow."

I remember entering the hotel, being seated at a table, and looking at the menu. I thought I was hungry. I ordered a Porterhouse steak.

But I never got to see it or to eat it. Because moments after the waiter departed, I started feeling ill. I excused myself and said I was heading for the washroom. I don't know how long I was gone. I would say it was a sizable amount of time.

When I returned to the dining room, Field was no longer to be seen. The table that I had been seated at was bare, and I was too embarrassed to ask any questions.

I probably didn't see Bryan again for another year. When I did, I acted as if no such incident ever had taken place. He, on the other hand, was considerate enough not to bring it up. He was a gentleman.

From that time on, I never had more than one drink—absolutely one has been the limit. And in the past few years, I haven't even had one. But I still drink cold milk, lots of it, and described it as the best beverage that was ever invented.[4]

---

[4] Editors' note: One aspect of the drinking culture of sportswriters during this time was that whiskey and other beverages were common presents. Michael never drank at home but built a locked storage room for this cache. However, he forgot about it when he moved out of his house in Oceanside, LI. The new owners had quite a liquid bonanza!

CHAPTER 12

The Boarding Schools –
Andover, Choate . . .

Bryan Field, our racing editor at the *New York Times*, was partial to thoroughbred horse racing, our prolific writer Allison Danzig was devoted to tennis, and our Robert E. Kelly was closely identified with college football and polo. I, of all things, found my heart the lightest and my interest the greatest every autumn when I was assigned to visit the East's leading independent schools—the boarding schools.

What impressed me most about that field of endeavor was not that students received the opportunity for a better education if only because they were put into smaller classes, thereby receiving more personal attention from teachers, but because every one of them was expected to participate in some sport during each of the seasons. This program was carried out diligently.

Even lower formers, weighing eighty and ninety pounds in some cases, would appear after a day's classes togged out in football outfits—pads, helmets, and all—or in shorts or shirts prepared for soccer or cross-country. In winter, it was hockey and basketball; and when spring arrived, it was baseball, track, tennis, and golf.

This all-inclusive program interested me because I had attended public grammar and high school. There, only those capable of making the interscholastic varsity teams were encouraged to engage in sports. Never was sports participation compulsory.

As a boy, I lived on the edge of Highland Park on the Brooklyn–Queens border of New York City. I found myself taking part in a "married men's–single men's" baseball game during the Daylight Savings Time season. This, of course, was years before Little League Baseball was conceived.

Fathers, coming home from their jobs, would happily take part in these impromptu baseball games. At age twelve, I was a full-fledged member of this group. As kids, we tried all the sports—baseball, touch football, and even ice hockey on a nearby pond which seldom froze solidly.

One winter's afternoon, I fell through the "ice." It was near one of our two hastily setup goals created from two sycamore tree branches placed on the ice, and a few feet apart, but parallel to each other. One afternoon, I was about to whisk my stick for a goal when the thin ice gave way. Into the water I dropped along with a teammate.

We clambered out of the water by grabbing a slab of ice. Soaking wet and freezing, I raced in my wet clothes to the nearby Highland Park YMCA, about a mile away.

"What happened to you?" the YMCA desk clerk asked me as I ran into the building. "You look as if you're ready for pneumonia."

"I fell through the ice," I answered. "I'd like to put my clothes in the boiler room to dry while I go swimming in the pool."

"Go right ahead," he said. "It looks like you know your way around here."

I never told my mother about my icy plunge, and she never found out because when I return to my home late that afternoon, thanks to the boiler room, my clothes were bone dry. My friend Harry, who fell into the pond with me, went directly home. He wound up with the grippe.

Years later, when I was twenty, I visited a boarding school campus for the first time. I was sent to cover a Choate School–Deerfield Academy football game at Wallingford, Connecticut.

Boarding schools, in those early years held a certain attraction for me. I knew, for example, that President John F. Kennedy and Adlai Stevenson were members of Choate's alumni. Franklin D. Roosevelt had attended Groton School in Massachusetts. The alumni lists of these boarding schools were loaded with distinguished personalities.

On that first day on the Choate campus, which is about twenty miles north of New Haven, I was greeted by the personable Cappy Leinbach, who was the head of the school's Press Club.

"We're delighted you came," he said to me. I later heard him repeat the identical words when Caswell Adams, the well-known boxing writer for the *New York Tribune*, subsequently appeared. Cas, being older, was a well-known figure on prep school campuses.

The game resulted in a scoreless tie, John Lehman, the son of the then Governor of New York, starring for Deerfield. When the contest was finished, Cass and I went to the Western Union office in town and wrote our stories then handed them to the telegrapher.

"Are you hungry?" Adams asked, as we left the telegraph office and began taking the short walk to the New Haven and Hartford Railroad station.

"I sure am," I replied.

"Would you rather have dinner in town here or on the train? The one we're boarding has a dining car."

"The train's for me," I answered immediately. "Actually, I've never eaten in a dining car," I replied. "I think I'd enjoy that."

Eating on the white tableclothed table and looking out of the window while the train swept past such stations in Connecticut as Bridgeport, Darien, Stamford, and Greenwich, was an experience I never forgot. I even remember my main course if only because I'd never heard of it before. It was lamb steak.

To round that weekend out, I received my first byline on that Choate–Deerfield game, thereby becoming one of the youngest writers ever to have had a signed story in the long history of the *New York Times*.

But it wasn't until a decade or so later, in the 1940s, that I started making the rounds of the boarding schools on a regular basis. Each fall, I would visit about thirty-five of them starting with St. Paul's School in Concord, New Hampshire, and winding up the tour with a visit to Mercersburg Academy in Pennsylvania. On Saturdays, I would report on college football games.

Apart from sports, there were many aspects of prep school life that I found intriguing. The small classes, which I sat in on from time to time, seemed made to order for boys hoping to reach their maximum academic potential.

The rapport between masters and students revealed mutual interest and concern. Almost all masters served as coaches. Those less qualified in sports than others assisted with the lower-level teams.

In the dining halls, I enjoyed watching students take turns waiting on tables. Many of these "waiters" came from some of America's best-known families—Dupont, Rockefeller, Warburg, Ford, Phipps, and Roosevelt, among many others.

From time to time, I would enjoy lunch or dinner at the school's dining halls, sitting at a table that had about ten students with a master in the head seat. What always surprised me was how quickly the students finished their meals.

"The students eat so quickly," I once said to John Boyden, the pleasant-mannered aide to his father Frank Boyden, the founder and headmaster of

Deerfield Academy. "I barely am able to remove the napkin from its napkin ring when the ten boys at the table are finished with their first course."

John smiled. "I don't know the reason for all the speed. Maybe youngsters eat faster than adults. I have trouble keeping up with them myself."

And I could make that observation from experience because in the fifteen years or so that I kept visiting these campuses, I probably set some kind of record for the number of boarding schools at which I broke bread.

Just from the top of my head, I can remember eating at Exeter, Andover, Kent, Saint George's, Governor Dummer, Williston, Vermont Academy, Winchendon, Mount Harmon, the Suffield School, Cheshire, Portsmouth Priory, Taft, St. Mark's, and Choate, all of which are in New England.

In New Jersey, I enjoyed dining with the students at the Peddie School, Blair Academy, and Bordentown Military Institute and while in Pennsylvania, Mercersburg Academy, and the Hill School favored with dining room invitations. There were probably some more.

I would keep visiting prep schools to do feature columns, usually on their varsity football teams or on any other phase of their sports programs I thought would make for an interesting story.

Upon reaching a campus, my first question to whomever the official greeter happened to be was: "What's new?"

Unless a new field house was being completed, a new football coach had been appointed, or a modern gymnasium was being erected, the answer was usually the same.

"Nothing's really new."

But there usually was something new or at least something that was newsworthy.

When I first began appearing at the schools, the faculty member attached to me, on occasion, made a request.

"We'd appreciate it if you would not focus on a student in your article just because he comes from a prominent or wealthy family."

I never did single out an athlete because of his family connection except in one instance. In that one exception, I had no choice.

It occurred during my first visit to the Westminster School in the quiet community of Simsbury, Connecticut. When it's varsity football team's practice was concluded, I met with Mike Micholini, the head coach. I told him I would like the name and positions of his probable starting lineup for his team's next game.

"Be happy to give it to you," he said. "But there's one thing I'd like to ask. Gene Tunney's son holds down one of the positions on our line. I'd appreciate it if you didn't identify him with his father."

"What's his name?" I asked.

"It's Gene Tunney, Junior," the coach replied.

I, of course, included young Tunney's full name in the probable lineup, knowing that just about everyone who read my story would know that he was the son of the famous world heavyweight boxing champion. However, I made no mention of his father.

In all my travels on the private school route, one of the most memorable personalities I ever met was Frank Boyden of Deerfield Academy in Massachusetts. Here was a headmaster who personally drove me around his school's far fields in his horse and buggy. We would watch the academy students going through practice sessions in football, soccer, and cross-country as the wagon rolled over the school's expansive greensward.

"See," he said to me the first day I met him, "now that classes are finished for the day, all of these students are out there doing what they like to do best—racing and chasing."

After visiting that campus several times each fall, I thought that here was one headmaster, aging as he was, who might make a superb subject for an American version of a "Goodbye, Mr. Chips" Hollywood movie. I suggested this idea to his son John.

"He just wouldn't be interested," John told me. "When it comes to major publicity about himself, he's on the shy side."

Anyhow, the Frank Boyden saga began early in the first decade of the twentieth century. This legendary schoolmaster, a graduate of Amherst College, decided that he would like to resurrect an academy, which originally had been founded in 1797, in the old Massachusetts village of Deerfield.

He arrived on the scene with his wife in 1902. Immediately upon taking over his new project, Boyden decided when spring arrived, that he would like to have his school represented by a baseball team. There was one hitch, there were only eight students enrolled in his school that first year. He was one player short.

I recall one afternoon, in particular, making the rounds of the playing fields in his buggy. It was in the same carriage and with the same bay gelding that he had lent to the Republican Party for Eisenhower's ride to the Convention Hall in Philadelphia to accept the presidential nomination in 1952. It was then that he told me his early baseball story.

"I decided I would ask the headmasters of our potential opponents in baseball way back then, whether it would be all right for me to become our school's ninth player."

When they agreed and gave him their blessings, he began wondering what position he would play. And although, he was short in stature, he chose first base. That position usually is occupied by one of the tallest members of a team.

Boyden never mentioned his academy's won-and-lost record during those early seasons and I never asked. It was for a good reason. Repeatedly, as he gave his opening semester talks to incoming freshman, I had heard him tell the "new boys,"

"We have a fine all-around sports program here. All of you will be taking part in it. You must remember, though, that the sport is the thing and not necessarily how many games are won and lost."

I often thought of that statement as I kept visiting the boarding school campuses because there was one stretch in which Deerfield's varsity football squads, under the coaching of Bobby Mar, triumphed in thirty-five consecutive games to be unbeaten for five seasons.

One of my most enjoyable schoolboy experiences occurred one afternoon in Exeter, New Hampshire. I was there to cover the traditional Andover–Exeter football game in the continuation of a series that began in 1878.

While seated in the small open press box on the Exeter side of its Plimpton Stadium, I heard a continuous clattering of a typewriter above me in the cement stands. What was causing it?

Members of Exeter's school newspaper were busy putting together a one-page paper focusing on that afternoon's play-by-play football contest. It was to be circulated right after the game—before Andover's students had departed on buses for their own campus.

"We'll have no trouble getting this paper out on time," one student who seemed to be overseeing the project told me. "We'll be able to distribute it less than thirty minutes after the game is completed."

It sounded like a highly ambitious undertaking to me for a school's newspaper staff. Its modus operandi, as it developed, did away with all frills and excesses in publishing a newspaper.

As the game progressed, these student newsmen who were sitting in the stadium's top row, typed without stopping. After one of them had written three or four paragraphs of play-by-play, the copy was placed in an empty cigar box.

Then the box would be lowered down the back of the stadium with the aid of a clothesline rope to students waiting below, on the ground. The recipient would mount his bicycle and rush the few paragraphs to the town's printshop about three blocks away.

"We have four boys below waiting with their bicycles," one of the editors on top of the stands explained. "When one of them leaves for the printshop, another takes his place. By the time our fourth bicyclist has taken off, the first and maybe the second are back on line waiting for another trip to the printer."

The scheme worked perfectly. Andover's students, sitting in their buses after participating in a brief campus reception, received a copy of the one-page paper just as they were about to leave.

When I received my copy of the "Exonian" extra, I thought it would make an interesting subject for my prep school column which appeared in the *Times* on Monday mornings.

I snapped a picture of that front page with my camera and headed for Bill Cox, the academy's secretary, to seek some advice about the possibility of getting the film to New York in time for our Monday morning edition.

"Bill," I said, "I've already sent my story of this game to my paper via Western Union. But I am also doing a Monday morning column on the way your Exonian student editors put out this one-page extra this afternoon. I have a roll of film here with a picture I took of the *Exonian*'s front page. How can I get it delivered to New York by tonight or early Sunday?"

"That's easy," Cox replied. "I know our stationmaster here on the Boston & Maine. He's done favors for me before. Not only will he get it to New York, but he'll also arrange to have it delivered to the *New York Times*."

However, there was one minor problem: that night's train from Portland didn't stop at Exeter. And so I asked the stationmaster whether the envelope containing the film plus a $5-bill could be placed on the station's flycatcher to be picked up while the train was speeding past the station.

"Don't see why not," he answered. "Just put down the name and address to whom it has to be delivered. He'll do the rest. After all, your paper is only a few blocks from Grand Central Station where this train ends its run."

Did it work out okay? A Secret Service courier couldn't have done it any better. That Monday morning's *New York Times* spoke for itself. The column and picture of the "Exonian Extra," as I had hoped, was there on top of a page. I received at least ten letters from alumni of both schools commending me for that bit of extra effort.

When I began visiting private schools on a regular basis in the 1940s, I soon discovered that ice hockey was an "iffy" sport even on such upper New England campuses as Vermont Academy and at Mount Hermon School in Northern Massachusetts. Staging games on ice in those days depended entirely on subfreezing weather since there were no artificial rinks at any of the schools.

Most gymnasiums, say at Andover, Exeter, Williston Academy, and the Suffield School, were bandbox in size. Such gyms were too small to accommodate entire sports-oriented student bodies when the weather outdoors was inclement. When there was a thaw, the hockey players were brought indoors to add to the crowded gymnasium scene.

Hockey coaches, in many cases, found space somehow, to have their players engage in "gill ball" practice sessions—a hard floor version of the puck-chasing sport. It was hardly satisfactory because skating is such an important part of hockey.

"Trying to fill all the dates in an ice hockey schedule without the availability of an artificial rink," Ted Harrison, coach of the varsity team at Andover, told me one day, "is like trying to take down big game with a water pistol. It's almost impossible."

A few years earlier, the Taft School of Watertown, Connecticut, had become the envy of boarding school hockey coaches across America. It was the first campus to have an artificial rink installed, but without a roof and on black hardtop.

The creation of an artificial rink without a roof proved to be a huge mistake because the school's artificially made surfaces kept melting as the sun beat down. The blacktop? As might be expected, its color, absorbing Old Sol as it did, helped in the thawing process.

One winter day, I arrived at Choate in mid-January. I asked friendly Bill Pudvah, the athletic director and hockey enthusiast and coach, how his skaters were doing.

"Terribly," Pudvah answered in a discouraged tone. "We've played only one game this season and we've had to cancel six. This has been a warm winter in Connecticut. My players are bored. Just look at our rink out there behind the baseball diamond. It's a small pond."

"What's the chance of having an artificial one built here at Choate?" I asked.

"Nil" was his taciturn reply. "The rink we need would cost about $100,000. And we have nothing even resembling that figure in our budget."

I thought for a few moments. I asked him whether he had any ideas on how to cope with the problem. Finally, we both arrived at a decision as we were standing in the school's field house. Lying in a corner was a canoe.

"Let's take that canoe out and put it on the rink," I suggested, "Then, let's get two of your players out in full uniform. We'll have them sit in the canoe while paddling along with their hockey sticks. It'll make a great photograph."

Pudvah was more than equal to the occasion. He had that entire scenario set up in about twenty minutes. I photographed the shot asking the players to paddle vigorously.

The picture appeared along with my prep school column in the *New York Times* on the following Monday. My column stressed the uselessness of natural hockey rinks on southern New England campuses. The caption read: "Choate's hockey players in a practice session on their rink." The photograph produced lots of laughs. But more important, it produced lots of cash.

Within a short time, alumni, in sympathy with the problem, began sending in donations for an artificial rink. Choate, thereupon, became the second boarding school in America, to boast this kind of luxury for its hockey players.

This Choate success, it seems, triggered similar responses from graduates of other private schools as well as support from their respective Boards of Trustees. Within six or seven years, students at such top boarding schools as Kent, Williston, Lawrenceville, Andover, Exeter, and the Hill School were enjoying such installations.

The newer ones, it should be noted, all were built with roofs or at least with facilities for overhead screens—and never on blacktop.

The mention of the Hill School recalls another of the "Headmaster personals" that surfaced during my lengthy tours. It was told to me by Ned Hall, just after he became the chief administrator at the Pottstown school. Remember Hall? He's the man who offered the great basketball playing Jabbar a scholarship, which the latter's father turned down.

"Hockey has always been my favorite sport," he told me one afternoon while he was squaring me around the school's busy practice fields. "I played on the varsity at the St. Mark's School in the so-called cold country of Massachusetts. But we had the same problem about natural ice that the other schools had. Thawing weather would repeatedly turn our rinks into a lagoon."

Since Hall was clean and trim even as the Hill School's headmaster, I said to him.

"You must have been a fast skater. Were you a forward, a wing?"

"It may come as a surprise," he replied with a grin, "but I was a goalie. I didn't have to be a fast skater."

"Talk about weather ruining drinks?" he continued. "There was one game in which all of the players in one of our interscholastic games at St. Mark's were skating on thin ice that was almost waferlike in quality. After the game's start, the sun came out and the temperature began soaring.

"As the game was nearing its end, I found myself crouching in front of our goal on a small, thin cake of ice with water almost up to my ankles. Minutes later, I found myself floating away from the goal that I was supposed to be guarding."

"That's a likely story," I answered. "You're kidding, it sounds like a Baron Munchausen take."

I just didn't believe him. I should have because when we returned to his office, he produced a photograph of the exact scene he had described—Ned Hall in a striped sleeved jersey and pads with hockey stick in hand, on a thin sliver of ice with water above his skates.

It was obvious from the picture that he actually had floated away from his cage. It was too good a picture story to pass up. Hall agreed to lend me the photograph. It appeared with my prep school column the following Monday.

In that story, I included the fact that the new the Hill School headmaster was determined to have an artificial rink at his school in the near future.

I didn't believe him because hockey never had been played at the Hill. I jokingly pointed out that Pennsylvania was virtually in the cotton belt. Hall proved he was no idle booster. The prestigious hilltop school did house an artificial rink within a short time, in the early 1950s. And, of course, with it, it also had a hockey team.

Stories about sporting life at private schools abound in my memory There was that fishing club at Governor Dummer Academy in South Byfield, Massachusetts, that had a small aquatic spread on it in which trout were plentiful.

A reason for that abundance was that club members, under the guidance of its faculty advisor, Edgar Dunning, used barbless hooks and kept returning the brookies to their private pond. As a result, their stock was never depleted. In fact, it kept growing.

I was on hand at the Choate School when its football mascot, an otter, on an inexplicable rampage, went berserk. This, after I had been told a few weeks earlier by Pudvah that the same otter was as tame as "a two-week-old pussycat."

However, the little beast, kept in a small shack, did get loose and just about destroyed everything around him. He was barred from the campus for life.

I was once the victim of a huge snowstorm in early October that began making its presence known while I was reporting on a football game played at the Kent School, which is near the western banks of the Housatonic River. By the time I had filed my story by telegraph in the Kent railroad station, the surroundings had taken on a distinct Christmas-card appearance. About four inches of snow already covered the ground.

To compound the problem, the day's last train from that small community of Kent had left for New York a few hours earlier. Aware of the railroad's schedule in advance, I had planned to take a taxi from Kent to Pawling, New York, a trip of about twenty miles, once my story was completed.

"I don't know whether our taxi driver will be willing to take you to Pawling," the stationmaster who also had doubled as my telegrapher, advised. "There are a lot of hills between here and there, and the road is going to be pretty slick. But I'll call him."

"It's rough out there," the cabby agreed once he arrived. "Sure you don't want to spend the night in one of our inns? I've never made that trip to Pawling with this much snow on the ground."

When I told him I would add a $10 bill as a bonus to the regular fifteen-dollar fare, he suddenly became eager and ready to go. And despite the slippery roads, we got to our destination just in time to make that night's last train to New York.

It was at Groton, one of New England's older schools that is operated somewhat along British traditional lines, that I was introduced to a new, for me, sport. It's the game of "Fives." During one of my early visits to this campus, I was taken to the basement of one of the buildings. There I found two students vigorously engaged in a handball match.

"It's an English game," I was told as I sized up what seemed to be a reduced four-wall handball court. The students were using padded gloves and whacking away at what seemed a "dead" ball, one that had little bounce to it. In a way it resembled squash, except that no rackets were being used.

"There's only one other court like this in the United States," advised my faculty escort. "The other one is in downstate Massachusetts at the St. Mark's School. We play against each other every year."

A few weeks later when students of both schools clashed in their annual match, I made the sport take on a little added importance in the *New York Times*, at least for a day. I described that match as being for the American championship. I thought it a justifiable statement. After all, teams from these two schools were the only ones participating in the sport on these shores.

Even after I stopped visiting the prep schools, I tried to keep abreast of some of the goings-on at the different campuses. My two children, both daughters, as sub-teenagers, had accompanied me, from time to time, on some of these trips. Among the schools they visited with me were the Hill, Lawrenceville, Mercersburg, Andover, Exeter, Williston, Pomfret, Blair

Academy, St. George's, Peddie, Hotchkiss, and the Northwood School in scenic Lake Placid. Did it make an impression on them?

Did it make an impression? It must have. I have four grandchildren. One of them attended the Rectory School, a grammar school, in Pomfret, Connecticut, and then went on to prep at Avon Old Farms. My other grandson was a student at Groton and finished up at Brunswick before matriculating on early admission to Princeton.

To round it all out, one of my granddaughters attended Choate–Rosemary Hall while the other attended National Cathedral, a fine private school in Washington DC. The two girls matriculated at Cornell and Princeton, respectively. The Princetonian young lady has just been admitted to Yale Medical, also on early admission.

Through the years, I continuously meet people who have attended some of these private schools. Our conversations always bring up fond memories. I spoke to one former student just the other day who had attended St. George's School in Middletown, Rhode Island. He had been a catcher on its baseball team probably during Coolidge's administration.

"When we played against Middlesex in Massachusetts, we'd sail on the Fall River Line to Boston and then take the train to Concord," he told me. "It was always a glorious trip."

"I knew about those sea voyages," I replied. "I was told about them by Headmaster Buell when I used to visit St. George's by the sea. That kind of journey, though, was a lark compared to some of the trips boarding school students and coaches sometimes faced in the World War I era.

"At many schools, the traveling was done by horse and wagon. In some cases, a thirty- or forty-mile round-trip was involved—a journey that included dinner and an overnight stay at the host school."

"Just think," I concluded, "today's leading prep schools have artificial ice rinks, large gymnasiums, tennis court complexes, and even school buses for interscholastic travel."

But the students? They're still enjoying their athletic programs just the way they did back in the pre-World War II days, when only bandbox gymnasiums with narrow running tracks hitched onto the sides of their upper walls provided the outlets for their youthful vigor.[5]

---

5 Editors' comment: Peter Boer attended the Nichols School in Buffalo, NY from 1951 through 1957. Although Michael Strauss never visited Nichols, much of the color in this chapter rings true. Nichols termed its grades "forms," and athletic participation was compulsory. Many faculty members doubled as coaches. By that time, Nichols had an ice rink and participated in an annual private school hockey tournament at Lawrenceville Academy. Ice rinks were still rare, and Peter first learned hockey on local ponds, especially the water hole on the South Park golf

CHAPTER 13

Clues to the News

Where did you get it, the editor, asked
The story you have in your hand?
I got it by asking questions, old boy
In a manner you won't understand.

There's no telling when and where a compelling story is likely to surface. I can recall some that I came upon merely by chance at unlikely places. A few questions asked, and I was on my way.

My favorite baseball story was triggered at a Long Island gasoline station. Then there was that taxi driver in Montreal who began telling me about a ninety-five-year-old skier who lived in the nearby Laurentian Mountains. Last but not least was an unbelievable tale about a runaway, full-grown diesel railroad engine that I heard about while standing on a line in a supermarket in Rutland, Vermont.

The baseball story surfaced in 1975 while I was having my car greased and oiled by my friend Frank Ferraro in Rockville Center on Long Island. We had been talking about the horse races at Aqueduct when he suddenly piped up.

"Say, Mike, did you ever hear of Steve Garvey?"

course. Thin ice could be a serious worry. The old Nichols school gymnasium had an indoor track right above the basketball court. Long shots from the corner were blocked by this structure, much to the disadvantage of some visiting teams.

———

"Are you kidding?" I answered. "Anyone who knows a baseball from a goal post has heard about Steve Garvey. He's the star first baseman of the Los Angeles Dodgers.

"Why do you keep asking me such silly questions?" I continued. "The last time I came into your station you asked me if I knew one of your customers, Mike Venezia, the jockey? Of course I know him. He's living right here in Rockville Center. I've even been to his house."

"But Garvey, Steve Garvey?" Ferraro persisted. "Do you know about him? His early story—back when he was a kid?"

I shrugged. I was not too interested. After all, there are lots of big leaguers. Few had had fascinating aspects that merited dipping into their pasts.

"This Garvey story," Ferraro persisted, "is worth hearing about. You just mentioned Mike Venezia, horse racing and betting odds. The Garvey story represents a success in big-league baseball that was a longer shot than was ever paid off at a racetrack. His story is just about a million-to-one shot come true."

Suddenly, I found myself listening carefully. A million-to-one shot?

"Steve Garvey is my brother's nephew through marriage," Ferraro explained, now obviously relieved because he sensed he had finally caught my attention. "I know the story in bits and pieces. Why don't you phone my brother Tiger—that is Mike—and get the details."

My interest in Steven Patrick Garvey had mushroomed. Through the many years I had known Frank, we had discussed lots of sports personalities. But he never had badgered me so much as he did about Garvey. When I reached my office, therefore, I found his brother, who had been an equipment manager for the New York Jets football team. Everyone called him "Tiger."

I had known something about Garvey's past. He had been a baseball and football star at Michigan State. And that, in his first season as a regular with the Los Angeles Dodgers, he had been named the National League Most Valuable Player. It was a highly unusual achievement for a first-year, full-time player.

Tiger, just as in the case of his brother Frank, however, wanted me to get all the details accurately. He said that he preferred having me speak to his talented nephew and gave me Garvey's unlisted phone number in California.

"He's a great guy," Tiger told me. "He'll be glad to talk to you. This is one fellow who has kept his head on his shoulders."

I made the phone call only to receive a monitored message.

"Good day," I heard. "I am terribly sorry that Cyndy and I are not at home now to speak to you. But I assure you that we will return the call as soon as we get back to our house. Please leave your phone number and name at the sound of the beep."

I did. Then I waited for at least a week to hear from the player. After eight days, I phoned Tiger at his Long Island home.

"I thought you told me that Steve was a regular guy, that he'd return all calls made to his private line. I phoned a week ago and still haven't heard from him."

Tiger? He was puzzled. But he still was amazingly firm in his stand that Garvey would get back to me. "Something must have detained him elsewhere," he maintained.

As it developed, something had. The Dodger star finally called me collect about nine days after I had tried to reach him.

"I'm really sorry for the delay," he said to me. "I know you phoned more than a week ago. But Cyndy and I were detained out of town. We both went to Tampa for a big class reunion. And in heading west, we stopped off at Michigan State unexpectedly. We stayed there for a few days."

Now anyone but a considerate Steve Garvey, I felt, would not have taken the trouble to do all that explaining. During the time I had been waiting for his return call, I had done some research. Steve, it seems, was considered by the not-too-easy-to-impress media, as a super human being—a gentleman, a do-gooder of the highest order. I spoke to him for about forty minutes on that phone call and obtained all the added information I needed.

The prelude to the unbelievable phase of the tale, I later wrote for a magazine, began with Steve Garvey's grandfather. Grandpa Garvey, who had been a sergeant in the Rockville Center Police Department, once had been an ardent Dodgers fan when that team represented Brooklyn rather than Los Angeles.

Through the years, his fervor for the team was such that he would manage to get to Ebbets Field a few times a week to see his Brooklyn team play.

The police sergeant's enthusiasm for the Dodgers stubbornly remained high even though he had sat through many seasons in which his "Daffy" Dodgers, as they were referred to by some, finished well down in the standings.

Woe was the lot of any policeman, however, on that village's force, who justifiably ridiculed the play of the Brooklyn team. Such an unhappy soul was certain to be assigned to the lobster shift—the midnight to 8:00 A.M. patrol.

Grandpa Garvey encouraged his son to retain the family loyalty for the Dodgers. The son, Steve Garvey's father, who developed into a semi-pro baseball player himself, was making his living driving Greyhound buses based in the metropolitan New York area. Eventually, he moved his family to Florida—to Tampa—where he continued to drive for the giant bus company. That move set the stage for the million-to-one dream realized by his own son Steve.

After a few years as a Floridian, Steve's father was assigned to drive the charter bus that carried the Brooklyn Dodgers to their different exhibition games during the spring training season.

One day, Steve's father asked Chuck Dressen, the Brooklyn team manager at that time, whether it would be "okay" if he brought his seven-year-old son with him on a few of the team's trips.

"He's a real big baseball fan," the father told Dressen, "and he loves the Dodgers. I know he'll cause no problems because he's extremely well-behaved."

Dressen readily granted permission. Before long, the team's players began considering Steve as a member of their club. Indeed, he eventually was made the bat boy.

"More than once, in the early years, just to break the monotony, Gil Hodges, the team's star first baseman, would entertain his teammates with a short skit as their bus rumbled over Florida's flat highways. He would prop young Steve on his knee.

"What do you want to be when you grow up, Stevie?" Hodges would ask the small-framed lad.

"I'd like to be a big-league baseball player," would be the answer.

"What team would you like to play for?" Hodges would continue.

"Why the Dodgers, of course," young Steve would reply.

"Now the position?" Hodges would ask. "Where would you like to play?"

Because Hodges, who played first base, was his idol, Steve would give the expected reply. "First base, just like you do."

The curtain for this little routine then would come down as Hodges released the boy from his knee. The other players, almost to a man, would chuckle. A kid with that kind of ambition? Such a hope? It had the makings of a fairy tale.

Thousands upon thousands of youngsters, of course, throughout the years, whether in big cities or country villages, have nursed the ambition of someday becoming a big-league baseball player. But to reach that goal while also naming the team and position they'd like to play and having all three materialize? That indeed was an impossible dream.

But the dream proceeded to become a reality. Young Garvey starred as a three-letter athlete at his high school. Matriculating at Michigan

State University, he turned out to be a standout performer in football and baseball.

At this early stage, however, there was only one inconsistency in this entire scenario. Garvey, at college, played third base instead of first. He was kept at third even though in football, he had injured his right arm, his throwing arm.

Even before he was graduated, the young Floridian decided to try and make baseball his career. He moved into the minor league ranks playing with such Dodger farm system teams as Ogden, Albuquerque, and Spokane. He finally was moved up to the major league Dodgers, who had moved their franchise from Brooklyn to Los Angeles in 1957. He was brought to Los Angeles as a reserve third baseman.

But Walt Alston, the manager of the team, became convinced that Garvey was no big leaguer at that position. His throwing arm wasn't strong enough. One day during pre-game infield practice, Steve had made a couple of wild throws toward first base. Upon seeing those errant tosses, Alston was reputed to have said in the dugout:

"We'd better get that kid out of there before he hurts someone."

The young player proceeded to give his manager a bit of a problem because, as a rookie, he showed lots of promise as a batter. Besides, he displayed a great attitude. He was willing to play at any position. After all, he WAS in the major leagues.

"We'll have to try him from time to time at first base," the manager finally told his aides early in 1972 after Steve had done part-time duty playing third and second base for two seasons. "He won't have to do much throwing from there. Let's hope that he eventually fits into that position."

For three seasons, starting in 1971, Garvey was a baseball player on the move, occupying positions at third as well as second and first base. In 1973, he even was tried in the outfield.

It wasn't until 1974, however, that Steve, at age twenty-six, clinched the first base job on a full-time basis. In that season he batted a career-high—high up until then—of an impressive .312. That year, he also clouted twenty-one home runs.

To make Garvey's long shot story seem more remarkable was that he didn't have the usual physical proportions for that position. Managers understandably have a stereotype notion about first baseman. They prefer them lanky and long-armed so that they can catch throws from their teammates that may be too high or too wide.

First basemen are also most desirable if they are southpaws. Left-handers, it is an established fact, can initiate double plays with more facility than right handers. Garvey? He was a right-hander and while officially listed as only 5 feet, 10 in tall, seemed at least an inch shorter.

Indeed, in his early years at first base, he was seeing helping himself attain more height, when possible, by standing on the edge of the base itself while taking throws from his teammates. Nevertheless, he proved outstanding at that position and seemed able to start a double play just as easily as a lean, tall, left-handed first baseman.

Garvey became considered by Allston as a valuable baseball property in 1973. During that season, being used mostly as a pinch-hitter, he hit safely ten times in twenty-four times at the plate. His performance at that gave him a sparkling batting average of .304.

"We can't keep a hitter like that on the bench collecting splinters," Alston finally had said. "We have to get him out on that field playing full time. We're going to put him on first base—to stay."

And so the last phase of a three-part fairy tale, uttered by a kid two decades earlier in light conversation, had come to pass. For those who knew the whole story, they put the Garvey story in the same category as a miracle: a seven-year-old who had dreamed of someday playing in the big leagues, with the Dodgers, and at first base, no less.

Once permanently installed at the position held earlier by his old idol, Gil Hodges, Garvey proceeded to have an outstanding year. He finished the 1974 campaign with a scintillating .312 batting average as a result of 200 hits. Then he batted an outstanding .389 against the Pittsburgh Pirates in helping his team capture the National League pennant playoffs.

The transplanted Floridian, then proceeded to cap it all. In the World Series that followed, he again was superb at the plate batting safely eight times against the Oakland Athletics in what proved a losing cause. However, Garvey's total hits in that championship series surpassed the number of any other player in that post-season get-together.

With Garvey's success as a ball player, other praiseworthy aspects about him began to surface. It developed that he was an amateur do-gooder, one who went to all lengths to help, whether it was to visit bedridden fans whose morale could be lifted by a major league player's visit or perhaps slowing down as he walked along at a downtown crosstown street to help an old lady get across.

To boot, his deportment on the field was of a such a high level that some of California's sportswriters, some often considered cynical, kept referring to the new Dodger's first baseman as "Mr. Clean" and "The All-American Boy." Typical were some observations at the time, by Bill Shirley, the highly knowledgeable sports editor of the *Los Angeles Times*.

"Hollywood would never buy the Steve Garvey story," he wrote. "Madison Avenue would run up its flagpole and say: 'Nobody ever will believe it.' Steve always is on time for practice, for the club's bus and for its plane. He never kicks the water bucket in anger the way some other players do nor does he throw his bat. What kind of story could Hollywood make out of that?"

My only reaction to Garvey's impeccable behavior after watching him in action one day at Shea Stadium? I subsequently, jokingly mentioned it in a magazine article:

"This guy has so much humility—and is so courteous on the field—that it wouldn't surprise me if someday after striking out, he would stroll out to the mound—not to complain, mind you, but to thank the opposing pitcher for having taken the trouble to pitch to him."

Garvey, after a distinguished career, was traded to the San Diego Padres where he continued to excel as a first baseman. Perhaps this transplantation had something to do with it. For suddenly, the whole Garvey image seemed to change—go awry.

I last spoke to him at a benefit celebrity tennis tournament of Florida's Palm Beach Polo and Country Club. He was his usual handsome self and in good spirits. We talked briefly. Shortly thereafter, however, word surfaced that Garvey and his wife Cyndy were parting. That was followed later by news of a paternity suit in which Steve was charged with being the father. It provided a disillusioning climax to what had been a happy Mother Goose story.

I once covered a yacht racing story in which one of the sailboats was named "Never Tu Yung Tu." That yacht's name came to mind one afternoon in Montreal while I was in a taxi taking me from the airport to my downtown hotel. En route, I was clued into a story by the driver, which by contrast, might well have been titled "Never Too Old To."

The driver and I were talking winter sports because he had just placed a pair of my skis atop his taxi, in its racks. The skis had been made by the Head Ski Company and his ears picked up. Why? Because I happen to mention that I had been in Colorado a short time earlier with Howard Head, the president of that famous ski corporation.

"Have you been skiing long?" he asked me in his French-Canadian provincial accent, once we were underway. "Those are good looking skis. Metal ones, no?"

"Metal ones, yes," I replied. "I've been into the sport for about fifteen years but my technique has never improved much. I'm on my way to Ste. Agathe and Mont Tremblant to write some stories."

"Ha!" was his reply. "You'll improve. Don't give up yet. You're still young for a skier. We have a fellow in our Laurentian Mountains, near where you are going, who is still skiing every day at the age of ninety-four. Apparently, he has no idea of stopping. His picture, it was in the paper just the other day."

I proceeded to find out where this old-timer lived, and I went up to speak to him. His story was a highly captivating one. It was so interesting that I wrote a column about him in the *New York Times* and also for the "Fitness for Living" magazine. It was that magazine's lead article in November of 1970. It was titled "The Living Legend of the Laurentians." His name was Herman (Jack Rabbit) Smith-Johannsen.

Jack Rabbit, it developed, had been a well-known figure in cross-country skiing, as an instructor at Lake Placid among other resorts back in the World War 1 era. Now, he was living in a log cabin in the Laurentian Mountains' community of Piedmont, about forty miles north of Montreal.

Despite his age, Johannsen was a genuine outdoorsman. His home was deep in a forest, near a wooded road. Maples, oaks, and evergreens enveloped his modest little building as if they have been placed there to protect the log structure.

"I'd like to do a story about you for the *New York Times*," I said to him after being invited to come into his tiny living room in which were cluttered books, newspapers, rustic types of furniture, and hooked rag rugs. "Do you mind?"

"Not in the least" was his answer. "I think such an article might make more people try the sport. But remember, I'm a cross-country man. I don't go for ski lifts that do all of the climbing for skiers. After all, how can people really enjoy nature, drink in the terrain, if they ski on slopes that have been carved by ski developers? Cross-country skiing, through the woods and over fields, lets you see nature as it was and still is."

During that short speech, I looked Jack Rabbit over carefully. He was tall and trim—no waistline. The only genuine sign of his age was a gnarled, lined face which I later found out broke into a half-toothy smile in response to remarks that amused him. He wore knickers, gray wool stockings, and a woolen sweater with designs on it.

Here was no doddering, timid, outdoor-minded old-timer forlornly trying to cling to an adventure-packed past, which I soon found out had begun in his native Norway. He was amazingly energetic. It developed that he had spent a good part of his life out in the forests with Canada's Cree and Ojibwa Indians.

"Is it too cold for you?" he asked. In answer to my questions, he had begun dipping into his past. But he took time out to head for his fireplace to pick up a heavy log. "I like the cold. I'm wearing a heavy Norwegian sweater. That is what really keeps me warm."

"Let me help you with that log," I said to him, keeping in mind his age.

"Help me?" he answered with a sort of a snort. "What's wrong with me?" Then he bent down and lifted the heavy log and placed it atop the fire with the care and ease of a parent placing an infant baby in a crib.

"That should make you feel more comfortable," he said, as he returned to his little wooden bench. "Would you like some tea? Would you prefer lemon or milk?"

It was while he was sipping the hot beverage from a mug that he really began talking of his earlier days.

"I've preferred the back country ever since I came to North America in 1894," he said. "I, like many Norwegian kids, learn to ski shortly after I learned to walk. I served in the Norwegian army and then went to college—to the University of Berlin—where I got a degree in engineering. Then came my trip to America. Suddenly, I found myself in Cleveland, Ohio, selling logging machinery."

Jack Rabbit said it didn't take him long to decide city life wasn't for him. Someone offered him a job as a salesman for heavy machinery in Canada's bush country, north of Lake Superior.

"That offer was like chains taken off me," he said with his toothy grin. "To me, it was like getting liberated. And off I went. I lived with the Indians up there, learned their languages and habits, and took part in their sports. I got accustomed, once again, to living outdoors—even in temperatures that sometimes sank to 30 below zero.

"In a way," he joked, "I taught them about rapid transit, not in cities but in the woods. Through the years, they had done their traveling through the forest, plugging along with slow-going snow shoes on their feet. I showed them how they could move faster, using cross-country skis."

In the years that followed, Johansson gained fame in Canada as well as in Lake Placid, as a leading advocate of ski touring—for sport and health. There he was, in that early era of recreational skiing for Americans, championing the slow-sliding sport more than two decades before the first rope tow was introduced in North America in 1934.

It was Jack Rabbit, who in those early days, created many of the touring trails that are still being used in the high as well as the low country of the

Laurentians. A peak in that range is named in his honor, and the trail that leads all the way west to Ottawa was blazed by him.

I asked this old-timer how he happened to come by the name of "Jack Rabbit." He glanced at a pair of his narrow skis that were propped up in the corner of the room.

"Those skis there are fast," he started. "And as for my nickname, people started calling me that because of a game I would play with them. To make skiing more interesting for my students at Lake Placid and other places, I would set up a game of hare and hounds in the woods. Naturally, I was the hare. Nobody ever caught me." He chuckled. "Those same skis sure helped me keep my distance."

I asked him whether he would pose for an action picture for me on skis. He readily agreed. He put on a thin, black parka, a black toque and replaced what he was wearing with a pair of long white woolen stockings.

"That's no problem," he said. "There's a trail right outside my door. I use it to get to the post office mornings. It's only half a mile away if you walk along the highway. But it's five miles if you go by trail. I go by trail. It's safer than having automobiles race past you."

As he headed for the door he grabbed those skis in the corner and a pair of ski poles. I looked at the poles and was surprised.

"What about them?" I asked pointing with my finger. "Aren't they apt to be dangerous as you come down that trail? One of them has no basket near the tip. Your pole may dip into the snow too deeply and cause you to lose your balance?"

"Pay it no mind," he replied airily as if he had just been told water is wet. "I'll make adjustments for that pole as I come down this slope. I've been skiing five miles to the post office with it every day for the past few weeks and it hasn't failed me yet."

Then he went out into the great outdoors, set his light leather boots into the toe bindings and off he went. He came down that short incline with the grace and ease of a champion woman figure skater going through her elementary figures.

I was impressed. And so, after he had finished that surprising exhibition, I asked him the obvious question.

"Can you give me any clues as to the reason for your surprisingly long, healthy life?" His answer?

"A good childhood. The ability to keep from worrying. Doing things in moderation. And last, but most important, exercising wisely."

His story and picture subsequently appeared in both the *Times* and in the *Fitness* magazine. He impressed me to such an extent that when I returned to New York, I contacted my friend, another experienced skier and famed news commentator, Lowell Thomas.

I suggested that we set up a luncheon in which Jack Rabbit was to be named "The Skier of the Year." The ever-congenial Thomas was a pioneer in the sport himself. A native of the high mountain country of Cripple Creek, Colorado, he really had become interested in skiing as a World War I correspondent. He agreed to head the committee.

The luncheon, with many members of the air and ink media present, was held with great success at a top midtown Manhattan restaurant. There was an amusing prelude to the affair. It was provided by the rugged Johannsen himself, whom I had led myself to believe feared nothing but perhaps the devil.

An hour or so before the affair, I found Jack Rabbit's room at the hotel we had secured for him. He had brought with him his daughter who was employed at Montreal's McGill University. It was about 1-2 blocks from the restaurant. I told him that although it was drizzling outdoors, it would be easy for him and his daughter to take the short walk to the luncheon.

The outdoors-minded nonagenarian proceeded to surprise me.

"I'd rather not walk in the rain," he said. "We'll take a taxi." They did. When he arrived, he explained that while he didn't mind skiing in blizzard conditions, "rain goes across my 'grain.'"

The last time I spoke to him was in Tony Wise's Mount Telemark ski area in Cable, Wisconsin, which is about fifty miles south of Lake Superior. Jack Rabbit had come by invitation to watch the trials for berths on the 1976 American Olympic cross-country team. He was then 100 years old.

Asked to don skis for photographers, he readily agreed. It was evident though that he had lost much of the zip he had displayed for me in those Canadian woods six years earlier.

In that original interview I had asked him how long he planned to remain a skier.

"Until I die" was his reply. "Golly you can't ski once you're dead."

Johannsen finally passed away at age 104. It is said that there are members of the Cree and Ojibway Indian tribes in Canada, however, who maintain that Johannsen, wherever he is, is still within the reach of a pair of skis.

One of the most interesting stories I ever stumbled on had nothing to do with sports. I heard about it in 1973 at about the same time that Steve Garvey was starting to create his niche as a big-league ball player. And it has an intriguing kicker at the end, involving a nationally prominent figure that has never surfaced—that is, until now.

It all began in the supermarket one Sunday morning in the city of Rutland. I was there to buy some groceries for my vacation home in nearby Danby, Vermont. I had covered a Dartmouth football game on Saturday in Hanover, New Hampshire, and was spending a few days at the house.

And now I was on the check-out line at the Grand Union on Main Street when I overheard a woman in front of me say to the cashier.

"Sue, did you hear about the runaway railroad engine? It went all through Vermont last night without an engineer. It was finally stopped in the northern part of the state above Essex Junction. No one knows where it came from. I heard that it went through about a hundred crossings without an accident."

The cashier was too busy to have the story sink in. She said that she hadn't heard about it and proceeded to bring up the charges for that woman's purchases. Sue had a line of people waiting and had no time for small talk.

But I was interested. I immediately went to that market's newspaper rack to pick up a copy of Sunday's *Rutland Herald*. I looked for the story. It was difficult to find.

When I did discover it, it was just a short piece, a paragraph or two. The engine, a diesel painted a fireman's red, had been spotted by police in Essex Junction and then stopped north of there.

"Gee," I said to myself. "This small article says that the engine traveled ninety miles without an engineer. The *Herald* certainly didn't do much with that story."

I concluded that the news of the runaway engine had arrived at the paper just as it was going to press, much too late to make much fuss for a Sunday morning edition which went to press much earlier than its weekday papers.

"This has the makings of a great story," I told my wife Ceil after I had made the twenty-mile trip back from shopping. "Just think: an engine traveling without an engineer. I wonder if anyone got hurt? It could be a great travel section yarn for the *New York Times* and even a magazine piece for a national magazine. I'm going to follow up on it."

"We have only two days left here in Vermont" was her reply. "Forget about it. It can't be that interesting. If it were, the *Rutland Herald* would have given it more space. It would have been on the front page, wouldn't it?"

Being the newshound that I am, I heard her not. The next day, on Monday, I was on my way, heading north. My plan was to make different stops on the way to find out whether anyone had seen the wandering engine two nights earlier. I drove along the highway that parallels the railroad tracks.

And right near the Brandon railroad station, about eighteen miles north of Rutland, I ran into an eyewitness whose house was near the railroad track.

"Yep, I saw it go past here at about eleven o'clock Saturday night," he said. "I had gone out to our front lawn to bring in my son's bicycle. I saw that red baby rattle by. I thought it odd. I knew the railroad didn't operate on weekends.

"Saturday night is my beer night in my kitchen," he continued. "I went back there and had another beer. Then I began asking myself how many beers I'd had? A Saturday night train? You know? I forgot all about that diesel until now."

After determining that the engine also had been noticed by a night worker in Middlebury, which is twenty miles north of Brandon, I headed for Essex Junction. It was in that town, according to the Rutland story, that the engine had first been spotted as a possible runaway. At the police station I met Lt. John Terry.

"Yes, I saw it," he said. "How could I miss it with its bright red color? It was clattering along at about six miles an hour as I was driving my prowl car next to it, on the highway that parallels the tracks. I thought it mighty strange. After all, it was about 3:30 A.M."

The police lieutenant, curious, proceeded to follow the engine. He drove down Essex Junction's Pearl Street which runs alongside the Central Vermont Railroad's trackage. As he caught up with the rattling diesel, he peered into the darkness at its cab.

"It looked empty," he told me. "I could see an engineer's jacket swinging on a hook by the window, but no engineer. I wondered if he was lying on the floor—dead. And then, when the usual engine's whistle didn't sound as the engine went through the Summit Street crossing, I realized I might be onto something."

Terry noted that the locomotive, number is 602, had a logo on its side that revealed it was the property of the Vermont Railroad, a company which operated freight about ten miles to the west, on a north–south route. He'd never seen one of that company's engines on his town's trackage, which is used by the Central Railroad.

"As soon as I saw all that, I did what I thought I had to do," he said. "I reached for my car's radio and instructed two of our policemen, Sgt. Wayne Bither and Patrolman Rodney Mills, to get into their car and to start following the engine, and to pull ahead of it so that they could protect the crossings from possible oncoming, unsuspecting motorists. As for myself, I headed for our station house."

He immediately found the Central Vermont's dispatcher to the north, at St. Albans. He wanted to warn him and remind him that if the engine was not stopped, it would soon be crossing the border into Canada and perhaps provide international complications.

"Apparently that locomotive doesn't have an engineer in it," he told the dispatcher. "Is there any way to stop it? I'm thinking of asking my man to try and forward it before some motorists coming through a crossing gets killed."

"That'll be easy," replied the dispatcher. "All your man has to do once he gets inside the cab is reach for the big lever over the engineer's seat and yank it. Then, the engine will stop."

Lt. Terry, now somewhat relieved, immediately radioed his men again. He informed them that if they could do so safely, to board the engine. He also told them where to find the lever that would stop it.

"Getting on it wasn't easy," Bither explained to me later. "We tried to climb on to it twice with no success. It was going downhill each time and was moving too quickly—maybe thirty miles an hour. The third time, we pulled way ahead of it at a point where it has slowed down because it was traveling on a grade that was uphill. We were now about eight miles north of Essex Junction."

Getting aboard was not easy. It was pitch dark as the diesel rattled along Vermont's hills and valleys, never sounding a whistle. To board it, the policeman had to shine their large flashlights in one hand so that they could see the engine's vertical handrail.

Then they had to grab the rail quickly, stuff the flashlights into their back pockets, use their other hand to grab the same rail and then swing themselves onto the engine's narrow boarding rail platform.

Bither, the much smaller of the two officers, succeeded in climbing aboard on his first try. But the much heavier Mills had difficulty in gaining a footing. As he grabbed the railing, he lost his footing and his legs went swinging precariously into the air. He finally got a toehold and boarded.

Bither immediately headed for the cab's left window and found it open. He looked inside. He was aghast. There was no engineer. There was no one in it. He wondered whether there had been any unreported accidents down the line, at one of the many crossings.

"We shouldn't have any problem now," he yelled at Mills above the noise of the pounding engine. "This should be simple from here on."

Bither had no difficulty climbing through the open window and reaching the engineer seat. He stretched over head for the lever. There wasn't any. Then he began yanking at the different gadgets in front of him to see whether one of them would start the engine. He had no luck. The diesel continued on its way.

Now that they had had so much difficulty climbing aboard, both men began thinking in terms of how they might get off the train—alive. It was now traveling on a downgrade, going around curves and was clipping along at about twenty to twenty-five miles an hour. It was too risky to just jump.

They were still contemplating their plan of action as the diesel approached the community of Colchester. There, all their fears were put to rest, because at that point, a local policeman climbed aboard. He knew something about locomotives. He merely turned the hand brake at the front end of the engine. It came to a stop just as it was reaching the community of Milton.

Soon, in the morning's early hours in the quiet pasture in northern, rural Vermont, at least a dozen cars began tooling onto the scene—automobiles belonging to railroad officials, local and state policemen, and members of local constabularies.

Now came the question: how had the engine gotten started and from whence it had come?

"I think I have some answers," volunteered one of the Central Vermont Railroad's representatives. "It's not one of our engines. That's why it doesn't have that big lever over the engineer's seat."

"Obviously, this loco had to originate in the Vermont Railroad's Burlington yards," he continued. "That's only twenty-two miles away. As to who started it? That's a police matter."

But the railroad official had made a wrong guess. A phone call to the Pinkerton special police guard stationed in the Vermont Railroad's yards in Burlington disclosed that no engine was missing from there.

"Maybe, you ought to try Rutland," the Pinkerton man suggested. "That's the only other place on our road from where an engine could come."

"Rutland!" cried a state trooper in disbelief. "That's impossible. Rutland is ninety miles south of here. It would have to go through such towns as Brandon, Middlebury, Vergennes, and Burlington. Do you know how many crossings that represents? Remember, we have no report of an accident.

"To boot, the switches in the Burlington freight yard would have had to be set perfectly for that engine to make the transfer over to the Central Vermont trackage," he explained. "Rutland! That's a real long shot," he concluded.

But the switches, somehow, happened to be perfectly set in Burlington and the city of Rutland, it developed, was the diesel's starting out point. Charles Bischoff, the Vermont Railroad's chief engineer, confirmed that one of its three engines based there—the 602—was missing.

"Our Rutland engine house has room for only two locomotives," he explained. "We keep our third one outside once we hit October with the engine idling so that it won't freeze on cold nights."

Who had started the engine? The culprit was never found. It finally was concluded that a prank-minded train buff probably had started it by perhaps thrusting the business end of a screwdriver into the locked throttle and had found only enough room to move it one notch. And, once he had the locomotive underway, he had jumped off it.

The bizarre night's events had one humorous sidelight associated with it. For, as soon as it was determined that the engine's starting place had been Rutland, that city's police department was notified.

On hand to take the message was the department's night dispatcher, a woman. She was the only one in the police station. She was hesitant about bothering Lt. Reginald Lafley, the small city's only detective, at that hour, at home.

Lafley had come into the station only two hours earlier, a weary man.

"This has been a tough day," he told her. "It's been a day that's lasted forever . . . seventeen hours. I'm dog tired and I'm going home to sleep. Please don't phone me for at least the next six or seven hours, no matter what." The dispatcher had nodded.

But convinced it was her duty, she phoned Lafley about two hours after the detective had departed.

"Didn't I beg you not to phone me?" he yelled at her. "I was fast asleep."

"But I have a story you won't believe," the woman said.

"I won't believe?" answered the police lieutenant. "Don't be ridiculous. I've been on this police force for many, many years. I've heard them all. Try me!"

"The Vermont Railroad just phoned," she told him, "to say someone stole one of its engines here in Rutland. The locomotive was stopped about ninety miles north of here without an engineer and it was headed for Montreal."

"You're right," answered Lafley. "I don't believe it. But I'll get right back to the station. Put some coffee on."

A few weeks later, I returned to Essex Junction to make sure I was accurate about all the details. I also wanted to photograph the policemen involved. When I got there, I was introduced to the chief.

"Would you mind posing with your three men who were involved in the engine chase?" I asked him.

His answer provided a surprise almost equal to the entire runaway engine story.

"No, I'd rather not be in the picture," he said. "I don't need the publicity. My name is 'Arena.' Ever heard of it?"

"Yes," I replied. "There is Emil Arena who used to be a sports editor at the *Hudson Dispatch* in New Jersey."

"No, there's no connection there," the police chief replied. "It so happens that I was the police chief at Chappaquiddick at the time that Senator Kennedy had that drowning incident with that young woman from Pennsylvania. I'd appreciate it if you didn't even use my name in the story. There's been enough trouble."

I didn't, out of respect for his feelings, use his name. Besides that drowning accident had nothing to do with the early morning ride of the 602.

But I did research that Kennedy accident and learned that on the morning after Senator Kennedy had driven his car into the creek, Chief Arena had demanded the senator's driver's license.[6]

Senator Kennedy received a two-month suspended sentence and a year's probation.

As for Chief Arena, he soon disappeared from that scene. Where did he go? We now know: to Essex Junction. It was evident he didn't want to tangle with the Kennedys again.

That part of the story hasn't been told until now. Before I decided to reveal it, I checked the Essex Junction police to find out if they still had the same chief. It was more than ten years later. Arena no longer was connected with that department, so then I felt free to use his name for this account.

The article, for which I was paid the usual freelancer's rate by the *Times*, won the "Best Story of the Month Award" in the *New York Times'* Travel section. *Reader's Digest Magazine* subsequently reprinted it for world distribution for which I also was paid. And about fifteen years later, that popular magazine used the story in one of its reading textbooks.

And my wife, remember? She had said at the outset that the story couldn't be interesting. It was one of the few times she had been wrong—dead wrong—in appraising the interest of a story.

Oh yes. The person who started the engine was never found. There weren't any clues—no fingerprints on or in the cab. Any chance of possibly finding such evidence was erased by Mills in his frantic yanking at the engine's different gadgets in his desperate attempt to stop it.

At least twice, in the years that followed, as I've walked through the streets of Rutland, I've spoken to young acquaintances—men who maintain they knew who started the 602 on that cold October night in 1973.

But no one was saying.

---

[6] For details see Joe McGinniss, "The End of Camelot," *Vanity Fair*, September 2003.

CHAPTER 14

Say It Isn't So – College Football

We called him Truthful Brown
'Cause he never let you down
He specialized in lies
And fooled a lot of guys.

It's in the terrible thirties—in the Great Depression years. The famed Babe Ruth is calling it quits. As a New York Yankee, the "Sultan of Swat," with more than 700 home runs to his credit, is nearing his fortieth birthday. And as might be expected, he has lost much of his ability as a slugger.

In that same decade, Maxie Baer and James Braddock are enjoying short reigns as world heavyweight champions. The New York Giants are dominating the National Football League. Margaret Mitchell has published *Gone with the Wind*, and Boulder Dam has been completed.

"Too bad about the Babe," writes a New York sports columnist. "But what a career! However even a baseball star's lights have to start dimming after a while."

Those were colorful and busy times in sports. The *New York Times* was interested in a wide assortment of them, ranging from badminton to yacht racing. In addition to the major sports, writers might be sent out to do byline stories on Gaelic football, hurling, fishing, archery, billiards, fencing, crew racing, horse shows, squash, all-breed dog shows, six-day bicycle racing, hunt meetings, and curling, among others

Ford C. Frick, the sportswriter who eventually became the High Commissioner of Baseball, for example, was into curling. He was a "sweep," the man who wielded a broom on the rink at a Yonkers country club. His job was to keep sweeping ice particles away from the steady advance of thrown "stones."

Such show business personalities as Groucho Marx, George Sanders, Daryl Center Oak, Moss Hart, George Abbott, George S. Kaufman, Richard Rodgers, movie director Samuel Goldwyn, and famed career critic Arthur C Woollcott, all were croquet-playing enthusiasts.

It was an era in which I would find myself, once the fall season arrived, up to my ears in football scores. Between the hours of 4:00 and 8:30 P.M. on any given Saturday, the *New York Times* Sports Department would take on the appearance of a bargain-basement rush.

There would be a dozen short-sleeved copy readers, some wearing green eyeshades, clearing stories arriving from all parts of America. Rewrite men, wearing earphones connected by a headband, would be taking dictation of stories or writing down incoming college and high school scores. Final results would be arriving from all parts of the metropolitan areas—dozens upon dozens of local scores.

Sportswriters, assigned to local games, would rush into the office and sit down at their desks to "bat out" their stories as fast as they could. Telephones would be ringing from all sides of the large room and copy boys would be rushing to and from our wire room, the copy cutter's desk, and the composing room to make each second count.

It did.

"Just keep remembering that on Saturday, our first edition goes to press at about six o'clock," Spiker, the head of our copy desk, emphasized to me on my first in the office football scores stint. "We get about ninety minutes to fill the better part of twenty or thirty columns. Don't let yourself get held up even if someone drops to the floor. Someone else will pick him up. Remember, the key word is 'rush.' Keep those scores moving to the composing room."

In those ninety minutes, 600- to 800-word stories would flow into the department giving accounts of football games involving Yale, Harvard, Princeton, Dartmouth, Army, Ohio State, Notre Dame, Manhattan College, New York University, Rutgers, Amherst, and Lehigh among many others. They would arrive by phone, telegraph, and from the wire services—the Associated Press, the United Press, an Hearst International News Service.

But on the far end of the rectangular room, telegraph instruments would keep clattering against small tobacco tins. The tins were used to make the arriving dots and dashes in the instruments sound louder for Western Union operators decoding and receiving them.

"This damn box has no sound," I heard Jim Rice, a telegrapher by way of Texas, sounding off one Saturday. "This is a Prince Albert tin. Shoulda' known," he complained. "Let me have that blue Edgeworth can lying over there," I heard him tell one of the copy boys. "Its tobacco is better than that Prince Albert junk, and so is the sound from its tin."

Regularly, above the din of it all, a copy reader, a rewrite man or a reporter typing a story at his desk, would call "Boy, boy." If the "boy" didn't show up soon enough, it wasn't unusual to hear an exasperated, "Where is that goddamned boy?" Everyone was in a hurry.

The hundreds of final college and secondary school football scores would keep arriving from all sources almost simultaneously. Handling them provided a lesson in geography because all of them were put into their appropriate sections. Gustavus Adolphus, Macalester, Winona, Cape Girardeau Teachers, Michigan, Indiana, and Kenyon, among many others would be slugged, marked "insert West" and sent to the composing room.

The Ivy League college games, naturally, were included under the "East" heading, while Texas, Georgia Tech, Louisiana State, and the University of Florida, of course, would be sent up to the composing room—one floor above us—in the "South" listings. Even high school results were divided into sections such as "Westchester," "Long Island," "New Jersey," and "Connecticut."

It was a tense scene. I would not only have to send up the scores received from the wire services and from the sports desk itself, but also take many of them over the telephone. I well recall the afternoon, at the onset of the football season, that I picked up the phone after someone in the office had taken an incoming call and shouted "Rewrite!"

The call was switched to my phone. A voice on the other end said, "I'm Jim Brown (or maybe it was Smith, I don't remember). I'm the sports publicity director of North Plainfield Teachers College in New Jersey. I have a football score for you. Our team won, 23–3."

I had never heard of North Plainfield Teachers or the name of the losing team he mentioned. As was our custom, I asked him for his telephone number which he gave me promptly. I typed the score into my long list of colleges "East" and then proceeded to take seven Long Island schoolboy scores by phone from one of our correspondents.

It wasn't until I was on my way home late that night—on board the Jamaica BMT elevated rapid transit line—that I suddenly began thinking of that New Jersey call. Why? Because it had struck and unfamiliar cord. I felt I knew suburban New York well. I was convinced there was no such thing as a college campus in North Plainfield which is about thirty miles west of downtown New York.

The next day, to ease my mind, I glanced at the scores printed by some of the other local newspapers. Their sports sections also had the North Plainfield score. I was somewhat relieved. But still, I doubt that there was such a college.

I, thereupon, dug out a Plainfield phone book. There was no institution with that name listed. Then I found the number the North Plainfield representative had given me. I was told there was no such number.

Came the following Saturday. And there I was in the office again handling the scores when that same person from North Plainfield Teachers phoned.

"We won again," he reported in an enthusiastic tone. "What a ball game! We did everything wrong until the start of the second half. Then we clobbered the other team. The score was—"

I never found out what the score was because I interrupted him. I said, "I'm delighted that you called. How many games have you won so far this season?"

"This is our third one and we're undefeated," he replied. "In view of our comeback today, I think we're really rolling."

"Maybe you are," I replied. "But where? I've tried to contact you several times this past week and I failed. Nor, for that matter, can I find a phone number listed for the North Plainfield Teachers College. How do you explain that?"

"Oh, that's easy," he answered. "We're a brand-new school. We're not in the current edition of the phone book."

"In that case, would you please give me the name and phone number of your college's president? I'll have to phone him to make sure this is all authentic."

The caller promptly disconnected. I didn't hear from him again for the rest of the season. But other newspapers did. It was then that I gave him the nickname of "Truthful Brown" and advised the people at my office to beware of him in case they heard from him.

Throughout the phone, on Sunday mornings, scores of presumed North Plainfield Teachers' games kept appearing regularly in the other New York newspapers. Here was a team that was consistent. It always won.

Sometime during the middle of the season, short stories about the ability of this "surprising" eleven began appearing in metropolitan New York dailies. Its successes had a peculiarly odd note. Why? Because its triumphs were scored against colleges unfamiliar to everyone in our sports department.

One afternoon, the *New York Post*, the city's oldest newspaper—at that time full-sized as compared to its later tabloid layout—ran the better part of a column, written by a staff member, about the surprising successes of North Plainfield Teachers.

This story featured the fact that this amazing New Jersey squad was quarterbacked by a Chinese signal-caller who also did the team's punting—barefooted, no less. Shortly after that season neared it closed, it finally was publicly revealed that it indeed had all been a hoax. There was no Chinese player, no such football team, and certainly no such institution as North Plainfield Teachers College.

It was determined that the entire scheme had been spawned by a Wall Street broker who had been at a bar drinking with some friends. During their light conversation, he had wagered that he could invent a team and get its scores printed in the newspapers. He proved that he was right on the money—but that poor *New York Post* writer—he was in shock.

Hoaxes, of course, are not new in the world of sports. There was that unforgettable Wood Field & Stream column I did for the *New York Times* exposing one that transpired along on the eastern shore of the Connecticut River just above the town of Bellow's Falls, Vermont.

It seems that late one spring afternoon, when the skies were overcast, the river's waters moving downstream at a slow pace and the temperature just right for trout fishing, two of that community's dedicated freshwater anglers suddenly found themselves marveling.

There they were, walking along the shoreline trying to find a spot where trout seemed to be rising, when they came to a dead stop. They stared in disbelief. Because lying just a few feet in front of them was a skeleton of a fish. They were not the bones, however, of a run-of-the-mill Connecticut River specimen, but the remains of a long finny creature that must have weighed at least forty pounds.

"Holy smoke," said one of the anglers. "What a giant that must have been. Never saw the likes of it along this stream, and I've been fishing this river, man and boy, for forty years. The best I've ever taken was a six-pound bass. I wonder under what rock this big baby has been hiding through all these years. Just think of what the boys in town will think when we bring them down here to see what's left of this fellow."

The "boys" were told and they came to see the evidence. None of them had ever seen a fish even "one-fifth" that large in the river. Finally, a local saltwater angling aficionado came along to solve the puzzle. He announced that that creature had never done its swimming in the Connecticut River.

"It's a striped bass," he reported. "You can find plenty of them once you hit the ocean waters. I wonder who put it there on the bank?"

It was subsequently confirmed that the big "critter" indeed had been a striped bass, captured by a Bellows Falls resident off Cape Cod, Massachusetts, about 200 miles southeast of Bellows Falls. The jokester had returned home, peeled the flesh from the fish, and set its bones down on the river side thinking it might prove a confounding conversation piece.

It did—but only for a while.

In an age when most communities in the United States treasure their historic backgrounds, citizens of Toms River, New Jersey, were convinced in the 1950s that they had uncovered an intriguing bit of their area's patriotic past. It came in the shape of a cannon ball.

The big round iron sphere was discovered in the town's sewer system shortly before I arrived in that southern New Jersey town to do a story on Admiral Farragut Academy's football team. Farragut, as was the case at all boarding schools I visited in those days, provided top athletic facilities for its students.

Stan Slaby, who had the physique of a pro football player, was the school's athletic director. He greeted me warmly and began telling me about some of the heavier players on his gridiron squad.

"We have one fellow who not only does a fine job at tackle, but he also is outstanding on our track team in field events," he said.

"Say," the genial Slaby suddenly added with a grin. "I know you're an American history buff. This'll interest you. Have you heard about the heavy Revolutionary War cannonball that was found a few weeks ago by a crew of our workers downtown? When it was brought up into daylight and cleaned, there was a partially obliterated number etched on it. The laborers decided the number was '76.'

"It didn't take long for some of our folks in town to decide that that heavy iron ball was a part of our town's early history," he continued. "Right here on one of our main streets is a New Jersey State historical marker. It states simply 'that a small naval battle between American and British vessels was fought a few miles east of Toms River in 1778.'

"New Jersey's Historical Society in Trenton was notified immediately," said Slaby. "The people there planned to put it on exhibit in their museum. But it never got there. It's still in Toms River.

"It's for good reason," he concluded with a dramatic pause. "What had looked like a '76' on that 'historic find,' was really a '16.' It actually was a sixteen-pound shot-put, the kind used in track and field meets.

"We had been missing a sixteen-pound shot here at the Academy for months," he concluded. "It looks as if someone lifted it from our equipment room and dropped it into the gutter as a gag. From there it must have rolled down a small hill into the sewer."

I asked him, "Who did it?"

"Probably we'll never know," he answered. "But one thing you can be certain about. It wasn't John Paul Jones."

Sometimes practical jokes take hours, perhaps days, to be resolved. Some are never brought to light. But there was one perpetrated in the Pennsylvania city of Williamsport that was begun and ended in less than a minute. The incident involved Dave Breshnahan, a catcher for the Williamsport club of the Eastern League.

That it happened in Williamsport sort of delighted me. I had fond memories of that northern Pennsylvania city which is the home of the annual Little League World Series. Where I once saw a twelve-year-old Mexican pitcher, a member of the Monterrey team, who could throw fast-moving strikes with either hand and who tossed a six-inning no-hitter in the series finale.

It was in Williamsport too that I met Ted Williams, the great Boston Red Sox slugger, after he had retired from baseball. It was here that I had some fun with Emmett Kelly, the renowned trampish clown for many years of the Barnum and Bailey Circus.

As for Breshnahan, the catcher during the 1987 season, he threw a potato to third base instead of baseball, as a gag, presumably to pick off a base runner. The latter, thinking that the potato was a ball, broke for home plate. There he was tagged out by the catcher who had retained the actual baseball in his possession.

Breshnahan, of course, had thrown the potato as a hoax to give the spectators a laugh. He immediately was released from his team.

"There was no alternative," said a league official. "Baseball may be an entertaining business, but it's not meant to be funny. The plate umpire of that game justifiably allowed the runner to score. The catcher received an 'error' on the play and received a fine of $50 as well as his walking papers."

And there was that little aquatic expedition in the back country of Florida that provided me one of the surprises of my life. It all took place on huge Lake Okeechobee in that state's central precincts.

Because I was unfamiliar with the area, I did what I usually do in such cases. I headed for the police station in nearby Clewiston. I went there to get some local information because I planned on doing a photo story for the *New York Times'* Boating Section.

I wanted to take shots of as many different types of boats that I could spot on this well-known freshwater lake, the second-largest freshwater in the United States.

The police chief, Ronnie Lee, who was half Seminole Indian, and who knew the region like an eagle knows its aerie, was most cooperative.

"What I'm after," I said, "is to rent a small boat with which I can putter around the lake and take shots of the different kinds of craft. I don't need anything fast or fancy."

"You've come to the right place," said the chief. "My friend, Jim Edwards, he's the principal at the high school, has a little boat—a twenty-five-footer—and I know he'd be happy to show you around the lake. After all, how often does a fellow from the *New York Times* come by here? In fact, I'll go too. It'll give me a chance to get out there and see what's going on."

So off we went. There were all kinds of craft afloat—sportfishermen, speed boats, glorified skiffs, motorized yachts, sloops, and even a yawl. They were scattered all over the lake, and I got plenty of good shots.

Clewiston is a well-known agricultural center for the production of sugar. It also is a front door to some productive freshwater fishing—for big-mouth bass, snook, mullet, bluegills, and catfish.

We had seen some bass captured by anglers, and we were about to return to our dock. But then, I saw someone in the distance—about 400 yards off our starboard bow, lowering a small rubberized raft equipped with an outboard motor onto the lake from a palatial-looking cruiser.

It seemed interesting, so we decided to approach the craft. As we drew near, we noticed that the man aboard the cruiser was wearing an unbuttoned shirt and wearing hand-scissored shorts that had originally been slacks.

He was about to get into his rickety-looking dinghy—it turned out to be—which was equipped with an outboard motor. The little craft was bobbing alongside the plush one. In his hand, the man had a fishing rod. He was smoking a pipe and was sprouting large sunglasses.

Here was a guy about to leave a gorgeous-looking sports cruiser, apparently intent on fishing from his pint-sized dinghy.

"He just wants to do his casting closer to shore," said Edwards, the high school principal. "He'll find more fish there, but he's apt to find more alligators there too. I guess he knows, though, that 'gators are spooky; if a person moves too close to them, they usually just take off and disappear."

"These two boats—a big one and the pee wee one—should make a great picture," I said to the chief with a laugh. "It's a shot that might well be titled 'changing boats in midstream—and doing so for worst.' After all, he could, if he wanted, cast his line from his big cruiser, sit on a deck chair and wait until he gets a strike."

"He probably knows the bass are closer to shore," suggested the chief. "But he'd better watch out particularly if the alligators have young 'uns in that area."

The sun was shining brightly—right in our eyes—as we approached the fisherman who was just about to lower himself to the raft. He looked up at us.

"Do you mind if I take a picture of your big boat cruiser and your small one?" I asked. "I'm from the *New York Times*. I'm doing a series of boat pictures."

"Help yourself" was the reply. "Take as many shots as you want."

"Gee," I said to him. "Did anyone ever tell you that you sound like Ralph Houk, the big-league baseball manager?" I asked.

"Yes," he answered with a big smile. "That happens on occasion."

I took several exposures. Then I explained that I wanted to take some from the other side so that my camera's lens would not be facing the sun.

"Go right ahead," he answered with a broad smile. "Help yourself. After all I don't want you to feel you came all of the way out here for nothing. You deserve good pictures."

"I'll be darned," I said in all seriousness to the chief as he swung his small boat around, and I got a better view of the fisherman. "I think I know you.

"You don't only sound like Ralph Houk, you look like him."

"Hello, Mike," he immediately replied with a wave of his hand. "I am Ralph Houk."

Then he called to his wife who was below in the galley.

"Come above," he said. "Mike Strauss of the NYT is here." And after we had exchanged hellos, he said to her, "You remember me telling you about Mike when I was the manager of the Yankees, and he was reporting the games for his paper?

"He's the fellow who kept making me envious. Because after the Yankees finished a trip heading back to New York, he'd perhaps be leaving us to go west, to one of those great spots to write fishing stories for his paper."

There were many reasons why I hadn't recognized Houk instantly. For one thing, the sun had been in my eyes and then again, I hadn't seen him for about four years because he had left the Yanks to manage the Detroit Tigers and subsequently the Boston Red Sox.

When I used to sit in the Yankees' dugout before games and talk to him whether it was at the Stadium in New York or in an out-of-town park, he'd usually be chewing on a plug of tobacco. And he'd be wearing sunglasses but not of the huge size he was wearing on the lake.

Also, I had never, absolutely never, seen him smoke a pipe. He smoked cigars—the best brands. Last but not least, Houk was living in Pompano Beach at least ninety miles south of Lake Okeechobee. Who'd ever expect to find him there even though it was well known that he was a fishing enthusiast?

"Sorry, I strung you along like that," the genial and well-known baseball personality said with a grin as I tried to get over my embarrassment.

"But I was wondering how long it would take you to recognize me," he continued. "If you had swung around to our stern instead of coming up to our bow, you probably would have known me at once. Go around and look at the name of our boat."

Edwards revved up his motor and steered to the cruiser's stern. There emblazoned on the boat's transom was its name. It read, "Thanks Yanks."

"Yes, my long stay with the Yanks as a player and manager sure helped me get this big boat of mine," Houk explained with a gracious smile. "Without them, I might have had to settle just for that little rubber tub of a dinghy."

I had gone out to take pictures and to write a routine tale about the boats on the lake. But meeting Houk, as I did, in the middle of nowhere, I felt deserved more interesting treatment.

The story appeared in our sports section along with a photo I snapped of Houk's "Thanks Yanks." Standing in the stern right above the two deep-sea anglers' chairs was the one-time major league baseball manager.

The three-column wide, two-line headline on the story read:
"THE SHOES OF THE FISHERMAN LACKED ONLY FAMILIAR SPIKES"

The headline didn't make sense to me. Even if Houk had been wearing spikes, I never would have recognized him with the sun in my eyes.

How about a hoax with a medical touch? This one began at the C-Lazy-U Ranch in Granby, Colorado, during a convivial and lively evening. Guests had danced, swapped stories, and sipped cocktails. Dick Schoenberg, formerly of New York, who ran the plush resort, had exchanged views about skiing with his guests through much of the evening.

"The American Olympic ski fund program needs help," he told us. "Money is being obtained for this purpose all over the United States. I've helped raise some, and I'm trying to get some more."

A visiting physician and his wife had listened attentively. Both had been impressed. Before the evening was over, the doctor, a slim, quiet-mannered sort of soul, had taken out his check book and donated $100 for the cause.

"I'm glad to do it," the physician said in a genial tone. "I've always been partial to amateur sports. This is an endeavor that should be encouraged. Movements like this, I'm convinced, help turn out better citizens."

Everyone there was impressed. The personable Schoenberg and his wife had found that their guests, in the past, had been generous in contributing to the ski team. But this physician—a stranger to them until his arrival a day earlier—seemed particularly heartwarming.

"It's amazing how many different ways fund raisers have obtained help for our ski teams," Schoenberg told the doctor. "Our National Ski Association has utilized everything from a letter-writing campaign to the sale of colorful pins. It's surprising how many dollar bills the pins, alone, with the red- and white-striped American logo on them, have produced."

"Say, I have an idea," the physician said as he lifted his martini from the rustic coffee table. "Do you mind if I explain it?" Since everyone seemed interested, the physician continued.

"I have a friend who has an oversupply of wild rice. He has so much of it that one of his favorite jokes is to tell people that he's going to use it to stuff his bedroom pillows.

"I know he'd be more than happy to donate the rice for fund-raising," continued the doctor. "The only problem then would be finding volunteers willing to bag it."

A young woman whose husband was a member of the Air Force Academy's faculty in Colorado Springs and who previously had shown a sharp interest in the money-raising project piped up.

"I think I could find a way to help," she said. "I'm sure the wives at our Academy Officers' Club would be happy to cooperate. They go for movements like this. We could bag the rice and make it ready for sale. How do we get it?"

The physician promised that he would be in contact with the Schoenbergs and provide them with the necessary information. The following day, he departed with his wife after paying his bill by check.

Gloria Chadwick, the blonde-haired skiing enthusiast, who at that time was the executive secretary of the United States Skiing Association, subsequently told me of the ensuing developments while we were driving through a snowstorm over a slick highway between Colorado Springs and Crested Butte en route to the NCAA's championship ski races.

"You remember that doctor at Katie's (Mrs. Schoenberg)?" she asked. "Well, he turned out to be a phony. The check he gave the Schoenbergs and the one he left for his stay at the ranch, both bounced."

"The FBI cornered him about three weeks later in a motel in Kansas City. Before the federal people could get to him though, he killed himself. It turned out that he had stolen his credentials from a physician."

As for all that wild rice, as might be expected, it was just part of a wild story.

It was while I was in Texas to cover a pro basketball game featuring "Dr. J"—Julius Irving of the Nets—that I encountered what seemed the most dangerous hoax of all. The morning after the game, I drove east from San Antonio to see my friend Dr. Harvey Resnick. Harvey, a Texas physician, and his family lived in Lake Jackson, about fifty miles south of Houston.

As I neared the Resnick home, I stopped at a small diner. I was enjoying my bacon and eggs when I heard a scary announcement come over the radio.

"Four wild lions have escaped" was the report. "They've gotten out of their cages and they're on the loose in Lake Jackson. Only a four-foot high fence on the end of a 115-acre farm separates them from complete freedom."

"Huh!" remarked a diner at the counter who was togged out in a wide-brimmed straw hat, dungarees, and a light blue shirt unbuttoned at the neck. "Someone's joking. Four wild lions! If they had said four wild steers, I'd have believed it."

It sure sounded like a hoax. After all, wild lions in Texas?

By the time I reached the Resnick home, the latest announcement on the radio was that the lions—two of them sizable cubs—apparently were on a rampage in a large field. They already had killed a cow, a calf, and a donkey.

I made a few telephone calls to the local newspaper and to the police. I found that J.W. Jackson, the city's acting chief, hadn't been sure whether it was wise to warn the public about the grave danger.

"I'm not sure whether I should take a hand in getting this kind of word out," he said. "I'm afraid that too many curious motorists will drive up to that property and clog the highways."

But he soon realized the public indeed had to be alerted and protected.

"Our key problem," he reminded two of his men, Ron Franco and Bob Turner, as he sent them out to patrol the area, "is that our department doesn't have the necessary armament to cope with wild lions. All we have are our service revolvers, a 30-30 rifle and a 30-0-6 caliber shotgun. Do the best you can but watch yourselves!"

An hour or so later, it was revealed on the radio that one adult lion, who had been snarling and acting unruly, had been shot and killed. A volunteer, who had been hiding behind a tree, had hit the animal after it had approached him in a "threatening manner."

The two cubs were discovered napping in one of the farm's many large sheds, but the other adult, a lioness, was heard roaring while dragging the stricken donkey along the ground. However, she didn't seem the least bit interested in doing much roaming although the four-foot high fence, at times, was only a few yards from her. She finally was captured and returned to a cage.

Deeply interested in why it had been possible to have lions running wild in that busy Brazoria County community, I sought out the farm's owner. He was Albert Friederich, an eighty-two-year-old retired building contractor. He lived in the neighboring town of Freeport in a home a few blocks from the Gulf of Mexico.

"Sure, I was keeping caged lions," he explained in a mild manner as if wild animals on the loose presented no major problems. "I've always loved animals. At one time, on that same property, I took care of as many as 400 stray dogs, a Bengal tiger, a llama, and numerous deer."

Friederich explained that his sympathy for animal life was well known in that part of Texas.

"People who can no longer take care of their pets have always brought them to me. They know I've always been ready to give them a home."

He grudgingly conceded that Brazoria County was no home where wild lions should roam.

CHAPTER 15

Lending a Helping Hand

It is well known that a good story must have a beginning, a middle, and an end. And so, as I made my rounds seeking good subject matter for a story, I would come across situations that had lots of potential but somehow didn't have an adequate beginning or in some cases a worthwhile conclusion.

For example, a big-league baseball player may pound out three hits in four times at bat during a game. That's outstanding but not unusual. But if he's the same batter who was held hitless in his preceding fifteen games, that provides the beginning of a story for someone who has emerged from a long slump.

Similarly, one might find himself doing an article about a crackerjack angler who sets out on a series of five or six deep-sea fishing trips only to be skunked—shut out—during each of the outings. However, if he then was to latch on to a 600-pound tuna or a 500-pound swordfish, that would be a great ending. But if on that last trip, he again had caught nothing? So what? For column purposes? He becomes just another guy who has run out of luck. He's no story.

I would run into situations, from time to time, that had the makings of a darn interesting piece. The only condition, in those cases, would be that the subject matter needed a little added investigation and, in some cases, prodding, to develop into a darn interesting article.

There was that December in St. Anton, Austria, for example, when the slopes surrounding that small Alpine village had virtually no snow on them. It was an economic crisis in the making for St. Anton. That cozy Arlberg community, at that time, had only a year-round population of 600. That is, except before the Christmas–New Years and February "high" seasons arrived. At these times, the town's head count would mushroom to 6,600. What caused such invasions? Skiers!

It was in the mid-1950s when I first set foot in this homey Austrian community. Only six days remained before Christmas. Hotel lodge owners, ski school instructor, and even the local small food market owners were beginning to sweat out. There was no snow on the nearby slopes. Such a condition if not remedied with the help of the heavens would prove costly to all.

"How about it?" I asked the clerk when I checked in that first night at the Post Hotel, the village's classiest hostelry. "What happened to the snow? The streets are almost bare. SA is famous for its early snow. What happened?"

The clerk looked up at the ceiling as if he was asking someone the same question up above, and shrugged.

"If I knew the answer to that question I would consider myself a genius," he replied. Then he looked at the ceiling again as if hoping an answer was coming through.

It was early to bed for me that night because my trip had been a long one. The next morning, I looked at the slopes on the jagged mountains opposite the hotel. They were loaded with brown, earthy patches. I had seen more snow in NY City's Central Park, even in early April.

My purpose for coming to this famed Austrian winter resort had been to do a ski story about this winter sports mecca. But as I looked at the snowless condition of the mountain out of my window, hopes for an easy-to-do article melted away. A stroll through the small village confirmed my worst fears. Shop owners were despondent. They feared many of the ski enthusiasts that were being expected from all parts of Europe and the United States for the yuletide season might head elsewhere.

It was after I had walked to the ski school's headquarters at one end of the town that a story idea began jelling. Hanging on the wall of a large room was a huge portrait of Hannes Schneider. Who was he? I knew the name well as did everyone connected with skiing.

Hannes was a famous head of the local ski school, who in 1939 fled to the United States with his family to get out of Hitler's clutches. Once in the United States, he had become American's first honest-to-goodness skimeister. His base of operations was at Cranmore Mountain in the busy New Hampshire community of North Conway.

I decided, since I was in his native village, that I'd do a story on Schneider who I knew had pioneered the Arlberg Technique, a manner of coming down a slope that made making turns on skis easier. In pre-World War II days, many of the sports devotees—nobility, military leaders, and bankers, among others, had come from all parts of the world to master the Skimeister's theories. Among them was Harvey Gibson, the well-known NYC banker.

My column on SA began shaping up as I continued to inspect the town. I found that across the narrow street from my hotel was the "Hannes Schneider Ski Shop," by far the largest store in town. In the Post Hotel's cocktail lounge, I found a sculptured bust of Schneider. It was on a shelf right above the table where in earlier days the Skimeister had enjoyed his daily glass of wine after ski school.

And then, to add to it all, I discovered a dramatic, life-size granite statue of the Skimeister opposite the town's Catholic Church, which had been founded in the sixteenth century. The statue depicted Schneider leaning on an elbow look up at "his" museum.

Yes, he was a natural for a story. But I felt something more was needed to give it added clout. Upon added investigation and some more questioning, I found that "something" in the church itself that could round out my tale. Up in the belfry were two large bells. One of them had been used traditionally for years as parishioners arrived for Mass. The other one, it developed, was the Hannes Schneider bell. That one, seldom, if ever, was rung.

"How come it's up there?" I asked Benno Rybyzko, also a highly respected ski instructor, who had taught the sport in the USA before returning to SA. His departure from the USA had been triggered by the death of his father, a local physician.

"As you know," the patient Benno, who was happy to see someone close to the American ski scene, told me, "Hannes never came back to Austria to stay. He prospered in New Hampshire. Mr. Gibson, who had helped him leave Austria, owned Cranmore Mountain, and that's where Hannes remained until he passed on."

The Schneider bell, in the church, it developed, had been presented to the ancient house of worship by some of the ski instructors who had taught under Schneider in SA. They had spearheaded a movement to raise money to create the bell that was given to the church in Skimeister's memory.

"Benno," I said, "I think we may have an unusually interesting story in the making. It's all based around the fact that there's no snow in the area. And here it is, only a few days before the Christmas rush of skiers."

Rybyzko, who graciously had agreed to make the town's rounds with me because I did not speak German, was puzzled. It was obvious from the look on his face that he didn't think I was making sense.

"Here's the idea," I explained, "I want you to take me to the priest at the church. I want to ask if he would agree to have the Hannes Schneider bell rung in the hope that it will bring snow in time for the holidays. After all, the bell in a way is a symbol for skiing.

"If the skies don't cooperate and produce snow soon," I continued, "it could develop into a financial disaster here for the entire winter. Come December 26, the hundreds of SA's bedrooms, instead of being loaded with skiing tourists, could be empty for the most part. I could contact the priest myself, but I'm told he speaks no English. I need your help."

"It'll never work," Benno said. "Our priest here is not an Austrian. He's Polish. People in town say he's not very cooperative, that he's only interested in raising money. He's not into skiing. I don't even know whether we could get him to listen."

"I know at least a dozen priests back home in the States," I answered. "I haven't run into one yet who wouldn't at least listen. Can't we go down and talk to him? Let him hear what I have to say. Try to reach him by phone as a favor to me and ask for an appointment for us."

Judging from his reaction, Benno thought it a hopeless case. He seemed reluctant to help. But because I kept urging him, he phoned the priest. The latter agreed to see us at 6:15 that evening. And when we went to meet him, there he was in his kitchen in a building next to the church. He was making tea.

I told Father, a gentle, spare balding man who was probably in his late thirties, about the bell and asked for his help, Rybyzko carefully spelling it all out for me. The priest stopped me halfway through my request.

"It doesn't make much sense to me," he said. "What does the snow have to do with the church?"

Nevertheless, he let us finish our presentation. Finally, he said, justifiably I thought,

"What if we ring the Schneider bell and it brings no snow. What will my people say? What will they think? Will they feel I have been foolish?"

"Nein, not so," I had Benno reply. "Even if no snow appears after the bell is rung, your people who come to church this Sunday will at least say, 'The good priest, at least he tried for us.' And just think, if the snow does come, there will be many who will think perhaps, 'The priest, he helped us.'"

Suddenly the patient clergyman's eyes seemed to widen and brighten. He thought about it for no more than a few seconds and said, "Let me think about it. Phone me tomorrow at about two o'clock in the afternoon. I'll let you know what I've decided."

The cooperative Benno agreed to make the call. And, as I had hoped, the priest said he was going to go along with the idea.

"I intended to have the Schneider bell rung tonight," the priest explained to Benno, "because time before the holidays is running short. But I can't do it then. We have a funeral tonight. It would be in poor taste to have the Schneider bell rung then. But tomorrow morning, a few minutes after morning Mass is completed, that bell will be rung. Let's see what happens."

I was more than satisfied because snow or no snow, I still had a story. If no flakes developed, I could write that in the event the Schneider bell had been of no help. And if it did snow, then I'd have a genuine success story—one that these out-of-town skiers, who would be arriving for the holidays, might even be put in the category of a minor miracle. In either case, the church was going to be placed in a good light.

That night at about ten o'clock I began playing nickel and dime poker with three people from Athens, Greece, and another gentleman who said he was from the American Embassy in Paris. About midnight, we agreed to take a breather. We weren't outside for more than three or four minutes when snowflakes, the size of half-dollars, began falling.

"Gee," I moaned to myself. "There goes the best part of my story. Why did it have to start snowing before my bell was rung?"

But I was lucky. The white flakes stopped dropping in about seven or eight minutes. It had merely been a squall. By that time, we had returned to the hotel to resume our game, the moon was out, and the skies were loaded with stars. I was relieved.

When I awakened the next morning, I noticed it had turned overcast outside. And as I walked to the dining room, I hoped that the priest had not forgotten his promise.

When I was having breakfast, I heard the church bell rung for Mass. About thirty minutes later, I heard the Schneider bell. It had a sound that was different from the earlier one. And unbelievably, as I kept anxiously peering through the window next to my table, within two or three minutes it began to snow . . . and snow . . . and snow.

The records will show that at least a minor blizzard ensued as the storm continued right into the next day. Indeed, when I awakened on the third morning, the white flakes were still coming down. I looked through my window at the mountain range. It was a complete white blanket. I was told that about twenty inches of snow had fallen, that the snow up there in some places was up to the thighs.

I now had the beginning, the middle, and the ending for my SA story. Out came my portable typewriter and I began writing it for the NYT. Its modest-sized headline read: "THE MIRACLE OF THE BELLS."

At about three o'clock that afternoon, I received a phone call. It was from the priest. He had found out from the hotel's concierge that I was leaving early that evening to head east for Innsbruck. Because I spoke only English, he asked the concierge to give me a message. It read as follows:

"Tell Mr. Strauss," the priest related, "that I'm delighted we followed his suggestion.

"Also tell him that we rang the bell a little too late in the season. From now on, we'll have the Schneider bell rung on every First Advent Sunday—well before the start of winter, in the hope that it will bring us a happy season. Tell him that he has started a tradition in SA."

Years later, in another December visit to the same quaint town, I did a lengthy story on Karl Schranz, the great Austrian Alpine ski racer who had been in that controversial slalom race with Jean Claude Killy at the 1968 Winter Olympics in Grenoble. I spoke to Karl in his impressive-looking, finely appointed ski inn and lodge. I asked him whether the Schneider bell was still being rung as the priest had promised.

Karl nodded his head. He said it was well known that the Schneider bell had now become a part of the town's First Advent Sunday observance. I told him that I, an American, had by chance started the tradition.

Friendly conversation and a little kidding by me in the early 1950s produced an almost unbelievable story in golf at the well-known Mercersburg Academy, a fine boarding school.

It is located in a small, neat, quiet community in south central Pennsylvania.

The story was triggered, of all things, by an innocent phone call that I made to Jimmy Curran, the academy's highly regarded track coach. I phoned one day to tell him that I was contemplating a visit to his campus as part of my regular annual tour of the private schools.

That private school swing, made each fall, was a pleasure. I would stop each day at one of the East's leading boarding schools. I would start at St. Paul's in Concord, New Hampshire and do a sports story at that prestigious campus. The next day, I would be down state at Phillips Exeter, and on the third afternoon, there would be a stop at Phillips Academy of Andover, Massachusetts.

In all, I would write about my visits to about thirty-five schools. It was all part of a promotion idea to get the youngsters attending those establishments interested in subscribing to the *New York Times*.

But to get back to Curran and Mercersburg and his quaint way of speaking which I can demonstrate only partially . . .

"Laddie boy, it's gang to be a delight to see you," said Curran, a Scotsman who, as a runner once himself, used to train by jogging though a cemetery in his native land. "We dinna have much of a track squad this season but we ha'e a football team that cae' cause woe to the inemy."

Curran, a short, wiry bundle of energy, loved by all on his campus, had no reason to make apologies about his track squad. Repeatedly, his teams would sparkle at the prestigious Penn Relays at Franklin Field in Philadelphia. In his day, he had turned out athletes at the academy who had become American Olympians.

Jimmy, in the 1950s, however, was no longer the spry, energetic individual he had been. But he still was loaded with enthusiasm. One thing that had slowed him down a little were varicose veins in his legs—a mean affliction for a man who still loved to jog and even engage in races with his school's runners.

Knowing that the academy had a short nine-hole golf course, and that Jimmy prided himself on being able to play a pretty good game, I said to him, "Did you read in yesterday's paper about a fellow, a senior citizen I think, who played ninety-five holes in one day? That's quite a stunt, don't you think?"

Jimmy, I knew, wasn't going to be impressed. He usually felt uncomfortable taking a back seat to anyone when it came to sports. If an old-timer, in those days, had traveled to the moon, and it had come to Curran's attention, chances are that he suddenly would have begun wondering whether he could make it to Mars.

"That golf stunt dinna be so great," he replied. "If I ha'e haff the mind to, I could do better. Indaed, it sounds interesting. I would gae out a prove it on the morrow, but I must gang awa' for the day and stay part of the night," his burring Scotch accent surfacing more than usual. "But I tell you wha'. I'll be gaeing out the day after to prove it."

"You're giving yourself a tough assignment," I said to him, not really realizing that such a statement to Curran was tantamount to waving a banner in front of him reading, "No one can beat that record."

And so, two days later, there he was, Curran with a friend as a witness, on the academy's first hole, at dawn.

Under his left arm, he toted a thermos bottle filled with coffee and a lunch bag filled with sandwiches. In his right hand, he carried a light putter—one that golfers use only for short shots when holing out on the greens. In his pockets were six golf balls.

The Scotsman placed one of the balls on the tee and swung. The ball lifted only moderately. It landed, bounced, and stopped about seventy-five yards up the fairway, about halfway to the green.

Then to the amazement of his friend, Jimmy didn't walk to the ball to make his second shot, he jogged, carrying the putter in his hand. He then swung at the ball and was on his way to a marathon golf exhibition.

Curran continued to jog, sometimes slowing down to preserve his energy, hitting the ball with vigor throughout the morning. Well before noon, word had spread around the small village of Mercersburg—it's a town whose claim to fame is that James Buchanan, America's fifteenth president lived on its main street—that Jimmy was on a day-long golfing outing.

"People in the village took it lightly for a while," Bob Black, the public relations director at the academy, told me a few days later. "They figured Jimmy would play thirty-six holes or so and quit. That was a lot of holes for a fellow his age to walk, let alone jog."

By the time the sun had reached its zenith, at noon, Curran's gallery had increased to about forty people. Spectators kept coming out in greater numbers as the afternoon progressed. And, after the few stores and offices in town had closed for the day at five o'clock, the village's entire population seemed to be on hand.

Everyone, it seemed, had turned out to see the popular Curran hit, jog, hit, jog, and hole out. From time to time, he eased up and walked to his next shot, and he even took brief rests. But the respites weren't exactly wasted. He used his time to take a few bites of a sandwich and a quick slug from his thermos bottle. By the end of the day, by his own count, attested to by his friend, he had played 129 holes.

"I tol' you I could do better than that other fella," Curran told his friend. "That other laddie probably was playing on a course filled with downhill braes. His was just a wee stunt. It's too ba' that the sun sets earlier this time o' year, or elst I could have gone on."

Since a short time remained before dusk, a few of the impressed townspeople urged Curran to keep going, to establish a record that might never be beaten.

"I ha'e no mind to play in the moonlicht," Curran answered. "Wha' I need naw is a hot bath rather than more holes to play."

Naturally, I wrote the story for my next prep school column in the NYT. I had no reason to rush. I had the exclusive. Black, the academy's publicist, had promised me that news of Curran's unusual golfing exploit would not be released until my story appeared.

On the day that it was published, Curran phoned me. He confessed that following his marathon, the aches in his aging legs had given him pain for three days. He said that he had spent most of them bathing in hot water.

"I dinna think I'll be trying that stunt agin," he told me. "Wha' would I be provin'? There's fellas already saying that I dinna played all those holes on a championship course. Besides, it's tiring."

The last time I saw Curran, he was sitting on a low bench in the infield of Franklin Field where the Penn Relays were in progress. Sitting alongside him was Emil von Elling, the head coach of the NYC University track's team. Both had stop watches in their hands. Jimmy had never seen me at the Penn Relays, and he was surprised. He grinned a greeting.

"Wha' are you up to now?" he joked. "Wha's the nearest golf course?"

Then he shook my hand and said he felt better than ever. I was sure he was telling the truth because he thrived when he was in his preferred surroundings—at a track and field meet.

The mention of Curran's legs brings to mind the legs of Sheila Young during the 1876 Winter Olympics at Innsbruck, Austria. Because of the rhythmic speed they showed during the women's speed skating events, she emerged with three medals—a gold, a silver, and a bronze.

Sheila was by far the standout American in that edition of the Olympics, her clocking in the 500-meter event representing a world record. Indeed, the only other woman to win a medal at Innsbruck was blonde-haired Cindy Nelson in the ever-dangerous skiing event.

I deliberately wrote a sidebar piece in addition to the account of Miss Young's successes to determine whether it would receive a reaction from the White House. President Ford didn't disappoint me. He reacted.

But it was Bob Paul, a long-time friend and then the knowledgeable director of communications for the USA Olympic Committee, who triggered it all. He was with me as a sizable crowd of enthusiasts surrounded Miss Young after she had finished third and won a bronze medal in the 1,000-meter race on the Olympic rink which lay in the shadows of the snowcapped Alps.

Following that race, a well-wisher in the crowd asked her whether she had received a congratulatory telegram a day earlier from President Ford for having captured a gold medal in the 500-meter event. The long-haired brunette shook her head.

"No," she replied. "Was I supposed to get one? What a thrill that would be."

Paul, having heard the question, provided an answer.

"As far as I have been able to find out," he said. "An American president never has sent a congratulatory message to one of our American Olympic Winter Games winners. I don't think it has a precedent. On the other hand, most of the heads of states of other nations do.

"That's interesting," I said to Paul sort of jokingly. "I wonder why it's never been done. Probably, our presidents never even have realized that they were being upstaged by the heads of other nations."

"I have an idea," volunteered Paul. "I'm positive that people on the White House staff read the NYT every day. Wouldn't it be interesting if you related in your story how delighted Sheila said she'd be if she was congratulated by Washington? And including that with other heads of state, such a procedure was more or less routine."

I agreed. I wrote about the post-race skating rink incident putting into strong focus the conversation I'd had with Paul and Sheila, dealing with congratulatory messages. We wondered whether it would have any effect.

It certainly must have. The story appeared in the NYT the next morning. That afternoon, a phone call from the White House was directed to Sheila. However, she wasn't near the phone. She subsequently received the message with the information that she should phone President Ford, "Collect."

I didn't learn what eventually happened to that exchange of phone calls because by the next day, my attention in Innsbruck had to be focused on skiing competitions. In fact, I didn't find out what had ensued between Sheila and the White House until three years later. It was then that I finally met her again at the Olympic Arena in Lake Placid. She was being crowned "Queen of the Carnival."

"Did the White House finally get in touch with you in Innsbruck?" I asked her.

"Yes, it did," she answered. "A White House operator finally reached me late that same day. After a few moments, the President picked up the phone.

"'Mrs. Ford and I want to congratulate you sincerely,' he said. 'We certainly enjoyed watching you skate on television. Also, please congratulate Cindy Nelson for finishing third in the downhill. You were both so great.'"

During the course of a year, I would enjoy writing the Wood, Field and Stream column for several weeks. It was a delightful change of pace because it did take me to the great outdoors, through forests, lakes, and even to the ocean. I found it more fun than sitting in a smoke-filled boxing arena or at a football game and without the pressure of a deadline.

The fishing and hunting beat never presented the opportunity of creating a tradition as in SA, but with a little extra effort by me, it did produce unexpected developments, from time to time.

The story that became a reality, with an assist from me, occurred in Nova Scotia when I was lucky enough to lend a helping hand for a fishing story at a time when it seemed I was running out of subject matter.

I had driven to Bar Harbor, Maine, and taken that long ferry ride across the Bay of Fundy to write about the week-long annual Walton B. Sharp International Tuna Fishing Championship tournament being held in the Atlantic off Wedgeport. The trip loomed as a sure lesson in frustration because it seemed that the big tuna, at that time, were doing their feeding elsewhere.

There hadn't even been a sign of one of those big piscatorial fellows. In the first three days of prospecting by competitors from such distant points as South Africa, Mexico, and Argentina, not to mention California and other distant American precincts, the anglers hadn't even had a nudge from a tuna. The local Chamber of Commerce people were embarrassed.

"This is terrible," a member of the American team said to me with a wry grin, after returning to port at the end of three expeditions in one of the gray lobster boats that was being used for the competition.

"I've been here when giant tuna weighing anywhere from 450 to 900 pounds were taken," he said. "The captains of our fishing boats are blaming it on any number of reasons. Some say it's because there are no small bait fish around in the sea. One keeps insisting it must be the hot weather we've been having."

At the end of that afternoon, I realized that continued stories to the *Times* about the absence of tuna in the area would no longer be making news. I began looking elsewhere for a possible change of theme. Convinced that tuna fishing, at least for the time being, had gone the way of dinosaur hunting, I asked about the quality of Nova Scotia's freshwater fishing.

"There's a real neat fishing camp and lodge, the Birchdale Camps, about thirty miles inland that caters to tourists," a member of the tournament committee told me. "That's near the Tusket River in Kemptville. Guests there are floated down that stream in economy-sized punts.

"While those little boats drift, the guests fish," he continued. "When the river nears its outlet, the fishermen are picked up and driven back to the camp. It's a setup worth seeing. Go! You'll enjoy it."

The next morning, I drove north to the camp's lodge hoping to find an interesting story. I had decided that, even if there were no fish to be taken in the river, I could always write about the pleasures of drifting, dabbling, and dreaming down the Tusket in a pint-sized boat, no less.

I arrived at the inland fishing retreat, it seems, just in time. A talented fly fisherman—a dyed-in-wood devotee, a purist who fished only with flies—named Bill Flemer, the only guest there, was about to leave. Where was he going? Not to the freshwater Tusket but to do some deep-sea fishing in the Atlantic. Puzzled, I asked, "Why salt water when you're at this highly rated camp where trout fishing is supposed to be an angler's heaven, where fish do everything short of jump into your boat?"

"Trout fishing on the river, as far as I can figure," he answered, "has been a bust this month. It's been so hot. I've been here for three days and haven't seen a trout worth taking. I figure I'll do better out on the ocean trying to make contact with some of the gamefish."

"But I've just come from that big tuna fishing tournament in Wedgeport," I said to him. "The only thing the anglers there have gotten are sunburns. That's why I came here."

At first, Flemer, who I learned was the head of a large Princeton Nurseries operation in New Jersey, acted as if he didn't hear me. He kept gathering his gear together as if determined to leave. I didn't want him to leave. He could be part of my story whether he caught any trout or not.

"Your luck may change in your stay here and try again," I suggested. "I know you've been around long enough to realize that every day is not fish day, except in the supermarkets."

Bill remained skeptical. He finally decided to stay put. I could almost sense the transition in his thinking. Because, in the final analysis, he didn't like the idea of driving all the way to Nova Scotia's coast and then perhaps being shut out there too.

And so he walked up to the lodge owner's office and asked for a punt and a guide.

"Bill has agreed to give that float-down one more time," I told the camp's operator. "But if we're going to be gone all day, how about putting in a stock of sandwiches?"

"Be glad to do it," he replied. "Ordinarily, on our trips, the guide stops at noon and fries the fish that's been taken that morning. But since the trout don't seem to be acting contrary, we'll stock you up with some chicken sandwiches."

Within an hour, we were ready to go, having been provided with a punt and all the other niceties that go with a float-down. A punt, anyone who can tell the difference between a motorcycle and a Cadillac knows, is not an ocean liner.

Ours was about two feet wide and probably between fourteen- and sixteen-feet long. Such a boat has no prow being broad at the bow as well as in the stern. Oh, yes, there was one modern convenience. It was equipped with a small outboard motor to propel us across three sizable lakes that led to the freshwater Tusket River.

The slow cruise through the lakes proved fascinating because each of them—they were quite large—were connected to each other by well obscured six-foot wide weed-choked streams. Our guide, I felt, deserved a master's license in navigation just for finding his way to the river.

In our punt had been placed all the necessities: tackle boxes filled with all kinds of flies and fishing rods. Oh yes. There was one other important item, the sandwiches. They were in a large, high-handled wicker basket. Also in it was a large thermos bottle filled with coffee. After all, such safaris as we were taking required from four to five hours.

"Let's hope we don't need many of these sandwiches," said Bill Goodwin, our guide, as we began puttering across the first lake. "Besides I don't like chicken. But if we latch on to any trout, we'll be stopping along the river when the sun is at its highest, make a fire, and dine on freshly fried fish. Now, that's eating.

"In the bow, I have a kit where I keep flour, grease, and skillets to do the frying," he continued. "But I haven't used any of that stuff nigh onto a week. The trout just haven't been biting. We haven't even been able to get a decent strike."

When we reached the Tusket, a slow-moving, twisting narrow river, Flemer, a left hander, lost little time in making a cast. It was obvious that he felt that he was wasting his time. It also was obvious that he was an accomplished angler.

Here was a fellow too, who no more would think of using a worm as bait than planting banana trees in New Jersey. His casts were made with uncanny accuracy as he aimed his fly for the tiny rivulets that trickled into the river from both sides.

Within five minutes, he had a strike. It was a modest-sized rainbow trout, about fourteen inches long. He continued making casts with his superb follow through as we floated down the river and kept latching, yes, to trout. The small ones, and even some of those that were "keepers," he tossed back into the river.

"They ought to be allowed to grow up," the guide joked to me. "It's in keeping with what the real sport fishermen do around here these days. Conservation! They feel angling should be done just for fun and sport, and only one or two big fish should be kept for on-the-spot eating or for the freezer."

Just before the noon hour, only a few minutes after the guide had announced that he planned to land the boat and start our fish fry, Flemer felt a strong tug on his line. It was a "whopper." The strike by the big fellow was made just as we were rounding a bend. We all had to duck under the branches of a young red oak to keep moving.

"We didn't need those branches as an added headache," said the concentrating New Jerseyite as he kept reeling in with his light rod while tugging intermittently ever so slowly. Soon he had the fish within eight feet of the punt. It was now that he finally showed some REAL concern.

"I'm probably in deep trouble here," he said quietly. "I thought the only thing we'd get today would be wet. I didn't bother bringing a net. And as for that hook at the end of the line, it's barbless. It's the kind I use for playing around with light fish for fun. It might be tough boating this one. Now comes the test."

Flemer proved equal to it. But it took all his skill, patience, and ingenuity to make the capture. Because just as the trout was being brought alongside, Flemer suddenly reached for our big basket of sandwiches, dumped the contents, and reached under the trout with the business end of the basket to scoop it up.

It was a brown trout and was large enough to provide for a small family picnic. It was determined by the lodge owner, after he had driven back to the camp by car, that the trout weighed about seven pounds.

"That's the biggest brownie taken in the Tusket this season," he said. "Latching on to one like that in view of the poor luck everyone has been having, comes under the heading of a major surprise. But capturing it with a barbless hook and no net comes under the heading of a fine accomplishment."

CHAPTER 16

Fun at the Home Office

There's so much good in the worst of us
And so much bad in the best of us
That it will behoove any of us
To find fault with the rest of us.

Who knows? I may be the only man alive who has had the distinction of playing baseball at the Yankee Stadium, the Polo Grounds, and Ebbets Field—the one-time home of the Brooklyn Dodgers. And I never signed a million-dollar contract to play in those ballparks.

Wait! Don't bother to dig into baseball's record books. I'm not in them—and for a simple reason. I was on the *New York Times* teams. Our sportswriters in the 1930s and 1940s had an ongoing informal rivalry with the sportswriters from such papers as the *New York Journal*, the *Herald Tribune*, *World Telegram*, and the *Brooklyn Eagle*.

We played our games, of course, when the major league clubs which tenanted those stadiums were on the road. And we enjoyed every minute of it.

For the record too, when we played at the Stadium, for example, it was before an empty house—57,545 empty seats. The only spectators at the field probably were the two men sent by the ball park catering firm of Harry M. Stevens to serve our eating and drinking needs, gratis.

As a result, we probably hold one record—that of being the best fed, on-field players in a big-league ball park, in the history of the sport.

The Stevens' ambassadors of goodwill would set up a long table next to the playing fields on which a large assortment of sandwiches and pastries awaited the sportswriters. In the back of third base, there would be a large keg of beer—also through the courtesy of Stevens. Any runner reaching third was entitled to help himself to a stein full of the "suds."

It was an era in which there was a great spirit of camaraderie in our sports department. Bernard Thompson, the sports editor, a former Canadian army officer, walked and sat as if he was commanding a brigade. His back always seemed stiff as a board, and his face had a serious expression. But inwardly, many felt, he had the gentleness of a pussycat.

"He has to act like the good executive he is," Phil Burke, the department secretary told me one afternoon. "You notice he often wears spats and carries a cane. That's because he wants to look like a boss."

Thompson countenanced almost anything that wasn't going to jeopardize the welfare of the paper. There were one or two deskmen who, while editing copy, would periodically rise and head for the washroom. Their destination was the adjoining locker room where they kept their liquor supplies. A quick nip and they were back at their desks.

As the first edition neared its close each night, it often appeared that these deskmen, having already been in the office for four hours, were becoming much the worse for wear. A giveaway for one was the ruddy face that started blooming once he had one too many. But nevertheless, they were still able to do their work. We never saw Thompson fret about the repeated paths they beat to "the washroom to freshen up."

Our sports editor, at first, had some qualms about his staff members participating in baseball games. After all, some of our players were in their forties. They hadn't fingered a baseball since their teenage days.

"He's given us his okay," Burke finally announced one day with a grin. "He says that if our people can get through all that traffic around Times Square to get to the office each night, they ought to be able to duck if a baseball is coming their way."

Suffice it to say, we never had an injury. And in keeping with the amiable spirit that prevailed in our department, even our top writers would appear to play. They included Arthur Daley, Bryan Field, James Roach, Joe Nichols, and John Kieran.

Daley eventually became a Pulitzer Prize Winner while Kieran became famous not only for his "Sports of the Times Column," but also for his encyclopedic mind. In his later years on the staff, he also became a key member of radio's popular "Information Please" coast-to-coast programs.

One afternoon, when an opposing team failed to appear because of a mix-up in dates, I batted against Kieran at the Yankee Stadium in what became an inter-department game. Considerably older than me, the gray-haired Kieran nevertheless struck me out with a sharp curve during the short stint that he chose to remain on the mound.

"What does he have on the ball?" our Pete Brandwein asked me as I returned to our dugout frustrated. "He made you look like a bum."

"If you can't hit a hook," I replied, "he'll make you look the same way. He's got a fierce outcurve that comes right up at you as if it's going to take a kidney out. But then it hooks right over the plate dipping a little. I never thought, at his age, that he'd fan me that easily."

When it came to sports, our players were versatile—willing to take part in any type of game. We had a bowling team and also played basketball against employees of the same papers. We'd oppose each other on the courts of the Downtown Athletic Club (AC), the New York AC, and at Union Temple in Brooklyn. We even played at Madison Square Garden—again, of course—before an empty house.

The best basketball team hailed from the *Brooklyn Eagle*. A few of its members attended St. John's College shortly after that institution of learning had housed what became known as "the St. John's Wonder Five."

And while the players, such as Harold Parrott, were not necessarily winners when it came to making baskets, some of the ability of their alma mater's varsity five must have brushed off on them. They were able.

I played on both our teams because I had been active in sports near my home at Highland Park, Brooklyn. It had a fine outdoor basketball court and six baseball diamonds. Probably my roughest experience of all came during a game with the *Herald Tribune* on Union Temple's court.

Stanley Woodward, the sports editor of the Trib who eventually became known as "The Coach" because of the illuminating columns he wrote on football, was assigned to guard me. Well, Stanley, a one-time intercollegiate wrestler, must have weighed about 235 pounds. I probably tipped the scales at 130.

As a forward, I had been a fairly good scorer with the team. But I didn't do much scoring in that game. I spent most of the time defending myself from his heavy arms. When he made contact against mine, I felt the pain right down to my heels.

"I've never been much of a basketball player," he confessed to me after the game.

But judging from the pounding I received, he must have been one heck of a wrestler. Both of my shoulders felt as if they had been mangled.

All of this inter-sports department rivalry came to a sudden and inglorious end one sunny afternoon at the Yankee Stadium. We were scheduled to take on William Randolph Hearst's *Journal American*'s team in a rematch. Up until then, most of our inter-paper games had been waged on fairly even terms.

But this time, the Hearst unit, led by a member of the publisher's family, started a pitcher against us who knew how to throw strikes with enough velocity to make us blink as the ball whizzed by.

It developed that the pitcher was a ringer, and had pitched for Yale University's varsity. He unquestionably established a new record for strikeouts in our sports department league while at the same time bringing an end to the rivalry between our two teams. We never played the *Journal American* again.

During those years, friends repeatedly would ask me how come our teams played in the big-league ball parks. The answer was easy.

"We found," I explained one afternoon over a dinner table at the Times Square Childs restaurant, "that whenever we scheduled a game for Central Park, which is much closer to our office than the Stadium or Polo Grounds, only the umpires and a few players showed up.

"On the other hand," I continued, "we soon realized that the big-league diamonds had a sort of mystique for our people. Frequently at game time at these stadiums, we'd have enough players to make up two teams. Everyone, it seemed, wanted to be able to say he had played at Yankee Stadium. You can include me in that group."

We had an out-and-out fun-minded copyreader on our desk, Jack Reardon. A former member of the University of New Hampshire's football team, he had come to New York to strike it rich. At the time I began working at the paper, he had yet to come up with many golden nuggets. And although in his forties, he played basketball with us and was our captain.

But it was in the office that Jack really seemed to thrive. Even under deadlines, when concentration over a story he was reading was essential, he was likely to glance at someone passing and joke with a remark that caused chuckles. Jack made a practice to use nicknames when addressing us, even if he was calling to us from across the room. And he gave many of us nicknames. He called me "Counselor" because I was attending law school. To him, Tom Haney was "The Sheriff" because Tom had once told him he originally had wanted to be a policeman.

He dubbed Frank Elkins, who did rewrite with me for the Brooklyn Queens Sports Section, as "Sven." Jack thought it was for good reason because Elkins was the first of our ski editors in that early era and because his column often focused on Norwegian ski jumpers.

Frank O'Reilly, who reported on the occasional rugby games held in New York, was known as "Rugger," while Tommy Deegan, who eventually became president of the Chesapeake and Ohio Railroad, and who was well known for his dedication to his church, was called "The Deacon."

Jack also went in for practical jokes. Whenever a new copy reader—an editor—was put on the staff, our New England friend would think up some early stunt to make the newcomers feel right at home, to be "one of the boys."

One of Reardon's routines was to wait until the new man, if he wore glasses, and most copywriters did, would head for the locker room perhaps to get some liquid refreshments. Reardon, with all his years of experience, knew that as a rule such "victims" almost always left their glasses on their desks.

As soon as the new man was out of sight, Jack would pick up the glasses and substitute one of a number of other spectacles that he kept in one of his desk drawers. If he didn't have a pair that had a similar appearance to the victim's, he'd borrow a pair from one of the other deskmen.

Eventually, the new man would return to his chair, pick up the glasses and put them on. Then he would take a sheet of written copy and a pencil and start to read.

In a matter of moments, the victim would start blinking. Then he would take off the glasses, hold them up to the light to see if they soiled and then wipe them with a handkerchief. The glasses would then be replaced on his nose and he'd start looking at the printed copy again.

Suddenly a look of concern was likely to appear on the new man's face. Off would come the glasses and again they would be held up to the light. We all would watch with amusement.

"If he's been out in that locker room drinking, he will have good reason to believe that the liquor has perhaps impaired his vision." Reardon observed one night.

By the time the new man had finished his second round of eyesight maneuvers, we would find it impossible to remain quiet and break out into laughter. The victim, almost always, took the stunt in good grace, realizing he'd been had—hazed, in a way, in good fun.

One night, however, a slim newcomer, who formerly had worked for a Connecticut newspaper, delivered some choice words regarding our ancestry.

"You sons of bitches," he blurted. "That's a dirty trick. I thought I was going blind. That's what I hope happens to all of you."

Thirty minutes later, however, he was laughing along with the rest of us.

Reardon, who eventually got a job as the head linesman for the Pro Football New York Giants' games, eventually did strike it rich. But it wasn't because of football. One afternoon I learned that although he was still young as deskmen go, he was retiring. Burke explained the reasons.

"He bought heavily into Grumman Aircraft and that stock has been skyrocketing," he said. "He's sold most of his shares. He feels that with the money he's made, he'd only be giving the salary he makes here to the Feds. He's going to buy a hotel in New Hampshire—the Bradford Inn."

About five years later, I stayed overnight at Jack's hotel on my way to do a fishing column for the paper. The Inn provided quite a contrast to Reardon's earlier surroundings on teeming Times Square. The hotel was on a quiet, narrowed two-lane highway and overlooked a pretty little lake on the other side of the road. The white clapboard building, which contained about fifteen bedrooms, was typical New England late nineteenth century vintage.

But what surprised me most was the loss of what had been Reardon's trademark—his ebullience and sense of humor. We spent the evening in the Inn's small bar discussing old times. As he was sipping the only drink he had that night, he said,

"Counselor, let's face it. This part of New England can get pretty cold in the winter. Come November, I'll be closing this shack and heading for Florida. They tell me they don't have snow down there. I plan to operate a strictly summer hotel."

To my regret, Jack passed away at a fairly young age. I felt, when I saw him at the Inn, that he regretted his decision to retire as early in life as he did.

But even without Reardon around, there were plenty of diversions in our third-floor department. Once summer arrived, we were privy to impromptu burlesque shows while at work. Our big windows overlooked the backstage dressing rooms, about 100 yards away, of a legitimate theater on West Forty-fourth Street.

And while there the back part of the theater was not in focus for us in the winter, come summer it was a completely different story. For, in that era before air conditioning, the chorus girls undressing in the adjacent theater found it necessary to keep their windows open. So did we. A newspaperman had to be blind not to watch this extra attraction.

While the *New York Times* prides itself in publishing "All the News That's Fit to Print," the language used by some if its staff members, particularly as edition times neared, was not necessarily printable. Of course, there was nothing unusual about that. Newspapermen have never been known for their discreet use of words under moments of stress.

The four-letter word that starts with an "f" was undoubtedly thrown about with more consistency than any other profane word. It often was used when two of our deskmen were feuding.

There was that night, for example, when Si Fishkind, an erudite alumnus of Columbia University making up our sports section in the composing room on the fourth floor called to his copyboy.

"Phone Frank Blunk downstairs," he instructed, "and tell him to cut fourteen lines out of the Briody story and twelve out of the Effrat piece so that I can make them fit the space we have."

The boy phoned, communicated his message, but failed to report back to Fishkind.

When the cuts in the stories failed to arrive, Fishkind, after waiting ten minutes, asked the copy boy to phone "the bastard" again.

"Another call is not necessary," replied the youngster.

"Why?" bellowed Fishkind.

"Because Blunk when I phoned him before, said for you to go f— yourself."

Even Joe Durso, one of the best-dressed, most competent, most patient, politest writers I ever had the good fortune to meet, found it necessary to engage in that same bit of profanity one day. It was after an evening in which only seventeen columns had been assigned to sports by the *Times'* bullpen (executive night editors).

The sports department had requested twenty-nine columns for that same night because of a big schedule of events. Durso, who in his zeal to do a good job on the night baseball game he was covering, sent in about 800 words as originally instructed.

As a result, his story had to be cut. Paul Durkin, who was on the desk, was asked to do that necessary hatchet job by Joe Prisco, the makeup editor at that time.

Angry when he saw his reduced story the next day, Durso left a note for Jimmy Roach, who at that time was the sports editor. His message was:

"That story I wrote last night read like a f——g telegram."

At first glance, a casual visitor to our third floor where the entire newsroom was located, had good cause to believe the *New York Times* was indeed a stuffy, solemn establishment. The editors on the cable, telegraph, city news, obituary, society, and sports desks, as well as the reporters and rewritemen, all would be concentrating on their work as edition times approached.

Three men, as I remember it, would often be seen walking into the office wearing spats. They were Edwin L. James, who became the managing editor in 1932; Thompson, our sports editor, and Henry R. Ilsley, our horse show and dog show expert. Indeed, all three of them often would arrive in the office with walking canes.

Sound starchy? It wasn't. James, for example, in charge of hundreds of newsmen, seemed to take a friendly interest in all of us. He had been a top World War I correspondent and subsequently had helped develop a vastly increased European coverage program which put the *New York Times* in a class by itself in that phase of journalism.

He amazed me one afternoon in the mid-1930s as I was walking down the corridor that led from the newsroom to the sports department. He stopped me. I didn't think he even knew my name. After all, I was little more than a cub reporter.

"Mike," he said. "You ought to think seriously of getting into the Ochs Pension Plan. I understand you're not in yet. You ought to take advantage of its benefits. If you find you're interested, go down to the cashier's office and let them know."

I was flattered to think that the managing editor had taken time out to tell me about that program. No one else had ever told me about it. Upon inquiry the next day, I learned that on his sixtieth birthday in 1928 Ochs had inaugurated a plan which was estimated to cost the *New York Times* $300,000 a year.

It became obvious to me that James really was one of the boys—one of us when I learned that he, like many, was interested in betting on horses. Indeed, his wagering was quietly done right in our office on the third floor with a member of the staff who did bookmaking on the side. It was an era in which just about every important office building in the area housed at least one bookmaker. Often it was a newsstand dealer.

From time to time, James would be found spending a few minutes in the *Times'* Syndicate Room waiting for a result from Jamaica or Belmont Park, to come over the race wire. With him, on occasion, was the gray-haired March, the head of the Telegraph Desk.

March was the brother of General Peton Conway March, who had been Pershing's chief of staff during World War I and who had taken an active hand in having more than two million American troops sent to France. Also watching for the race results from time to time were much less important members of the staff. James didn't seem to mind that in the least.

One day I asked the lean, gray-haired March why he was interested in betting and watching the race results. He smiled.

"It's still many hours before edition time. At this time of the day, I can't think of anything better to do."

Dave, who worked for the *Times* for many years as a copyboy—the least important category in the newsroom—had demonstrated more than once that he knew nothing about the word "intimidation" or about popping a question at the wrong time.

As he was closely watching the machine, almost head to head with James, while waiting for a race result to be flashed on the printer machine, he must have felt somehow he was not the managing editor's chum.

"Mr. James," he asked. "Do you think I can get a raise? I can use the money."

"Later, see me later," the boss replied with a surprised grin. "Maybe your horse will win in this race and you won't need the raise."

Dave never got the raise. We weren't surprised. We guessed that it was probably because James's horse had failed to win.

CHAPTER 17

Home Plate – The New York Times

Everything seemed to be going wrong in the world when my career at the *New York Times* began in 1929. The disastrous stock market crash had just occurred, the Great Depression had been spawned, and Albert B. Falls, the supposedly respectable former Secretary of the Interior, had been sentenced to a year in jail for his part in the infamous Teapot Dome scandal.

For me however, it seemed like happy days. I was a freshman in college. I attended classes in the morning and although I had never written for my school's newspaper at Brooklyn's Thomas Jefferson High School, I was receiving weekly checks—albeit small ones—from the great *New York Times*. I was paid on space—forty cents an inch for my stories. I felt like a lucky miner of the '49 era. I had struck gold.

The only one who didn't seem happy about my alliance with the *Times* was my father. He was a successful artist and a commercial photographer. He wanted nothing to stand in my way of becoming a lawyer.

"Remember, Mike," he said to me as he saw me more immersed in my work at the *Times* than at the college.

"I'd like to see you finish law school. You'd have a profession for life. You never can be sure with a newspaper. We need a lawyer in the family. Your newspaper work could sidetrack you."

It did. A shining example was my indifference. After I received my law degree, I signed up for the cram course that everyone at school took to prepare for the bar exam. It consisted of thirty-five lectures given by Harold Medina. He later became a New York Supreme Court judge.

Those nightly reviews were presented in a New York Theater on West Thirty-ninth Street, a few blocks from the *New York Times*. The charge was only $35, only $1 per session. I paid the fee to keep my father happy. But I attended only four or five lectures because I was too busy working for the paper.

It was now 1936. I recall that John Rendel, assignment editor for our main sports section, saying to me,

"Mike, can you go to Atlantic City for a four-day horse show? It's going to be held at the Convention Center. Whoever goes," Rendel added, "will be staying at the Haddon Hall Hotel on the boardwalk."

The plush Haddon Hall Hotel? There was no way I could resist that assignment even with those bar exam lectures in progress. And so I went, having determined at least a year earlier, that in no way, did I have any burning desire to be an attorney.

I had attended trials at Brooklyn's Supreme Court as part of my senior year's curriculum at law school and had heard lawyers tearing into each other in anger during the hearings. No! That wasn't for me, not when I could go to a baseball game or a horse race and just have to write about it, and even get paid. There was no comparison.

In Atlantic City, I had a most enjoyable time. The gracious lady who was the chairman of the show—from Ohio—approached a group of us as we waited to interview a winning rider and asked,

"What papers do you represent?"

The reporters gave such answers as the *Newark Evening News*, the Cleveland Plain Dealer, the *New York Herald Tribune*, the *Philadelphia Inquirer* and the *Baltimore Sun*. She nodded with each answer.

Then she turned to me as I said, "The *New York Times*." It was then that she made her first comment. It was "Oh, the *Times*," and she smiled and moved on.

That horse show was one of the first times I had been on an extended assignment out of town. Each evening a feature of the show was a jousting contest held between two long pole-bearing riders. They were attired, as in days of old. I felt pain each time one of the riders became de-horsed. It was for good reason. Both men finished the show with injuries.

Overall, though, I had such a good time that after I returned from Atlantic City, I gave my father the bad news.

"I am definitely not interested in becoming a lawyer," I told him. "I really enjoy working for a newspaper. I'm working for the best paper in the world. I could never become the best lawyer in the world. I'm going to stay with the *Times* as long as they want me." Who knew at that time that the paper would be willing to put up with me for forty-six more years?

Getting a job with the elite *New York Times* in those early days was in the same category as a kid from Brooklyn becoming the star pitcher for the Dodgers—a long shot! And, even more surprising, was that, at my age, sixteen and a half, I was not being asked to be just a "gopher" or a messenger but rather a reporter and rewriteman for our suburban sports section.

Sam Grubman, a member of my pre-law class, asked me one day.

"Mike, how did you get hired by the *New York Times*? After all, we're in the Depression, none of my friends can get jobs."

I wasn't so sure myself, so I answered.

"Maybe it was just luck."

By the time I finished my college freshman year at St. John's downtown cement campus on Schermerhorn Street, almost everyone in our class of about 250 knew me. I was singled out as one who was working for pay. How did they know I was working?

Because many of them came to borrow money from me. By the middle of spring semester, I had loaned out a few dollars to perhaps two-to-three dozen students. It was "to tide me over for a few days," they would say. They always paid me back.

"That's one way to win a popularity contest," a classmate told me one day. "The boys are thinking of having you run for president of the sophomore class."

I had no time to become a politician at the college and thought no more of it until the following fall when I received a letter from the convention manager of the St. George, Brooklyn's largest hotel. He suggested that as president of my class, would I consider hiring the St. George Hotel for our sophomore ball. I was so busy, it seems, that I didn't even know I had been nominated and elected president of the class.

At the *New York Times*, however, I was far from being a big wheel. I enjoyed working for our editor Joe Gephart and his assistant, Tom Haney, both Pennsylvanians who were Columbia University graduates.

If on rewrite, I would put on ear phones, along with the staff's Lou Effrat and Frank Elkins, to take details of incoming games played all over Brooklyn and Long Island. In those early days we had eight columns to fill. To rewrite the reports on these incoming games, we were paid twenty cents per inch.

"How are you on boxing?" the ever considerate Gephart, asked me one night. "Since you're at college in the daytime, how would you like to go on assignments for us at night instead of coming into the office and staying so late? We'll still need you for rewrite some nights."

"Anything you say, Mr. Gephart," I replied. "As for the rewrite, I'm happy to help."

As a result of that conversation, I was soon reporting to the *New York Times* via telephone or telegraph, at ringside, the developments at local boxing shows. On Sundays, I would cover the then popular semiprofessional baseball games. Such Long Island teams as the Bushwicks, Farmers, the Springfield Club, and the Elmhurst Grays would draw sizable crowds for their weekly double headers.

Brooklyn, Queens, and Long Island were loaded with boxing clubs. In those days, it became routine for me to spend several nights a week covering fight programs at such establishments as the Broadway Arena, Ridgewood Grove, Mitchel Field, Fort Hamilton, Freeport Arena, the Coney Island Velodrome, Dexter Park, Queensboro Arena, the 106th Regiment Armory, the Long Beach Arena as well as the Golden City Arena in Canarsie.

I got to know and recognize many of the fighters, and I followed their careers. Most of them hoped someday to box at Madison Square Garden. Few of them ever did. Fighters in those days in four-round preliminaries received only $10 per round for being pummeled.

As early as April in 1932, however, it seemed that my career with the *New York Times* was about to end.

"Because of the Depression," Eddie Fisher, the night head of the *Times'* Syndicate Department told me one day, "everyone's pay is being cut 10 percent. Some of our newer employees may even be let go."

Newer employees! That could include me. We all knew that Adolph Ochs, the esteemed publisher of the NYT, had refused to cut wages until reluctantly compelled to do so as he watched the paper's advertising lineage decrease. Other newspapers already had reduced their salary scales. Ochs had been a holdout.

As it developed, I was retained by Mr. Gephart, but worked on a more limited basis.

"Just hold on, Mike," he said to me when the news about the pullback first broke. "I'm sure we'll get over this hump. We'll keep finding things for you to do although it may not be much."

And so I held on. Within a year, things began returning to normal, and I had no more problems about my future at the *Times*.

Ochs, it should be noted, in keeping with his reputation in the outside world for having great integrity as well as compassion, was highly respected by members of our paper's staff. He would be found doing some of those little things that were foreign to many of the other publishers.

For example, he introduced the Ochs Pension Plan for staff members. He fathered a program that provided virtually free meal tickets for the paper's copyboys in the *Times'* spacious cafeteria. The "boys," who received only about $12 per week to start in an era when salaries were low, paid only 10 cents each time for a full-course dinner.

As might be expected, I found that working for the *New York Times* was much more stimulating than college classes. However, my attendance record at school was excellent. I never missed a day unless it was for illness. At that time, I was on a rigorous routine getting by with only five to six hours sleep a night.

As a teenager, I was aware of the many temptations that came with the job. I was repeatedly asked by some of the older men whether I cared to go to a speakeasy with them.

One afternoon, as I accompanied the popular Joe Nichols to the Childs Restaurant across the street from the *Times*, he asked,

"How come you don't drink or smoke?"

"Never will," I answered. "I made up my mind when I was still in grammar school."

Nichols laughed.

"I've heard that before from fellows your age," he sort of chuckled. "Wait'll you see all the free drinks offered. You'll probably change."

I never did.

But I did go in for poker games. The cards came out almost every night in the office after our first edition went to press. There was little else to do for some of us otherwise except sit around until the time came to head for home.

On Monday nights, there always was a card game at the Newspaperman's Club located a few blocks north of our office. The timing was perfect because that was payday. As a result, players would have plenty of cash for that night's action. And it wasn't unusual at the end of that session for a player to ask to borrow a quarter to get home because he had lost his entire salary.

My problem with this type of recreation was that I virtually had been weaned on card playing. As a youngster of eight or nine, I had played penny-ante poker with kids my own age. Sometimes the stakes were baseball cards or even matchbox covers. At the office, the limit was considerably larger, ranging from a dime to a quarter.

There were times when I remained with the game until dawn. It was for an obvious reason. I didn't want to go home a loser, and I felt that by lingering, my luck might change.

In the earlier days of my marriage, I would come home with the sun shining and my wife awake.

"Where were you?" she asked me early one morning as I arrived at the same time as the milkman.

"I was playing cards," I answered.

"But why so late?" she asked.

"I was trying to get even," I replied.

"What a waste of time," she said. "Did you ever stop to think that you were even when you started?"

You know. She was absolutely right except I had started playing that night not to get even but to win.

CHAPTER 18

Sneezing and Freezing

Of all things, I was made ski editor of the NYT in 1953. It came as a shock because I never had been on a pair of skis. But for that matter, no one in our office had.

I now became so occupied with ice and snow sports for the next twenty-five years, that I sort of lost track of basketball heroes. As a result, I only saw Alcindor play a few times at Madison Square Garden.

However, I did watch him in action many times on television. This loss of contact with basketball came after I had reported, in earlier years, on scores of college and pro contests. When the NYC Knicks were first organized and were playing at the 69th Regiment Armory as well as at Madison Square Garden, I wrote about their games regularly.

As ski editor, I attended the major college Winter Carnivals—at Williams, Middlebury, and Dartmouth. I also reported on ski racing and jumping events held in Stowe, Aspen, Iron Mountain, Squaw Valley, Crested Butte, and Sun Valley—from Maine to California.

At the college winter carnivals, other sports besides skiing remained key attractions at these colorful fixtures. I remember being amazed one night during a basketball game at the Dartmouth Carnival in Hanover, New Hampshire.

An Ivy League basketball game was in progress there. During it, I saw young Bill Bradley of Princeton, who was to become a Knicks' star and a US senator, foul out in the first half. He was out of the game with five committed penalties.

At the time, Bradley was undoubtedly the best player in the Ivy League circuit. I was so disappointed. I could hardly believe it.

Once I got into the snow country, New York City, where I was raised, seemed like the tropics with its bare winter sidewalks. I recall one afternoon, on my first ski jumping assignment, standing at an outrun of the ski hill in Lebanon, New Hampshire. I was shivering in temperatures that were in the 20 below range.

I think I would have died had not Pat Harty, the ski writer for the *Boston Herald*, come to my rescue. He had been watching me from inside his warm automobile which was parked nearby.

Pat was properly dressed for the occasion, with heavy boots, a fur-lined coat, down mittens, and a beaver hat.

I had no car. I had arrived on a New York & New Haven Railroad sleeper attired in a light winter coat, leather gloves, and rubbers worn over my dress, laced shoes. Whoever had expected that I was going to encounter arctic weather in Lebanon? The temperature was, by far, a record low for that part of New England.

Harty spotted me after I had been standing around for a short time, sneezing and freezing.

"You there, come on over to the car and warm up. This is no day to be standing outdoors."

I was grateful. I had been about to retreat, to look for someplace to get warm. I never forgot Harty's kindness. We often laughed, in the years that followed, about my introduction to the ski beat, the day I nearly froze.

How did I happen to get this ski beat? It really came as a big surprise. It was offered to me after the near Lebanon disaster. As often happens in a metropolitan newspaper, there are unexpected personnel changes. Suddenly, the NYT needed a ski editor.

"You're married to a Vermonter, aren't you?" Mr. Kelly, the sports editor said to me one evening in 1953.

"Yes," I answered in what must have been a puzzled tone. "Why do you ask?"

"How would you like to be in charge of the ski beat?" he said. "Do you think you can get to all those offbeat places in New England where they ski?"

I nodded my head. But at the same time, I made it sound evidence that I wasn't particularly interested in hanging out in the snow country. I candidly told him that if I had to take the job that I had no intention of learning how to ski, that I considered that "damn fool sport too dangerous."

"That will be up to you," said Mr. Kelly (I always used "Mr." when addressing him). "We need a ski writer. You'll need some special clothing to keep from freezing. Go out and get what you want and bill us."

I took him at his word. Recalling what had happened at that ski jump in Lebanon, I went to Sig Buchmayr's fancy winter sports shop off Fifth Avenue and bought everything that was offered. I said to the salesman,

"I'm new to this game. Get me everything you think I'll need."

He got me everything. He turned out to be a golf pro from Dorset, Vermont. I thought he knew more about breaking par than breaking me into this new way of life.

In my new arctic wardrobe I now found I had ski boots, heavy pants with elastics at the bottom of them to tuck under the soles of my feet, a heavy fireman's red shirt, a hand-knitted Norwegian sweater, long johns, a gray half-length overcoat, and a hind knit ski hat.

As an afterthought, he had me buy sheep-lined flight boots—World War II surplus.

"You'll need them for standing around on cold days." I knew what he meant.

The bill came to more than $400—very reasonable by latter day standards.

When Mr. Kelly saw the bill, he didn't utter a peep. He was just happy to know, I imagine, that he had found a snowbird.

Actually, I did learn how to ski but only well enough to ease myself down an intermediate trail at an easy pace. I was forty-one-years-old when I began that winter beat and not nearly as agile as I had been ten years earlier. But I soon found out that to be able to ski was a necessity for this new job. To report on some of the Alpine races—downhill, special, and giant slalom—it was much easier often to ski down to the finish line than trudge over snow to get to it.

I arrived at this unhappy conclusion during my first season as a ski writer. It was on a bitterly cold day while I was at Mad River Glen in Waitsfield, Vermont, reporting on a giant slalom event, a competition in which skiers tear down the mountain through gates and race against the clock.

When I arrived there, I was greeted by Jack Murphy, the manager of that challenging ski resort, I told him I didn't ski, he looked at me and asked, "How are you going to get to the finish line of the races?"

"I'll walk over to it," I said. "Isn't it at the bottom of the mountain?"

"In no way" was his answer. "To get there, you'll have to do some climbing on foot—maybe 400 yards in deep snow and it's all uphill. I'll have Tom, one of my assistants, show you the way."

Tom, who it turned out was a rugged mountaineer, did. He took the ascent right in stride. But I, wearing heavy flight boots that Murphy had loaned me, was in a dead sweat by the time we reached our destination. I had removed my heavy short overcoat and was carrying it over an arm.

There they were, the official timers on the side of the finish line and someone inside a tiny wooden structure, that look like a misplaced outhouse, writing down the times as each racer finished.

"The last one is coming down now," Tom said to me.

I watched him skim across the line and pulled my notebook out of my coat to copy some of the times that were posted on a small, nearby bulletin board that was propped in the snow.

In about three minutes, when I had finished my last note, I looked up. The only person remaining was Tom. The ten-foot long finish line sign, that had been spread above the end of the course, was no longer there, the bulletin board was gone, and all of the race officials had left.

"Where did they all go?" I asked Tom.

"Oh, they skied down the mountain to the base lodge," he answered.

"How long did it take them to get down?" I asked.

"I'd say about forty-five seconds" was the answer.

"How long is it going to take us to get down, walking?" I asked, with a little concern.

"Probably twenty minutes" was his response.

When we reached the base lodge, I again was perspiring freely. I soon found that picking one's way down a snow-covered mountain was almost as trying as climbing up.

After we reached the bottom and I had phoned my story to the *Times*, I did what now seemed the obvious. I asked Murphy whether I could take a ski lesson? He arranged for one for the following morning. My instructor was the head of the resort's ski school, Bud Phillips.

By the end of a forty-five-minute session punctuated with plenty of tumbles, I had mastered the elementary phases of the snow plough. This fundamental technique is an approach to skiing that might best be compared to a toddler learning to crawl before he's able to walk.

People who read my stories kept asking me through the winters that followed how well I skied. They thought I must be an expert. I wasn't. My usual answer in later years was,

"I've been skiing for twenty-five years, and I can safely boast I've never improved."

Actually, it was difficult for me to do much skiing. My priority at any winter resort, of course, was watching the downhill plunges which usually began before noon and then writing a story for the *Times*. By the time I finished filing my story, the ski lifts were being closed for the day.

When on sporting assignments, I usually also would be on the lookout for an 800-word Travel section story and photographs to take with my camera.

That meant extra income. I've been told that I've had more freelance stories in the NYT Travel section than anyone. There've been hundreds of them.

When I began hitting the road for the NYT on sports assignments, I thought it sort of a waste to travel to some distant point, perhaps on a football assignment, or way out to Aspen in Colorado or Heavenly Valley in California just to write about a ski event. I recall well one weekend when I was assigned to report on the Army–Nebraska football game on the latter's gridiron.

After the game, I chartered a small plane in Lincoln and headed for Grand Island, Nebraska. I had heard that in that river town, a re-creation of an old Union Pacific railroad community was in progress. I thought it might make a good story for our Travel section or perhaps a national magazine.

Then there was that year preceding the 1960 Winter Olympics at Squaw Valley, California., when I took advantage of a day's lull in the Olympic trials to drive to nearby Virginia City just over the border, in Nevada. I took photographs and did a story that was made into a generous spread by our travel editor.

Many weeks after the Virginia City story appeared, the person who had been my host, a delighted mayor of the small, colorful, old mining town, wrote to me asking what he could send me as a "reward" for the story I had done. Reward? That sounded outlawish. I wrote to him.

"There's nothing I really need," I wrote back. "Besides, it's definitely against our paper's policy for anyone to receive gifts. But I'm pleased you liked the story and spread."

Almost by return mail, a little package arrived from the mayor with twenty silver one-dollar coins in it. I suppose he had remembered that we had talked about those coins—also known as "cartwheels."

At that time they were freely being used in Nevada's slot machines. I didn't bother returning the coins. I didn't feel like repackaging them and hiking to our local post office. After all, the amount involved was small. In those days, a silver dollar was worth only a dollar. They became worth much more in the years that followed.

As the *Times'* ski man, I traveled to the wide-open spaces all over the United States, reporting on ski jumping events being held coast to coast—from Leavenworth in the state of Washington to Rumford in Maine.

There were Alpine (downhill, giant slalom, and special slalom) ski races staged on New England's slopes as well as on the lofty trails of the Rockies. These winter events found me meeting many people of prominence. It was during a racing weekend at Sun Valley—during the Harriman Cup races, I believe, that I met Ernest Hemingway and famed actress Norma Shearer.

At Lake Placid, I became friendly with the popular Lowell Thomas, the well-known voice of the news reels and coast-to-coast radio news broadcasts. And at Jackson Hole, Wyoming, I became well acquainted with Jean Claude Killy, the celebrated French skiing star. There were others.

"Be sure you look me up when you come to France," Jean Claude told me one afternoon. "We have a small hotel in Val d'Isere. Come there and we'll treat you right."

As for Thomas, gracious as ever, he arrived at the Accreditation Office of the 1968 Winter Olympics in Grenoble, France, with a young girl, a little more than a teenager in tow. He greeted me warmly as he noticed that I was wearing one of my Scotch plaid fedora type hats.

"Still got the Scotch on the top of your mind," he joked. "Actually," he laughed, "I should be wearing a turban because I've just come back from India.

"Maybe you can help me," he continued. "I promised this young lady's father, who is one of the top people in the American Embassy in India, that I'd see to it that she would get a close look at the Games. She wants to be a journalist. She plans to send a story or two back to a paper in India.

"But she has no accreditation because those arrangements had to be made in advance," he added. "Is there some way to get her accredited?"

"I sure can try," I answered. "I've gotten to know all the people in that office. I think they like me because of the way I speak broken French—and with a Brooklyn accent. They may make an exception in this case particularly in view of who you are."

I thought the matter over carefully. I knew that a freelancer, such as this young woman seemed to be, from a Bombay or a Delhi newspaper in India, would make no impression on the officials. I also knew that the *New York Daily News* was not being represented at the Olympics by a staff reporter.

So with fingers crossed, I approached the appropriate desk, introduced Thomas and gave them the story about this youngster without credentials. I was amazed by the readiness of the officials, in view of how strict they had been previously with others, to cooperate. The young lady had her photo taken and had her credentials in her possession within ten minutes.

Thomas, who in those earlier days kept particularly close to skiing, subsequently showed his appreciation.

Shortly after I had returned to New York from Grenoble, I received an invitation asking me to join him as his only guest at the annual formal dinner to be held by the prestigious Explorers Club at the Waldorf Astoria Hotel.

He followed this up with a phone call.

"Mike, you just have to come," he said. "I want you to meet some of my fellow club members. Many of them are extremely well known."

Of course I accepted. And before and during the dinner, I did meet many men of prominence—an admiral, a few generals, and two who seemed as familiar with the Arctic Circle as I was with New York's Times Square.

My friendship with Killy came in particularly handy during the 1968 Winter Olympics held in Grenoble, France—on the slopes of the Chamrousse. The French star, having already gained gold medals in the downhill and giant slalom events, became a principal in a rhubarb. Through no fault of his, complications developed following the special slalom held in a dense, icy fog—ideal flu weather.

The snafu stopped the typewriters of hundreds of international sportswriters who were on the scene for well over two hours. The reason? A victory in this slalom meant a noteworthy sweep of that Olympics' three Alpine events for Killy. The controversy became major news and later that day, I did a special story on just that mix-up.

It indeed seemed that the French racer had made the sweep, that is, until the highly competitive Karl Schranz of Austria was granted a third try in the slalom after finishing his second one. The reason? He alleged interference by a spectator crossing the course during the Austrian's second plunge down the mountainside.

As it developed, Schranz's third try enabled him to turn in a two-run time that bettered Killy's combined two-run effort. Surfacing immediately was a controversy as to whether the Austrian should have been allowed to make that third descent. French fans were irate.

Killy? He was as cool about it as a sixth-grade schoolboy reciting the twenty-six letters of the alphabet.

"I have heard that Karl, he missed an earlier gate as well as the one in question. 'Je ne le comprends pas'—I don't understand how the officials, they can have allowed him that extra run. The fog, it was the same for everyone. I was down at the outrun (at the bottom of the course) when Karl made that second run. I could see nothing from there. It was too foggy."

I tipped off Fred Tupper, our NYT Olympics' chief in downtown Grenoble, who as usual, was about to do the wrap-up story that covered all that day's events.

"That bit you've told me about Schranz missing that earlier gate as well as the second one, no one seems to know about that," the ever-alert Fred said to me. "I'm going to write my story and assume Jean Claude wins that triple. But I won't send it until the officials make their final decision."

And so, he began writing, thereby saving valuable time. As a result, when the race jury's official decision was made, perhaps two hours later, Tupper's complete story, thanks to the tip, was transmitted to New York immediately, thereby saving valuable time.

By making Killy the winner, the race's jury soothed the feelings of the angered local fans. For it had appeared, after Schranz's third run seemingly had made him the winner, that they were ready to start a second French Revolution.

"Thus a possible split in the relationship between the French and the Austrian governments has been averted," joked a colleague after the official announcement was made public. "Luckily, Killy was named the winner. If he hadn't been, de Gaulle, as France's president, probably would have declared war."

The decision by the officials had been preceded by a packed press conference in a shack, at the base of the mountain. I sat on a small, cracked wooden bench. On the "dias" were Killy and Schranz. The interview received worldwide coverage. Killy, not aware yet that he was to be named the winner of that third gold medal for a sweep, had little to say. He listened while Schranz was interrogated.

"Tell us about the episode with the spectator on the course?" Schranz was asked.

"I was descending, and I saw a dark shadow ahead of me," he replied. "I wanted to avoid it and I stopped. It was apparently a ski policeman."

"Did the officials on top see what happened?" was the next question.

"No, it occurred down the slope at about the 10th gate. The Soviet's trainer was there, and he suggested that I return to the top for another start. He climbed up with me."

"It is being said that you missed a gate before that incident with the spectator. It that true?" was the next query.

"It is possible, but if I did, I didn't realize it," answered the Austrian. "I was hypnotized by the dark shadow of the spectator that I saw ahead. It is possible that for the moment I missed a gate to avoid it."

That day sure was a busy one for me. That same evening, I was scheduled to cover the hockey game in downtown Grenoble between the

Soviet Union and Canada in the Olympics' final game for the medal. I reached the arena just in time to see the opening face-off after having been driven on the roundabout, one-way detour around Chamrousse set up for the Games to expedite traffic.

My chauffeur was one of the 500 gendarmes from all over France who had been assigned to drive station wagons for the convenience of media and officials.

"This is a great day for our 'nacion,'" he said proudly to me in French which he mixed with a little English, so I could understand him better. "Never has one of our skiers won three gold medals in one Olympics. Jean Claude, I think, we should build a statue for him."

I visited Schranz, several years after the Grenoble Olympics, at his impressive public ski lodge in his home town of St. Anton, in Austria's Tyrol. I wired a long piece to the *Times* about my interview with him putting the focus on the controversial Olympic slalom event in Grenoble.

Schranz, as gracious as could be, still maintained that he had been victimized by the race committee on that foggy day in Chamrousse.

"It's right in the rule book," he pointed out. "FIS (International Ski Federation) regulations stipulate that a racer who suffers interference on a course is automatically entitled to a rerun."

There was no doubt that Schranz was capable of still being a winner even though he failed to win at Grenoble. He proved it in the two years that followed—in 1969 and 1970—by finishing first each time in the highly competitive, winter-long, World Cup series championship.

The last time I saw Killy I was with my wife at Shawnee-on-the-Delaware in Pennsylvania's Poconos. Jean Claude, who by that time was doing television commercials and other similar work, was at Shawnee to help promote the expansion of that resort's ski area.

"Let's take a picture together," he suggested as he saw the resort's photographer approaching. I've kept that photo in my scrapbook.

"What do you remember most about that controversial slalom at the Grenoble Olympics?" I asked him. He turned on his familiar, gentle smile.

"Mostly the fog," he answered. "Mostly the fog."

Chapter 19

Show Business in Snow Business

It used to be in days of Old
That people didn't like the Cold
But now that some have learned to Ski
It's Thaw that brings them misery.

In the fall of 1959, I received an invitation for a "dessert party" from Oscar Hammerstein, the famous lyricist, to be held at his brownstone home in midtown Manhattan. This was one invitation I accepted with alacrity. I wanted to meet him.

I not only knew the tunes from his hit musical *Show Boat*, but I also knew the words. Hammerstein, of course, also wrote the lyrics for such other hit shows as *Carousel* and *The King and I*. Why the invitation, I wondered?

I found out, as my wife and I were enjoying some ice cream and cake at the Hammersteins' spacious dining room. Their son Jimmy Hammerstein, we learned, was opening a ski center at Hunter, New York, in New York's central Catskills. The official unveiling was to take place on January 12, 1960.

Jimmy, it developed, had obtained financial backing from some of Broadway's and Hollywood's top names—Paul Newman, Joanne Woodward, Ross Hart, Kitty Carlisle, Lawrence Harvey, and Kim Novak, among others. He announced he was giving his ski trails—in honor of New York City—such names as "Broadway," "Fifth Avenue," and "Belt Parkway."

Of course show business people were not new to the skiing scene. In earlier years, such Hollywood stars as Clark Gable, Gary Cooper, Tyrone Power, and Norma Shearer, had taken up skiing in Sun Valley.

It was at that Idaho retreat that I met Ernest Hemingway. He was in the restaurant up on the mountain with a scarf wrapped around his shoulders. In earlier years, he had been an enthusiastic skier. He looked frail to me and he wasn't doing much talking.

Yes, the Hollywood set was really getting into the act. Hugh O'Brien, the actor, and I had dinner at the Lake Placid home of the owner of a New York City theater chain—just a party of four, to talk skiing. O'Brien, it may be remembered, played Wyatt Earp in the long-playing television series *Dodge City*. Among his chief charitable interests through the years was the Hugh O'Brien Foundation.

An important skiing event was in progress at the time. O'Brien, at the dinner, reminisced, with a grin, about his "short career" as a boxer. It had some of the familiar overtones of the story Dempsey had told me about his three-round exhibition on a troopship. As an aging former world heavyweight champion, in World War II, it may be recalled, he managed "to last" three rounds in winning the contest.

"When I was in the US Marines," O'Brien related, "our outfit would take part in 'smokers' in which a boxing program would be featured. One night I found myself matched against a fat guy. He probably weighed twice as much as I did.

"And so, there I was standing in my corner before the fight hoping this fellow wouldn't fall on me and squash me, when who steps into the ring to be a guest referee? None other than 'The Duke' John Wayne.

"After we all had moved into mid-ring to be introduced, Wayne said to us, 'You fellows are on your own. I'm going to ring the starting bell. After that it's a fight to the finish. None of that three-minutes-to-a-round stuff.'

"Do you know?" concluded O'Brien with a grin. "That fight must have lasted from ten to twelve minutes without a break. I only won it because that guy, beefy as he was, became weary. He dropped to the canvas out of just sheer exhaustion."

At the Hammerstein party, the famous lyricist had no such colorful stories to tell. He played it low key. We discussed mostly politics and sports although details about his son's new ski area eventually surfaced. The invitation from the celebrated Mr. Hammerstein had had its expected result. There were about a dozen news media and magazine writers there.

"We have high hopes for this new project," his son finally said. "Our ski area at Hunter is only a two-hour drive from the George Washington Bridge, and it has a northern exposure—the best. Now New York and Jersey skiers won't have to travel all the way to Vermont and New Hampshire to enjoy the sport.

"Our mountain," continued Hammerstein, "which actually is known as 'The Colonel's Chair' because of its high-backed hump, has a base elevation of 1,600 feet. Eventually, we'll be offering a vertical drop of about 1,500 feet. That means that even the expert skier should be attracted to it. Last, but not least, local statistics reveal that about 100 inches of snow drop on it each winter."

And that's where the younger Hammerstein went wrong. In the winter of 1960 and the two that followed, there were no natural snowfalls worth mentioning. Without snow, the area could not sell lift tickets. And without sales, Hammerstein's dream had to go under.

This venture was taken over by the Slutzky brothers, Israel and Orville. They were natives of the village of Hunter, who not only were familiar with just about every blade of grass on "The Colonel's Chair," but also possessed a much bigger plus. They were in the construction business, having built public buildings and outdoor theaters. Their firm had had the contract, among others, to lay down new road surfaces for the George Washington Bridge.

Well aware that winters and large snowfalls in the Hunter area were by no means synonymous terms, they soon introduced snowmaking machines to their slopes. They succeeded in getting the most out of them because of their engineering and construction expertise. Within a few years, Hunter Mountain was doing a booming business.

Snowmaking, incidentally, had been introduced successfully on a commercial basis in the early 1950s at the small-sized ski area operated by the mammoth Concord Hotel resort in the southern Catskills. It came into being then, through the stubbornness of Ray Parker, the hotel's general manager, who insisted on continued experimentation.

It was Joe Tropeano who personally provided me with the precise information about snowmaking's early history, He knew, because it was his firm, the Larchmont Farms Company, located in Lexington, Massachusetts, which Joe operated with his brother Phil, that accidentally discovered late in the 1940s that snow could be created on a substantial scale.

"As you know," Joe said to me, "we have been in the farm irrigation machinery manufacturing business for years. One of our services has been to create artificial fog for crop protection from frost. Our procedure calls for driving live steam and compressed air through pin-holed nozzles.

"One day when the temperatures were below freezing," continued Tropeano, "we experimented. We soon found that if we substituted water for steam, snow would come out of those nozzles. But once the thermometer went above 32 or 33 degrees, only water would spray. However, there were still problems.

"If it wasn't for Ray Parker," Joe Tropeano wrote to me in later years, "the practical application of man-made snow for skiing might have been delayed for years. I was present when the idea was originally tried on several fronts," he concluded. "But all that those early entrepreneurs got for their efforts was mostly cold water."

Parker, in reminiscing about his resort's success with snowmakers, smiled as he revealed,

"We made our first skiable snow with equipment that probably was worth much less than $500. We used a small second-hand compressor, a tired-sounding water pump, some old rubber hosing, and a few iron nozzles with pin holes punched in them. At first, we had some trouble at the contact points because of freezing, but treatment with a blow torch took care of that."

From that little acorn, snowmaking has mushroomed into what amounts to mountainsides of oaks. It is estimated that more than $300 million has been spent by operators of ski areas across America in installing machines capable of making snow artificially. They can even be found at the lofty ski retreats in the Rockies, the Sierras, and in the Green and White Mountains of New England.

"Just how necessary snowmaking was," said Cal Coniff, just before retiring as the executive director of the National Ski Area Association, "is that approximately 85 percent of our member ski centers now have the facilities to make snow. And that's a lot of snow, because we have 440 members in our organization. And Europe, and even Japan, are finally getting into the act," he concluded.

The decision by the sport's major entrepreneurs to include snowmaking in their formats was made after long years of delay. They knew about the success at the Concord, but they were convinced that their areas were in a colder climate and at higher elevations, and so, they felt they had no need for such extra help. They were convinced nature would take care of them. They were wrong.

Many of them learned from the near disaster at Innsbruck, Austria, where frantic preparations for the 1964 Olympic Winter Games were being made. That historic city, on the Inn River, surrounded by the mighty Alps, did not have enough snow on its mountain surfaces to provide for adequate ski racing courses. Many athletes were forced to train elsewhere—where there was snow.

At just about the same time that a major snowstorm was blanketing metropolitan New York, a four-column picture appeared in the sports section of the *New York Times*. Austrian soldiers were depicted—in Indian file—toting large baskets of snow up an incline to be used for Innsbruck's Olympic Games' special slalom courses. The accompanying story stated:

"Innsbruck, Austria, Jan. 18. — The sharply slanted slopes of the Olympic ski runs were jammed today—but not with Olympic skiers.

"Instead, hundreds of Austrian soldiers clambered over the hillsides, packing them by hand with snow that was transported by a truck from a nearby valley and hauled up the ski courses, in some cases, by wooden sleds.

"This city in the Austrian Alps, where the Winter Olympics opens January 29, lacks only three things at this stage: athletes, spectators, and snow."

Only two days before the winter classic got underway, Fred Tupper, on hand to handle the lead articles for the *New York Times*, on January 27 wrote:

"The downhill course at Innsbruck is in perfect shape, the snow having been virtually hammered into place by 500 Austrian soldiers of the Jager Brigade. They transported about 5,000 cubic feet of snow from a valley near the Brenner Pass, carted it up the mountain, froze it, and then tramped more snow on top of the lower layer."

Suffice it to say, while coming up with an unusual number of injuries and even a death, the skiing events all were completed by the time the quadrennial winter jamboree wound down. Without the help of Austria's military, however, the original schedule would never have been completed. Way back then, there wasn't a single ski area in Europe with snowmaking facilities.

Those ski operators in the United States who had originally arrived from European points, naturally sat up and noticed the goings-on in the Alps Mountain country. Among them were two prominent Vermont ski area directors, the imaginative Hans Thorner of Magic Mountain and the hardworking Sepp Ruschp of Stowe. Thorner originally was from Switzerland while Ruschp was from Austria.

Still they and other American ski entrepreneurs seemed in no hurry to install snowmaking machines. By 1971, some twenty years after the successful experiments at the Concord, Stowe had only forty acres of its vast two-mountain complex serviced by man-made snow while Thorner was into the act with fifty acres.

Fred Pabst, of the well-known Pabst Blue Ribbon brewing family of Milwaukee, with a major area at Bromley—a Vermont ski center plagued with slopes that had a snow-melting, sunny southern exposure—by this time had borrowed $750,000. The new equipment enabled him to have 80 percent of his terrain serviced by snowmakers.

189

"I just had no choice," Pabst told me on a sunny January afternoon as he looked out to watch his snow guns giving his lower Lord's Prayer slope a treatment. "When I first came to this region more than two decades ago, I was sure the scarcity of snow would be the least of my problems.

"I must have been looking at horse-drawn sleds on Christmas cards romping through highly banked snow roads," he continued, "the Currier and Ives stuff. Do you know? A few winters ago, I had to shut down in early February because there was little more snow than there was in Florida."

Why did it take so long for American's major ski area operators to decide that snowmaking machines were necessary? One of the main reasons, I always felt, was pride. Those who ran the affairs of high mountain resorts were reluctant to concede that their ski areas, touted so highly in their advertisements, needed outside help. For years, for example, Stowe's Mount Mansfield Company chronicled "When you think of snow, think of Stowe."

By the time the real biggies got into the machine-made snow act, just about every area in the Midwest, dozens of them, were being serviced by snowmakers. For those establishments, the artificial snow was "a must" because of their low base elevations and verticals drops that averaged only between 400 and 500 feet. The operators of high mountain resorts, it seemed to me, found difficulty in admitting the need for snow-producing machines.

"Another obvious reason," John Mattison, a snowmaking machine salesman for Tropeano's Larchmont firm, told me while flying with me in his small plane from the Catskills to the Poconos, "'hope springs eternal.' Ski area operators start a season hoping that heaven will provide them with plenty of snow.

"The hardest sell," he continued, "is to owners whose resorts are in the high-altitude areas—in the Rockies, the Sierras, and even in New England's Green and White Mountains. Some, with derision, point to ski centers in the Catskills and Poconos and maintain that only establishments there need them because they are located in the 'banana belt.'"

It was statistics that kept misguiding skiing entrepreneurs the most. Pabst once opened a book and showed me a figure that revealed that his Bromley Mountain was said to average 144 inches of snowfall each winter. In no way was that true.

There were some winters that not even half that figure dropped on Bromley, the year 1989 being a case in point. That season all of New England's skiing complexes were drastically shortchanged in that department. Only the presence of snowmaking machines enabled them to keep open.

Of course, a third and a chief reason in many cases for the reluctance of skiing's operators to embrace snowmaking, was the expense. They were well aware that when the snow fell from above, it cost nothing. The alternative of spending hundreds of thousands of dollars for snowmaking machines was hard to accept.

The first ski area in the Rocky Mountain country to install the machines, early on, in the late 1950s, was the Broadmoor Hotel in Colorado Springs. Like the Concord in the Catskills, it had only a few short slopes.

"It's been a great thing for us," the personable Steve Knowlton, the former American Olympic ski racer who was in charge of the Broadmoor ski center, told me. "Our hotel complex sits well below Pike's Peak and so we don't have the high altitudes that you start finding around the Great Divide to the west. Owners of ski centers up there don't feel they need snowmaking." As it developed in later years, even they did.

News of the first earnest attempts to make snow was revealed in the Travel Section of the *New York Times* in 1950. Two stories appeared from two different regions—Massachusetts and the Poconos of Pennsylvania. History tells us that both trials, for practical use, were unsuccessful.

"Sure we were able to produce some snow thirty years ago at Big Boulder where I was the manager," John Bush informed me when I revisited him in the early 1980s, "but only in patches. So we concluded that the Poconos might be too far south for snowmaking. We decided to try our luck farther north. We headed for the Mohawk Ski Center which is located at Connecticut's rooftop, close to the Massachusetts border.

"We felt that since it was usually colder there, we might make plenty of snow. But we didn't. All we got out of those nozzles in three days of trying was cold water. The result was that our crew spent almost all of its time out on that slope enjoying a binge, just out of frustration."

Walter Schoenecht, the promotion-minded operator of Mohawk, however, was not about to give up that easily. Technically, his was the first area to provide skiing for its clientele on other than natural snow. But he used the system employed at Bear Mountain Park in New York State for its ski jumping meets. He had ice cakes pulverized and spread over two of his trails.

"It was too expensive doing it that way," Schoenecht, who later was to develop Vermont's huge Mount Snow complex, said. "Ice cakes and the use of pulverizers didn't come cheaply even in those days. And the skies did little cooperating. Add to our misfortune was a toasting sun that melted much of our expensive 'snow' a few days after we had carefully put it down."

Schoenecht, thanks to a system devised by the Tey Corporation, continued to experiment with snowmaking in the months that followed.

But he finally dropped the entire project. In his first effort, the compressors in use created such a din that they had to be shut off. Neighbors complained, declaring that when the pumps were operating it sounded as if an air raid was in progress.

"And on my second try along a slightly different tack," Schoenecht said to me years later, "we tried another variation of the system. It was quieter, but it evidently emitted a supersonic sound. It caused all of the dogs within a two- or three-mile radius of our area to keep howling whenever our guns were in action."

Tropeano and his brother Phil, while on an irrigation project, had accidentally discovered one morning, that a water sprayer, unintentionally left functioning one cold night on a field, had provided a layer of snow on nearby ground.

Impressed with the potential of what he had discovered, Tropeano bought the patents that the Tey Manufacturing Company owned and brought the entire concept to the attention of Parker at his huge Catskill hotel.

"It was a hard sell," Tropeano remembered. "Parker's plush resort was well known for its spacious everything, from dining rooms to night clubs; but his ski area was small by New England standards. However, he finally agreed to give it a try if it didn't cost too much."

Once into the proposition, however, Parker became more and more intrigued about the whole idea. He had Frank Eck, his maintenance superintendent, keep trying to make snow on one of the holes of his international golf course until success finally was attained.

As a result, as many as 200 would be attending ski classes at the Concord on weekend nights while lifts were not even running at resorts farther north because of the lack of snow. In the years that followed, such Vermont ski area heads as Pabst at Bromley, Thorner at Magic Mountain, and Frank Snyder at Stratton Mountain, were among the many to the north, who held out against snowmaking.

"Those machines aren't for me," maintained Pabst. "They're too expensive. Besides, they aren't needed in a cold winter state like Vermont. Heavens! We usually get enough natural snow for skiing—and that kind costs us nothing."

However, artificially made snow became the life saver for the entire industry, coast to coast. Today, it is well accepted that without man-made snow, the entire industry would find it difficult to survive even in the giant ski resorts in the Rockies and lofty Sierras of California.

The introduction of snowmaking was the key factor that attracted one of Hollywood's outstanding choreographers, the trim Michael Kidd, to the scene. An ardent skier who had done lots of his downhill slope sliding in California's high mountains, he began appearing in southern Vermont. He was convinced, after much thought, that there would be skiable snow at Stratton Mountain, where snowmaking facilities finally had been introduced.

Kidd, who had directed the Broadway hit musical *Ben Franklin in Paris* among others, and created the dancing sequences for such major Hollywood productions as *Bandwagon*, *Guys and Dolls*, and *Seven Brides for Seven Brothers*, made it a practice to fly his own Cessna plane and land on a small field in Bennington, about eighty-five miles south of Stratton, Magic, and Bromley. Then he'd drive a rented car to his skiing destination to enjoy a day's sport.

"But that system didn't work out," Kidd told me one day in the winter of 1965 after finishing a run at Stratton. "This rushing up here and rushing back is too much of an ordeal. I guess I have to buy a place near these mountains where I can keep my ski gear and stay overnight."

And so he purchased a small farm complex in Bondville which sits at the base of Stratton Mountain and created a ski lodge. Almost immediately, thereafter, he had a crew working on laying out a landing field for his plane. Those two projects completed, he was ready to sit back and take full pleasure from the recreational aspect of his life. But it didn't work out that way either.

"The first thing you know," he related, "I found myself with some friends I hadn't heard from in years—dancers, actors, and directors among others. They came to see me. I was sure that some of them weren't necessarily interested in finding out about my health. They came to ski.

"Before long," he continued, "I was hosting strangers who were friends of my friends. I realized then that the entire arrangement had to be changed. I had a sign placed over the entrance of my spread that read "Red Fox Inn." Now, I began taking in friends and strangers who became paying guests. The only trouble was that I no longer had much time to ski. I was in a new business, and had become a host who had to worry about my clientele's needs."

I visited Kidd at his skiing retreat twice and had dinner in his farm's old barn which he converted into a tastefully arranged rustic restaurant. He had provided it with loads of nostalgic trimmings such as old-fashioned kerosene lanterns and milk buckets hanging from the ceiling. Diners ate in what had been the hayloft. The area under the dining room, previously used for cow stalls, had become the establishment's lounge. The cuisine was excellent.

The first time I arrived, there was Kidd, who it developed was extremely handy with tools, busy with saw and hammer putting wood paneling on the walls of one of his Inn's bedrooms.

"My next job," he told me, "is to improve our lodge's small reception room for arriving guests. Just as in the first act of a musical, I think it's very important to make a good first impression. Yes, I'll be doing much of the carpentry. I enjoy it."

But what Kidd undoubtedly enjoyed more was schussing down trails, and he wasn't finding much time to do that. It was all a familiar story in the world of skiing. Right in his immediate area, there were lodge owners who had come to Vermont primarily to ski but who weren't doing it because of commitments to their inns.

Harry Littleton, a former heating engineer, was operating the Magic Blue Gentian Inn. His previous vocation indeed came in handy because on some of Vermont's winter days, the thermometer was apt to go down to 20 and 30 below zero.

Also in the Magic Mountain region was Erwin Dostal, who had earned his doctorate degree in chemistry. He was the proprietor of a lodge in the same Londonderry village that bore his name. Up the road apiece, the Inn in Weston was being operated by Jack Straw, a one-time actor.

There were many more within a fifteen-mile radius of the Stratton, Magic, and Bromley triangle who were in the same category—all work around the lodge and no play on the slopes.

Only the late musically talented Louis Weissman, who had climbed the heights of the Alps from Yugoslavia with his wife to escape the Nazis, seemed able to make a daily pilgrimage to the ski areas, that is, except for weekends when the lift lines were likely to be too long, and it was too busy at the motel he operated in Manchester.

There came one winter when Kidd found he'd only gotten to the slopes at Stratton six times during that season. He realized that having his airfield and home near Stratton's base hadn't given him the pleasure that he had expected. He hung up his hammer and saw, threw away his coveralls, and returned to the west.

Thorner, whom I considered one of the most colorful ski operators ever to come my way, was still wondering how he could afford the installation of snowmaking machines at his Magic Mountain "paradise," when Kidd first appeared on the local scene.

The imaginative Thorner major domo had come to the United States from his native Switzerland in 1933. He had set out for "The Land of the Free," he explained, because he had seen so many pictures of snow-covered elevations in the Rockies and even in the Appalachians. He felt certain that the USA was the place where he could strike it rich as a top ski instructor fresh from the Alps.

Soon after his arrival in America, however, he found that the number of skiers at that early date was not plentiful and that openings on ski school staffs were few. It took him more than two decades to realize his ultimate ambition—that of being in charge of his own large ski center.

"After going across the country and stopping in different spots in an effort to find a proposition that was worthwhile," he told me when I first met him in Weissman's motel office, "I've finally realized my ambition. It came into being so suddenly that I've decided to call my area 'Magic Mountain.'"

To prove that he thought it all had happened by magic, Thorner went about giving his slopes and even his base lodge names that dealt with the art of legerdemain. His slopes received such tags as "Hocus-Pocus," "The Wand," and "The Wizard." The base lounge he called "Abracadabra."

His recollections about his earlier nomadic experiences in America rate among the most interesting tales about a ski teacher trying to make good in a new land.

"As a young man, I had heard back home that college professors, football coaches, and baseball managers were making big money," he explained to me after he had opened his office at Magic, "as much as $15,000 a year.

"Why not a skimeister? I asked myself. I can start a chain of ski schools from coast to coast. In ten years, I'm back in the Swiss Alps a rich man."

But as might be expected, he found that he had painted too rosy a picture for himself. When he arrived, he was offered three ski teaching jobs, each of which paid miniscule wages. He finally hung his hat in Lake Placid where he felt he had received his best offer. He was promised $250 a month.

"I realized then, that it was going to take me much longer to get rich than I had thought," he told me many years later with a broad grin while looking out of one of his windows in his Magic Mountain office. "How could I think otherwise? At the end of my first month at Lake Placid, I unexpectedly received a bill for $200 for room and board. There was no profit in that, so I immediately started looking elsewhere."

The determined Thorner trekked all the way across the country to teach at Paradise Valley on Mount Rainier in the state of Washington. But even that lofty retreat didn't work out.

"The snow was great," Thorner told me. "The people were great, and the mountains out of this world. But so help me, skiers were scarcer than sightseers on a lion hunt. On weekdays, the staff and I were alone. On weekends, we barely had enough people for a small tea. We starved."

Thorner thereupon went to Hollywood, where he tried to interest movie moguls in ski films. That failing, he opened a small ski shop on Hollywood Boulevard.

"All I got from that venture was experience," he said. "True, there were a few movie stars who eventually found their way to Sun Valley, but they didn't find their way to my shop in enough numbers to make my store operation worthwhile."

As it developed, the movie atmosphere did have some influence on him as he returned east. He landed in the White Mountains of New Hampshire where he operated a modest ski shop and a ski school. But he also collaborated with the famed sports columnist Grantland Rice and others in producing ski films.

Thorner, however, always was in search of slopes on a mountain that had the preferable northern exposure and appealing sloped terrain. After trekking through New Hampshire and Vermont over a considerable span of time, he finally found his Magic Mountain.

"You know, when I was in Hollywood," he reminisced, "I kept visiting studios trying to interest them in making ski movies. It was hot out there—95 degrees on some days. One of those casting directors once took a look outside on one of those stuffy afternoons and pointed to the sweltering sun.

"'What else can you do besides ski?' he asked. 'Do you know how to ride?'

"'Ride what?' I asked.

"'Horses, of course,' he answered. 'If you can get yourself out to a ranch and learn how to handle a mustang or a pinto, come back. Then we may be able to cast you in a Western.'"

"That was no way to talk to a fellow who had been into skiing all his life," concluded Thorner.

"The devil with show business," I said to myself.

That's when I headed back East to the ski country—to Franconia and found the magic in Magic Mountain.

CHAPTER 20

Muscling in on Mussolini

I had just arrived with my skis in Rieti, in the Abruzzi region of Italy, when my driver, who worked for the National Tourist Bureau, looked out at the falling snow and said,

"Mike, how would you like to take a lesson from Benito Mussolini's ski pro up in the Apennines?"

I was surprised at the question. I had seen pictures in old newsreels, many years earlier, of Il Duce being ushered down a small slope on skis. I had never dreamed, of course, that someday I would be asked whether I wanted to take a lesson from his ski instructor.

Mussolini used to ski here at Monte Terminillo, my driver said. "His pro, who is now in his early seventies, is still around. Maybe you'd like to go out on the slope with him."

"I sure would," I answered. "I have a question to ask him."

Within the hour, I was at the old ski teacher's side in back of his home. Overhead, a large cable car, loaded with skiers, was making its way up the side of the mountain. Without further thought, I asked my question.

"What kind of a skier was Mussolini? When I saw him in newsreels years ago, I noticed he only was skiing slowly on an easy slope. Could he ski?"

"Si," was the reply from the wrinkle-faced pro. "He could ski but one practically had to hold him by his hand. Just a snowplow in coming down the slope, like a child's first step."

I wasn't surprised. In the films I had seen, I had been convinced that the Italian dictator looked like no Jean Claude Killy to me. He even had bared his chest after his short run in that film to show how virile he was. I could tell too, as I had watched in that New York theater, that Mussolini was no Eskimo.

"Did Il Duce like cold weather that much?" I asked the teacher.

"No," was the answer. "He grabbed for a warm coat as soon as the pictures were taken.

"Mussolini only was here during the early part of the war," he told me. "Toward the end, our town here, it was used by Canadian and American soldiers as a rest camp."

I enjoyed my conversation with the old pro, but I quickly felt that it would be asking too much for him to go out on the slopes with me. So I thanked the old montanero and went on my way.

Two winters later, by coincidence, my trail, in a return trip to Italy, crossed Mussolini's again. I had gone to the ancient city of L'Aquila, which is east of Terminillo, to examine the skiing terrain on the nearby Gran Sasso d'Italia ski area in the same high Abruzzi mountain country.

"No sense going there now," the Italian newsman who accompanied me said to me. "This has been a poor winter here for snow. The Gran Sassos practically are bare."

I had just about made up my mind to head north for the Alps. But my friend happened to mention that Mussolini had been imprisoned high in a mountain hotel at the top of the Gran Sasso cable car lift. It was felt that no one ever would be able to rescue him from way up there.

"That makes it altogether different," I told him. "I want to go there. I've met his ski pro. Now I just have to see the place where he was held captive."

So off we went. Our driver took us to the base of the cableway, and we rode up the mountain climbing lift. At its top was the old hotel where the nation's Fascist Grand Council—and also Royal Command—had ordered Mussolini incarcerated in the summer of 1943 after the Italians had become disenchanted with him.

The hotel's manager took us through the dining room, into the kitchen, and around to the musty-smelling parlor. I looked about. I tried to picture how the one-time chest-beating Il Duce had felt in this lonely, isolated lofty retreat as a prisoner.

"But Mussolini?" I asked my host. "Where was he kept while he was here?"

"Oh yes," he replied. "I will show you."

Then he took us up a long stairway that led from the hotel foyer to the guest room. On the second landing—I'm pretty sure it was the second—he turned to the right and after a few steps opened the door to a bedroom.

The room was small, dark, and dingy. There were two chairs, a bed, and a little desk in one corner.

"Here's where Mussolini stayed," he told us.

I looked around. It didn't look like a prison to me, spare as it was.

"There are no iron bars, no nothing here," I said to the manager. "Weren't the Italians afraid that he would escape?"

The manager laughed.

"Not in the least," he replied. "They felt he was more than secure. After all, the only way to reach this hotel was by the cableway. And that was well protected. They had many security men placed at the base of the lift guarding it."

History tells us, however, that after a fortnight or so in that mountain retreat, Mussolini was rescued in a dramatic effort by the Nazis. They crash landed gliders on the slopes behind the hotel and their commandos rescued him. He was then flown to Munich to meet Hitler.

Subsequently, however, he was recaptured by Italian partisans and shot and killed along with his mistress Claretta Petacci, who had insisted on remaining with him.

I thought that the visit to the former dictator's mountain prison would be the end of a two-sided Mussolini sequence for me. But there was a third part. This time it dealt with my meeting with Count Silvio Alfieri in Cervenia, in Italy's lofty northwest Alpine country. Alfieri, trim looking and with a mustache, was the son of the man who had served as treasurer as well as in other cabinet positions for Mussolini.

I was introduced to Alfieri by the pleasant-mannered Luigino Galleia, who with two brothers, operated three high-rise hotels in Milan as well as Cervenia's Grand Hotel. The Grand was one of the finer hostelries in an old village best known for its skiing facilities.

My first meeting with Count Alfieri was at a lunch in the hotel's spacious dining room from which could be seen the mighty, towering world-known Matterhorn. It was a bright, sunny day.

We had barely sipped water from our glasses after being seated, when Alfieri suddenly left the table. He hurried to a far corner of the room, held one hand over his eyes, and peered into the distance. I thought nothing of it until the Count began bobbing up from the table every four or five minutes and heading for that same spot.

"What's he doing?" I asked Galleia. "Is he all right? What's going on outside that window?" Galleia laughed.

"Alfieri has always been fascinated by the Matterhorn," he explained. "He lives in a little shack at the base of that mountain and claims that when the sun's rays hit it, that Matterhorn never looks the same twice. He doesn't want to miss any of the changes.

"Get used to it," Galleia said. "He'll probably jump up a dozen times before we finish dessert."

I counted eleven times. In the days that followed, I got to know Alfieri well and indeed did a story on him for the *New York Times*. He was a dedicated skier—enjoying downhill travel over steep slopes as well as cross-country skiing over rugged terrain. But to me, he seemed close to being impoverished.

"He's sort of a nice smuggler," a maintenance man at the base of the cable car terminal, told me with a grin.

"As you know, this lift takes skiers up to the top of our area. From there, it's easy to ski in the opposite direction down to Zermatt, which is in Switzerland. Alfieri makes this kind of trip frequently. There he buys cigarettes and the famous Swiss chocolates. When he returns here, he sells them at a profit."

A local postman talked with me about the Count.

"A few years back," he said, "Alfieri, after looking at a road map realized that Chamonix in France was a long trip by automobile from Cervenia. He figured out, however, that if he skied up and down the mountain passes, it would be much shorter. And that's what he did. Others have done the same thing, but it takes a stout heart and strong legs."

I spent some time with Alfieri, whom I liked because he was pleasant. But there were times when I thought he seemed a little pushy.

"I'd like to show you more of our country, maybe go to the other end of the Aosta Valley to Courmayeur, " he said to me one afternoon. "Some of us here have used cross-country skis to travel the entire length of this valley, high over the mountains."

"I would like to go," I answered, "but I don't have transportation."

The Count had a ready answer—too ready, I thought.

"I have an idea," he said. "I own a little British-made Hillman—an old one. I haven't driven it since last spring. It's probably buried under snow. I think it needs a new battery. If you could help me buy one, we could manage the trip."

I agreed. My contribution for the battery came to about forty dollars. It was well worth it. I enjoyed the trip. That valley was filled with scenic vistas and vineyards. Near its other end was the old city of Aosta. It was there that I saw, for the first time, an old Roman arena—an amphitheater with stone seats, in remarkably good condition.

We finally reached the end of the valley where the ancient Italian community of Courmayeur is located. Overlooking the town is the high-rising, spectacular Mont Blanc, the highest peak in the Alps which rises to 15,781 feet.

Since the town in Chamonix in France—the 1924 Winter Olympic Games were held there—can be reached by taking a cable car which travels about a mile above the ground between mountain peaks, we headed for it. But there was a long line of people waiting to board that big cabin lift, and we decided to pass it up.

"It's just as well," said Alfieri with a grin. "The snow on the French side is just the same as in Italy. Over there it's just as white as it is on this side of the mountain."

By the time we returned to Cervenia, Alfieri and I were good friends. He proved an entertaining companion particularly since he spoke English well, with only a trace of an Italian accent.

I subsequently saw him for a short time in Milan at the Hotel Continental, one of the three there owned by the Galleia family. It was in the afternoon.

"Have you ever seen La Scala, our big opera theater, which is next door to this hotel?" Alfieri asked me. "It's beautiful. You should see it."

Then he virtually took me by the elbow, and we walked to the famous theater's lobby. There was no program in progress.

"My friend, here, he's a journalist from American," he told the clerk servicing the advance ticket window. "He would like to see the 'splendor' of the theater. Is the front door open?"

This was one time that Alfieri struck out.

"We're not allowed to have visitors enter the theater when no show is in progress," the ticket seller told him. "Insurance reasons, you know."

Alfieri was chagrined. When we returned to the hotel, I again brought up the subject of Mussolini, a topic I had broached with him several times earlier. But as in my past references, he lived up to his previous form. He shrugged his shoulders and promptly changed the subject. I assumed he didn't like him.

As for La Scala, I did get to see its interior in a subsequent visit to Italy. Once again, I was staying at the Continental when the friendly Galleia approached me and said, "They are playing *The Barber of Seville* next door tonight. Would you like to see it?"

"I'd be delighted," I answered.

"I understand that the house is sold out," he continued. "There's been a lot of excitement about the program because the leader of the Soviet Union, Leonid Brezhnev, is to be in attendance."

"I understood he was in Italy," I said to the friendly Galleia. "I know he'll enjoy watching the opera in such a famous theater."

"Would you like to attend it?" Galleia asked. "One of our bellmen just told me he has a ticket for the fifth-row center seat in the orchestra that he wants to sell. He would let you have it for only 9,600 lire, about sixteen dollars American. Would you be interested?"

"I sure would," I replied.

And so I did see *The Barber* in action. I also enjoyed the sensation of feeling that I had a better seat than the Soviet leader. He watched the show from the lower balcony.

In Europe, at times, I needed assistance when I was walking to a destination. And I walked often because I needed the exercise. Besides, I was never happy about sitting in a taxi in heavy traffic.

"Do you speak English?" I would ask a passerby.

All too often the answer would be, "a leetle."

And so I would pose my question. The person, in his genuine effort to be of assistance, would listen attentively and all too often tell me, "Say it slower."

I would ask the question more slowly.

"One more time, please," would be the request.

I'd repeat the question.

This time, my patient listener would ask me to repeat my question with a motion of his hands.

By that time, I knew I was going to get no help, only because I wasn't able to make myself clear. And so, I would move on.

By my third trip to Europe I had that particular problem solved.

In Milan, Italy, one afternoon, I stopped a pedestrian and, with a smile, asked, "Can you lend me $10,000?" When his face remained blank, I said, "Excuse me," and walked off.

But after two more encounters on the same street moments later, I hit my target when I asked that same question. The man I spoke to broke into a grin. It was obvious he spoke English. I explained the joke to him and he helped me immediately. I had no problems thereafter in obtaining similar help all over Europe, in the Orient and even in South America—in Chile, Argentine, and Peru.

Perhaps my greatest triumph in using this easy-does-it method occurred one night during the 1968 Winter Olympics held in Grenoble, France. I was walking from a downtown Olympic site to my room in a nearby new housing development when I happened to see Lloyd Garrison, who was working with us as part of the *Times'* three-man team. A policeman had stopped him in his rented car.

"But how was I to know? I'm only visiting here. I'm a newspaperman from the *New York Times*," I heard Lloyd tell the officer as I came within earshot. "I'm only here for the Olympics."

It was obvious to me that Lloyd, who had told me only that afternoon, after I had put the question to him, that he was descended from William Lloyd Garrison, the Civil War era abolitionist, was a little worried.

The policeman replied to Lloyd in French while pointing to a nearby sign printed in French with a one-way directional arrow. I wondered if I could help. Never dreaming that I really could, I walked up to the policeman and asked, "Can you lend me $10,000?"

The officer turned to me quickly with a surprised look on his face. Then he smiled.

"But I do not have it," he replied in almost perfect English. "Why do you ask me?"

I thereupon explained the whole scenario to him, why I went around asking people to lend me $10,000 and that I had asked him the question to determine whether he spoke English. This time he chuckled.

After I had told him that I also was from the *New York Times*, he told me that he had been raised in New York—in the Bronx. Apparently, he hadn't intended to let Garrison know that.

Why was Lloyd stopped? Because he had driven down a street that usually was a two-way one. But after 8:00 P.M., it became one way. Why? Apparently, an important politician lived in a house that faced the street, and he didn't want to be disturbed by too much traffic after he went to bed. I thought THAT was funny.

There was no question, thereafter, about whether Garrison was going to be ticketed. The three of us wound up talking about New York, the policemen being eager to hear what we had to say. Finally, he stopped oncoming traffic, had Garrison make a U-turn, and waved him on with a smile.

CHAPTER 21

Getting Places – November 22, 1963

Though it is by footsteps that you do it,
And hardships may hinder and stay,
Walk with faith, and you're apt to get through it,
For "Where there's a will there's a way."
—*With apologies to* Eliza Cook

The year of 1963, as it entered the month of November, politically had been one marked with great national and international accomplishments. In June, President John F. Kennedy asked Congress to enact far-reaching Civil Rights legislation. A "hot line" emergency communication link between Washington and Moscow had been installed in August.

Neil Simon's *Barefoot in the Park* was proving to be a big hit on Broadway and the Beatles—yes, the Beatles' first US smash—"I Want to Hold Your Hand" was keeping the feet of young folks tapping. Older Americans were still wondering why such old Irving Berlin standard tunes as "All Alone" and "Remember" were no longer being hummed by the new breed.

On Thursday, November 21 of that year, I arranged for a next day plane ticket that would take me to the important Big Ten football game between Michigan State and the University of Illinois. The itinerary called for me to board my plane Friday afternoon, change in Detroit, and to arrive on Michigan State's campus in East Lansing Friday night. That was an easy trip.

But I never boarded that Friday jet. After traveling by subway and reaching my office off Times Square that Friday afternoon, there was

---

shocking news. President Kennedy had been assassinated in a Dallas motorcade.

Phil Burke, our department's personable assignment sports editor, had added reason to be dismayed. "At least a dozen of our other staff writers already have been assigned for Saturday afternoon's out-of-town football games," he said to me in a harried tone. "Many of those games, because of the tragic news, already have been postponed. And here I am up to my ears in phone calls. I've been trying to tell the assigned writers to stay home.

"It's been a terrible job," Burke added. "No one seems to be home. Some of our men undoubtedly will phone me once they hear about the assassination. I hope our whole country isn't in for even bigger trouble. There already has been talk of the President having been the victim of a conspiracy."

I waited around for an hour or so until Phil seemed ready to take a breather. Then I discussed my projected trip to Michigan State.

"That game hasn't officially been called off yet," Phil said to me. "You'd better think in terms of making the trip."

"But I think it will be along with all those other ones," I answered. "Actually, we can gamble on that trip. I can wait until the first thing tomorrow morning before taking off. The game is apt to be postponed by then.

"But if it isn't," I continued, "there's a plane leaving LaGuardia at about 7:00 A.M. It connects at Detroit with a North Central flight for East Lansing. That could get me there on time."

"What about the weather?" Burke asked. "What if that plane can't take off because of poor visibility?"

"I've checked that out," I told him. "I've contacted what I consider is America's best bureau—AccuWeather. My friend Dr. Joel Myers as well as his partner Elliott Abrams, who own the company, both assure me the skies will remain clear tomorrow. I'm sure I can make it even with that late start."

"I suppose leaving tonight would be foolish at that," Burke said. "After so many games have been called off, why not the one at Michigan State? Let's gamble. If by some long shot chance the game is played and you haven't arrived there, we can always pick up the reports from the Associated Press or the UP wires."

Friday night came and passed and still that game hadn't been postponed. And so, I was on hand the first thing next morning at LaGuardia to fly to Detroit. AccuWeather had called the conditions right on the nose. There wasn't a cloud in the sky as we took off.

Once in Detroit, I hurried to the other side of the airport and made my connection with North Central. I was in East Lansing by 11:00 A.M. about three hours before game time. I had gotten to the game on time, but had I?

Despite the early hour, crowds already had begun to gather around the campus's huge stadium. Tailgaters were getting set up for their Saturday foodfests. Anticipated by them was the regular invasion of friends who would be served from the rear of station wagons and from the side doors of motor trailers.

Then came the announcement. It was as if the university's authorities had been waiting for my arrival to make one. Because just as I reached the press gate, I was told the contest, only a few minutes earlier, had been called off. Biggie Munn and Doug Mills, athletic directors at the two schools, had just emerged from a meeting to announce the decision. It would be played the following Thursday—Thanksgiving Day.

The game, it should be noted, was a crucial one from the standpoint of Big Ten significance. A standing room only crowd of about 70,000 had been expected to turn out for it because it not only was for the Conference's championship but in addition, the winner was to be the invitee for that year's prestigious Rose Bowl Classic on New Year's Day.

The announcement created a gigantic traffic mix-up in several departments. For one thing, early arrivals, aware of the postponement, began heading for home. They ran smack into approaching motorists on highways not yet aware of the postponement. Those arriving by plane, in most cases, had no choice but to seek reservations—unavailable in many cases—for their return to their starting-off point.

More than 500 of the game's expectant spectators, aboard the "Grand Trunk Western Railroad's Football Special" which had left the Illini's home base in Champaign, Illinois, early that morning were flagged down at downstate Michigan's Battle Creek, only about forty-five miles southwest of East Lansing. The train was made to do the obvious. Turn about and head back from whence it had come.

Duffy Daugherty, the colorful gray-haired head coach of Michigan State's eleven, who had squired me around the Spartan's campus in his car earlier in the season while telling me how happy he was to be there, was among the most disappointed over the sudden turn of events. He felt on the day of the postponement that his squad was all tuned, in just the right mental and physical state to score a victory.

"This news about President Kennedy is devastating," he said to me. "I know we had no choice but to call this game off. But it still has to be played, and we still have to be ready for it. And so, I'm going to take my team indoors later this afternoon and run it through a light session—mostly signal drills—in our field house."

The decision by the two "M's"—Munn and Mills—late though it was made, was merely in keeping with determinations made on most other campuses across the United States. Only about one-fourth of the fifty major college games scheduled for that Saturday were played. Pimlico in Baltimore was the only one of five eastern thoroughbred race tracks to stage its program. The third round of the pro tour's Cajun Golf Classic at Lafayette, Ind., was among the many other sports events called off.

At Michigan State, there developed another type of false start. It was reported in some quarters later that Saturday, that the rescheduled contest had been rescheduled for the following Monday. The announcement left many ticket holders in a confused and indignant state. They had jobs and would not be able to attend the game on that day. Finally, Thursday was the date that came out of the foggy situation.

When I finally collected all the necessary facts on that Saturday, I hustled up to the stadium's press box. My Western Union operator was waiting for me. There I began writing the details of the eleventh-hour postponement. The story appeared on the front page of the following morning's sports section.

In that article, I included some interesting trivia such as the fact that, because of the postponement, 400 gallons of coffee had to be dumped by the stadium's concessionaires and that 1 ½ tons of hot dogs were left howling for takers. The franks finally were turned over to the campus's food service agency for sale to dorm students.

Once I finished that chore, I had to start thinking in terms of a revised itinerary. My original arrangement with Burke at the office was that I was to remain on the university's campus until Monday in order to report on the NCAA's cross-country championships, also being held on the Spartans' campus.

But that title run, in which collegians from across the United States were scheduled to compete, was moved ahead to Tuesday. Monday, it was announced, was to be a day of mourning for the late president. The question, therefore arose, whether I was to remain in East Lansing for the Thursday football game.

Anticipating a siege of idleness, a state that I seldom appreciated while on the road, I phoned Burke at the *Times* late Saturday afternoon. I suggested that rather than spending the day on Sunday as well as Monday seeing the sights, which I had seen a dozen times, that I fly to Milwaukee where the Green Bay Packers were hosting the San Francisco 49ers in a National Football League game on the following day, a Sunday.

I received the go-ahead. But there was one proviso. I could cover the game providing I could obtain the needed press credentials on so short a notice.

Short notice never had bothered me. Five phone calls did the trick.

"Calling kind of late," the Packers' publicity director said to me once I reached him. "We usually get such requests a week in advance."

"I would have been happy to have let you know a month in advance," I answered. "But not even you could have predicted that we were in for troubled times this weekend. Are there any problems?"

"Glad to have you come" was the reply. "It'll be a change. We usually don't get a *New York Times* man here except when the Giants are playing. If you run into any problems when you get here, let me know. Your press badge will be at the 'Will Call' window. We'll be glad to see you."

Burke arranged for a telegraph operator to service my story in the press box. I made a reservation on a North Central Airlines plane scheduled to arrive in Milwaukee Sunday morning. Came game time and I was comfortably seated in the press box—on the forty-five-yard line.

My story of that pro game appeared in Monday morning's paper. It was not a contest that was calculated to keep the crowd of about 46,000 spectators spellbound. Led by famed quarterback Bart Starr, the Packers clinched the game with a big first-half scoring display. Then after seemingly playing "dead" in the last two periods, they provided the 49ers with a gift—an easy touchdown—in the last four seconds that enabled San Francisco to cut its final deficit to eighteen points. The score was 28–10.

I returned to East Lansing that night and on Monday, I did do some sightseeing in the state's capital city of nearby Lansing. On Tuesday, I reported on the NCAA cross-country championships at Michigan State and watched the late finishers huff and puff over the last part of the course which was known as "Cardiac Hill." The winner of the race was Vic Zwolak of Villanova.

Wednesday arrived. I sent an advance story on the delayed Big Ten championship game between the Spartans and the Illini. I pointed out that while the previous Saturday's postponement had provided its share of snafus, that rough times lay ahead for Michigan State's stadium officials.

It was suddenly realized that they were going to be short of help on the new game date. Most of the students usually manning the parking and barricaded areas as well as other game day assignments, were gone. They had left for the long Thanksgiving Day holiday weekend.

The result? Hours before the contest's start, highway approaches to the stadium were one long parking lot of automobiles moving bumper to bumper, whenever they indeed, moved. There were plenty of ticket holders who never saw the game's first quarter.

Those Spartan fans who did arrive late didn't miss much. Fumbles by their team cost heavily as the home eleven went down to a 13–to–0 defeat. Prominent in pacing the Illini were 152-pound halfback Sherm Lewis who included in his breakaways a spirited 80-yard run, and Dick Butkus.

For Butkus, a defensive starter, that victory over Michigan State, paved the way for him eventually to attain a great career in the gridiron sport. Illinois went on to defeat the University of Washington, 17–7, in the Rose Bowl and Butkus went on to become a super star in the pro ranks as a member of the Chicago Bears. He subsequently was named to the pro game's Hall of Fame.

The only department at Michigan State that reaped at least a wee bit of benefit from the entire proceedings was its Sports Information Office. The editors of the game's official football program had given its front page cover a big Thanksgiving Day theme, even though the contest originally was to have been staged five days before the holiday.

Those same programs, of course, were used on the day of the actual contest. As a result, the cover page of these attractive booklets, with their colorful pictures, was perhaps the only part of the entire proceedings exactly on target.

Of course, there were many other times that it wasn't easy getting places while in pursuit of assigned stories.

There was that year when Phillips Exeter Academy in Exeter, New Hampshire, was my destination—also on a November day—but in the late 1960s. I boarded a Northeast Airlines plane at LaGuardia heading for the small airport at Lawrence, Massachusetts.

As in earlier years, for this trip, once in Lawrence, I planned to take a crack Boston & Maine train for Portland, Maine, that stopped at Exeter. I had done it at least five times.

I was scheduled to cover the annual football game between the Exonians and their traditional rivals, Andover. These two schools had been meeting each other since the late nineteenth century, and because I had made it a practice to visit boarding schools for the paper, this game fell into my lap each year.

Reaching Exeter, in previous seasons, had been routine. I customarily would take a taxi from the Lawrence Airport to the Boston & Maine's downtown railroad station. Lawrence was once a thriving woolen-textile center as well as an important railroad hub. The Great Depression of the 1930s, however, had helped send the city into a period of decline.

After leaving the taxi, I went right to the station's ticket window where a clerk was in attendance.

"I'd like a round-trip to Exeter. The train leaves in about an hour, doesn't it?" I questioned.

"Leaves?" was the reply. "It goes right past here. It doesn't stop."

"How come?" I asked. "I've been taking this train to Exeter for at least ten years."

"Well," the man replied with a smile. "You may have, but times have changed. The B&M is cutting down on its passenger service. That train still stops at Exeter, but it races past here—usually as if it were jet propelled."

I was in a dilemma. My first thought was to rent a car. I suggested it to the ticket agent. He said that that would be difficult if not impossible. He explained there was nothing that even resembled a Hertz or Avis agency in town.

"There would be no call for it around here," he added. "Besides if you were to find an agency down at Lowell or over toward Boston, you'd never get up to Exeter on time to see the game."

I pondered over the problem for minute or two and then a thought came to me.

"Who's in charge of the train operations in this area?" I asked. "Can he be reached?"

"He'd be the towerman at the Reading station, about fifteen miles down the line."

"Do you have a phone number for him?" I asked.

The agent nodded, reached into his desk drawer, copied the number and handed it to me. He was eyeing me curiously undoubtedly wondering what I was up to.

I hastened to one of the station's pay telephones and called the Reading dispatcher. He picked up the phone after only two rings.

"I'm in sort of a fix," I explained to him. "I'm a *New York Times* sportswriter and I'm at the Lawrence station. I'm in the area to report on that big football game in Exeter. I arrived expecting to board the train here. Now I'm told it doesn't stop at Lawrence anymore."

The dispatcher began giving me the same explanation I'd heard from the ticket agent. When I told him that I had had no way of knowing about the change in the railroad's schedule and that my editor was going to be pretty peeved, if I missed the game, he offered to help.

"Okay," he said. "I'm going to help you. I will send orders to the engineer of the train to make that unscheduled stop at Lawrence to pick you up. I want you to know, though, that this is highly irregular."

Grateful and relieved, I headed for the ticket agent's window. I told him that the train was going to stop, and I bought my ticket for Exeter. Then I sat down in the large waiting room to read a newspaper.

Five minutes later, however, there was bad news. The ticket agent hailed me through his window.

"The Reading dispatcher just phoned me," he said. "He's had to change plans because that train can't stop here and pick you up. There's a waiting freight train occupying the track right next to our station's platform. You'd be blocked. You'd have no way of boarding. He says he is sorry."

Distressed, I mulled over the situation for a few minutes. Then I phoned that Reading dispatcher again,

"Would it be possible to have that train stop at North Andover which is only a few miles north of here," I asked.

"North Andover!" the dispatcher exclaimed. "That station is smaller than a peanut stand. It's used only by slow trains as a commuter stop. The baby we're talking about is an Express." He paused for a few moments. "How would you get to North Andover?"

"By taxi," I replied in a tone that had to reveal I was worried.

"Get going," he said. "Hustle up there and I'll get the train to stop."

I hastily found a taxi and had no problem reaching the tiny North Andover station. I got out of the cab about thirty yards or so in front of the black-and-white-striped railroad gates that protected the crossing.

With my portable typewriter in one hand and my small overnight bag in the other, I proceeded to walk to the gate. I was about to proceed up the track when I noticed the gate tender—a grizzled faced old-timer, obviously near retirement age—standing on the far side of the gate.

He looked at me with what seemed a perplexed expression. He touched the peak of his cap with his right hand and then seemed to work up enough courage to ask,

"Where are you going?"

"I'm going up the track a bit to wait for that Portland Express that's headed for Exeter."

"What did you say?" he queried with a rising voice as if he didn't believe what he'd heard.

"I'm waiting for the Portland Express."

"You're waiting for what?" he asked. "That train doesn't stop here. I've been working at this crossing for almost twenty-five years, and it hasn't stopped here yet."

"That doesn't surprise me in the least," I answered, as I glanced at the small bench with a roof over it that served as the station. "But this train is supposed to stop for me."

Then I strolled up the track while the gate tender kept staring at me. As I walked, I looked backward once or twice. He was still watching me. I thought he might be thinking I was planning suicide, that I might jump in front of the speeding train.

In about five minutes, I could hear the Express approaching. It slowed down as it neared the station and then stopped.

A conductor hopped down on the car's steps and placed a small boarding stool on the ground. I stepped on it and boarded the train.

As the train was coming to a stop, I had glanced up at a window. Of all things, there was Eddie Samuels,[7] a well-known sportswriter from the *New York Herald Tribune* staring out at me. He also, I realized, must be heading for the Andover–Exeter game.

Once inside the car, I sat down alongside Eddie, whom I knew well. He had been a World War II pilot and was plagued, it was said, by shattered nerves. It apparently had caused him to become a drinking man. And he evidently had already been imbibing that day. He seemed shocked that the train had pulled up for me.

"How come this train stopped at this dinky station?" he asked me as soon as we had exchanged hellos. "I had to board it at its starting point at North Station in Boston. I was told that the next stop would be Exeter."

"It's a long story," I answered. "We'll probably be in Exeter before I could finish it. I'll tell you about it later."

I didn't tell him the story because, at the time, he seemed a little hazy. And, although Eddie and I covered many subsequent sports events together, I never did give him the details. I kept having unusual experiences with him. Once at the Aqueduct race track in New York and again at a baseball game in the Yankee Stadium, he brought up the subject.

I brushed him off because both times, we were writing near deadlines. The train story? He probably never would have believed it.

One of the many other times Eddie and I covered the same event was at a Colgate–Dartmouth football game in Hamilton, New York. There were no flights from New York to that small campus. To get there, one had to fly to Syracuse and rent a car.

I arrived at Kennedy Airport in New York that morning an hour ahead of time to await the departure of a Mohawk Airline plane for Syracuse. I had only been there for about ten minutes when none other than Eddie, impeccably dressed as usual, sat down beside me.

---

[7]   Name altered by editors

"How'd we ever get assigned to this game?" he asked. "No one likes to travel to Colgate. It's so much out of the way. Now take a Yale game or one at West Point. An hour's drive, or so, in your own car, and you're there."

Eddie was a nice enough guy when he wasn't drinking, but even when he wasn't, he seemed nervous. It was obvious to me that he already had had a few nips that morning. I agreed with his feelings about the complexities of a trip to Colgate.

"It's not going to be so rough getting to Colgate," I answered him. "It's an easy one-hour flight to Syracuse. After that, I do the driving for another hour and we'll be there."

I was confident that we'd have no problems, that is, until an announcement came through the airport's public address system.

"Mohawk Airlines is very sorry, but our 10:30 A.M. departure for Syracuse has been canceled due to equipment trouble. We suggest you rebook immediately at one of our counters for our next scheduled Mohawk flight for Syracuse, leaving at 4:30 P.M."

Four-thirty! Naturally, that new departure time was going to be of no use to us. Game time was at 2:00 P.M. The announcement seemed to bother me more than it did Eddie. He took it right in stride.

"Guess that means I go home," he said in a matter of fact tone. "I'm going to spend my afternoon at my house in Suffern watching some of the football games on television."

But as always has been the case in similar situations, I was not willing to give up the chase. I said to Eddie,

"Let's not call it quits that easily. I know American Airlines also services New York and Syracuse. It's a long shot that American will have a flight that will do us any good. But let me call on the phone."

I phoned American.

"Yes," said the voice on the other end of the line. "American does have a flight departing for Syracuse at noon but it leaves from LaGuardia."

Well aware that the uneasy Samuels might need some direction, I took charge. I ordered reservations for two and hurried with Eddie outside the terminal. I hailed a taxi.

"Get us to LaGuardia quickly," I told the driver. "We have to make a twelve o'clock flight."

He raced down the Van Wyck Expressway and got to LaGuardia in about twenty-five minutes. We reached the American Airlines counter only about fifteen minutes before departure time. After picking up our tickets, I said to the counter clerk,

"Please, I am with the *New York Times*. The gentleman with me is from the *Herald Tribune*. We're heading for the football game at Colgate

---

213

this afternoon. We'll be getting to Syracuse so late that we'd never make the ball game on time if we drove a rented car. Is it possible for you to contact Syracuse and ask if a small charter plane can stand by to fly us to Hamilton?"

Without another word, we rushed for the American Airlines Convair that was waiting at the gate with its engines already revving. I spent the hour's flight to Syracuse explaining to Sinclair what I had done. I got him to agree to pay half the expenses for the charter. I also told him that we couldn't be sure a small charter plane would be awaiting our arrival in Syracuse.

It was. Its pilot was standing near our Convair plane as it rolled up to the ramp with a cardboard sign. Over his chest he had the name "Strauss" scrawled on it. We entered his small Cessna and were airborne within ten minutes. I saw Eddie, devout Catholic that he was, take out his beads and start kissing them intermittently as we began flying over the hilly countryside.

"Hope we're doing this right," he said to me in a little bit of a perplexed tone. "All I know is that I was supposed to be on a big plane, and here I am in a small puddle jumper."

It could be that Sinclair's devotions helped. We landed on a rustic, grass-covered strip just outside of town. The pilot, before leaving from Syracuse, had someone wire for a taxi to be waiting in the mowed hayfield in Hamilton.

Anticipating the possible difficulty of getting home after the game, what with no rented car, I asked the pilot, who had been extremely cooperative, just before we touched down, a question.

"Have you ever watched a college football game while sitting in the press box?" I asked the pilot.

"No, never had occasion to," he answered.

"Well, we could get you into the press box here," I told him. "Then after the game and after we have written our stories, you could fly us back to Syracuse. We'd pay you for that trip too. And if you haven't had lunch today–"

"But I haven't had lunch yet," the pilot answered. "And I had breakfast early this morning, at 7:00 A.M."

"That would be no problem if you stayed with us," I replied. "There's always a free feed in the press box at halftime."

"That sounds good to me," he said. "I'll go for that."

The taxi to take us to the football field was waiting at the end of the grassy landing strip. After a short drive, we reached the press box about ten minutes before kickoff time. When the game was finished, we wrote our story and taxied back to the waiting Cessna at the far end of town.

We landed in Syracuse about twenty minutes before an American Airlines plane was scheduled to depart for LaGuardia. We were back in New York by 7:15. Had we flown Mohawk that morning and gone through our original itineraries, we could not possibly have gotten back to New York until 10:00 P.M. or later.

Oh, yes, the pilot of the Cessna who had dined in the press box as a guest of the university, saw us write our stories on our portable typewriters, and then he watched the telegraphers transmit our accounts by dots-and-dashes Morse Code?

"Do you know," he remarked as we paid him at Syracuse for our passage, "This has been one of the most remarkable and enjoyable days I've ever had."

There have been times, naturally, when trips—lengthy ones included—have failed to work out. There was that week in July in the early 1960s when I went with Marty Glickman, the well-known radio and television sports commentator as well as a former American Olympic trackman, to Santiago, Chile. We flew there on the now-defunct Panagra Airlines, then a joint venture of Pan American and W.R. Grace & Company.

Our goal was to enjoy the skiing high up in South America's lofty Andes Mountains—at Portillo—at about two miles above sea level. I expected to ski but I primarily was interested in doing stories for our sports and travel sections as well as for a magazine. But while we reached Santiago—after a trip of more than 6,000 air miles from New York—we never reached the ski area.

A blizzard, one of the largest in Chile's history, had wiped out part of the railroad and the highway leading to the high altitude, colorful resort. There was absolutely no way of getting up to the ski area.

Indeed, even the power lines leading to the big ski lodge were down. We spent the entire week in downtown Santiago sitting in the hotel's lobby, looking at the distant snowcapped mountain peaks, or walking around downtown shopping.

For a time it was feared that disaster had struck the skiers who already had gotten up to Portillo. The routine way of contacting them by telephone had been eliminated because all wires were down. One gentleman, a well-known skiwear manufacturer from New York, was worried. His wife and daughter were up on the mountain, and he had heard that there was no power up there—no heat. Since he knew that I was a newspaperman, he approached me.

215

"What can I do?" he asked. "I've tried everything. My family may be in trouble."

"I'll tell you what," I answered. "The US Ambassador's headquarters is only a few blocks from our hotel. Maybe he can figure this out."

We both went over to the large building that had an American flag flying over it. The ambassador was out but one of his aides came to our rescue.

"I think we can help. We have a radio telephone immediately beamed up to Portillo because there are always so many Americans skiing up there."

The embassy official's efforts did the trick. Contact with the lofty ski area revealed that power indeed had been lost but that the resort had an auxiliary plant that was taking care of its needs nicely. Our friend, the New York clothier, was relieved. His family returned to him in about four days.

Only a little disappointed because of our failure to go skiing because he had enjoyed his sightseeing, Glickman, after we had patiently waited down in the city hoping that highway conditions would change, finally shrugged his shoulders.

"There's always the next time," he said. His ability to take disappointment in good grace was characteristic of him. After all, hadn't he been the track star who had been on the same American Olympic team with the great Jesse Owens and hadn't his chances of competing at the Berlin classic been eliminated?

It was explained by some at the time that, it was because he was Jewish, and that his possible appearance might displease Adolph Hitler, who was to be an observer at the Games. And so Glickman took our inability to ski at Portillo right in stride.

"This airline still will be flying next year, and the Andes still will be towering above Santiago," said Glickman. "As for the snow, it makes this area a regular stopover once winter arrives in Chile. We've got here once," he concluded. "We'll get here again."

He spoke the truth. I returned to Santiago about four years later. I skied at Portillo on deep snow bases. This time, my big problem was to stay healthy. There was an epidemic of the flu and nearly everyone I knew became sick—that is, except me.

An entirely different type of frustration dealing with getting places found me on a small four-seated plane—a charter—en route from Kennedy Airport to Bradley Field, which is just north of Hartford, Connecticut.

"I've been invited to speak at a journalism clinic that's being held at the Mount Hermon School in Massachusetts," I had told my wife that morning. "It's an easy trip because Mount Hermon is sending a driver to Bradley to meet me. I'll be back tonight."

216

Originally, I had booked a scheduled flight from Kennedy to Bradley. The charter had been provided for me by TWA, free of charge, when the official in charge of the boarding areas had unintentionally misinformed me about the departure time.

We had just taken off from Kennedy in that small plane, and we were flying across nearby Long Island Sound when I got a little uneasy. It was a heavily overcast day, and I noticed that we were soaring immediately below the cloud cover—not more than a few hundred feet above the Sound's waters.

Below, I could almost make out the large, identifying numbers on the sails of about a dozen racing sloops.

"Isn't it rather dangerous to be flying this low?" I asked the pilot who was seated alongside me.

"It sure is" was the laconic reply. "But I have no choice."

"No choice?" I questioned. "How come?"

"My radar has blinked out. It's out of order. It happened right after we took off from Kennedy. If I went above the clouds I would lose my bearings. I'm flying this low so that I'll know where we are. I plan to land on the other side of the Sound, at Bridgeport Airport in Connecticut."

"Aren't you afraid that some other plane might suddenly come down from this overcast and hit us?" I asked. His answer was not what I thought reassuring.

"NO OTHER PILOT WOULD BE STUPID ENOUGH TO FLY THIS LOW" was his reply.

We did make it into Bridgeport without any problem. There I boarded another charter, one that had been requested from my first pilot by his radio while we'd been in flight. From there I was flown the remaining sixty miles to nearby Bradley Field where I was met by the Mount Hermon School driver.

But by the time I reached Mount Hermon School, the seminar had been concluded.

"What happened?" Axel Forslund, the school's athletic director, asked me when I arrived.

"This modern age is being held back by radar," I joked. "This is one time I should have taken the train instead of the plane."

When I was traveling with the New York Yankees or Mets big-league baseball team, getting places ordinarily was easy—and comfortable. Players and press usually arrived at their destinations with the help of jet planes and buses following carefully prescribed itineraries made out by the teams' road secretaries. But a writer, out on his own, had to learn to improvise when it came to a trip.

217

In 1966, I was asked to interview Nancy Greene of Canada who, two years later, became an Olympic champion, an unusual distinction for someone from the Maple Leaf nation. But there was a problem. Nancy was in Schruns, Austria, preparing for World Cup races while I was in Milan, Italy, with Marty Glickman and his son, no less, plus a motion picture crew doing a promotion piece for Alitalia Airlines.

To keep up with prior commitments and interview Nancy, it meant making the round-trip in one day.

Schruns is just north of the Italian border, only about 125 air miles from Milan. But the mighty Alps separates the two places. To reach Schruns, it was necessary to travel by plane and train more than twice that distance via the Swiss city of Zurich.

"You'll never make it in the time frame you're allowing yourself," Glickman said to me. "We're all going to be moving on to Rome from here. And we're not going down there to see the Pope. There's no telling where we'll be photographing."

Nevertheless, I set out for Schruns. And as it developed, getting there posed no major problems. Arising shortly after down, I flew to Zurich via Alitalia Airlines, taxied downtown to the railroad depot, and boarded a train. It took me east for about sixty miles. There, I made a direct connection with a one-car shuttle train that took me on a short ride to Schruns.

Nancy, a petite brunette with large eyes, wasn't too happy to see me although I had phoned a night earlier from Milan to tell her about my story assignment. Always extremely agreeable to me, however, she consented to the interview.

After my arrival, I waited an hour for her in the hotel lobby. Where was she? She was still doing training runs on the mountain. She still seemed a little nervous about our appointment. I thought she might feel our interview might prove a jinx for her World Cup race the next day.

"I'm really not sure I'm doing the right thing," she told me. "Tomorrow we race, and I don't like to be interviewed at a time like this. After a race, it's fine."

But when I told her about my deadline—that I wanted to get her story into the following Sunday's *New York Times*—she seemed ready to cooperate. I finished our pleasant conversation by taking out my camera and photographing her on skis. The film was sent by express mail to the paper along with my story, which I wrote the next day.

But that Schruns trip wasn't to be completed that easily. Because by the time I returned to the village's tourist bureau, it was late afternoon. I knew that I already had missed the early afternoon train shuttle and asked the director when the next one would leave.

"There is no next one today," she replied. "After all, Schruns is not a major city. You'll have to wait until tomorrow. Even if there were another shuttle today, it would be of no help because it would have no train to meet that would be leaving for Zurich. Shall I arrange for a hotel reservation in town for you tonight?"

To say I was nonplussed is putting it mildly. I had to get back to Milan that same night. If I didn't it would mean one great mix-up for the rest of my itinerary. After all, I had other appointments to keep in Italy for the rest of that week.

If I were in the United States, I told myself at that point, I probably could come up with some kind of a solution. But I knew nothing about Austria's railroad system except that its trains always seem to be on time. Suddenly I had an idea.

"Do you have a map of Austria's railroad system?" I asked the tourist director.

She looked puzzled as she took one out of a drawer. We looked at it together.

"Isn't there another railroad line that runs reasonably close to the one on which I arrived?" I asked.

"Why, the nearest one is about 30 miles from here," she answered. "Nobody from Schruns ever uses it because it's so far away and on bad roads . . ."

"Will there be a train for Zurich coming through there in the next two hours or so?" I questioned.

She checked her train schedules. "Yes," she replied, "in about ninety-five minutes—from Bludenz," I think she said.

"Is there a taxi driver in town who can drive me to that station in time for me to catch that train?" was my next question.

"There is, but it probably will cost you about forty dollars to make that trip," she volunteered. "Nobody ever goes that way for a train."

"Please get the taxi as soon as possible," I requested. "I want to make that train."

I did make it with about fifteen minutes to spare after a bumpy automobile ride over roads that were snow covered and barely two lanes wide—two lanes, that is, for compact cars.

Once in Zurich, I whistled for a taxi that took me to the airport. The plane to Milan, the last one for that night, was waiting to be boarded.

The day was saved and for that matter, so was my subsequent itinerary.

CHAPTER 22

I Knew Them When

Of all the good words from tongues of men,
The best can be, "I knew them when"

Through the years, veteran sportswriters have had occasion to recall great athletes who were still in their teens when first spotted by them; superb performers, for example, as baseball's Mel Ott and Bob Feller, tennis' Steffi Graf, and versatile Babe Didrikson Zaharias. Babe won two Olympic track and field medals when she was only eighteen years old.

The story which I've taken pleasure in relating, through the years, concerns Kareem Abdul-Jabbar, the famous basketball player. It's a tale that's never been told. I don't think that even Kareem, to this day, knows its full details.

I was the first sportswriter, certainly, at least from a major newspaper, to discover Kareem when he was only, mind you, a twelve-year-old and was known as Lew Alcindor. Kareem, sports fans know, was considered, at the time of his retirement, by almost all, as the greatest player in basketball's history.

When Kareem, at age forty-three, quit the game as a professional in 1989, he held the distinction of having broken many of that sport's records. Aided by his great height, he not only had been a fantastic scorer and rebounder but also a tremendous team player.

My first encounter with Jabbar was in a chance meeting I had been sent by Phil Burke, our assignments editor, to a Boy's Club center on Manhattan's east side to report on special awards being given to three outstanding young people.

"It probably won't get much space in the paper," Burke had said to me as I left the office. "Maybe, it won't even get past the first edition. But it's being held at a Boy's Club, and we like to pay attention to such worthwhile groups every once in a while."

Alcindor, it might be noted, stood head and shoulders above the two others. He was a six-footer. I don't remember the names of the other two youngsters, and I wouldn't ordinarily have remembered Lew's, except that I was so impressed with him that I immediately tried to get him a prep school scholarship.

"There's a great kid," one of the observers at the Boy's Club ceremony said to me as he watched me scribble some notes. "He's not only a fine basketball player for his age, but he's also a great student. I understand he has a 98 average in school. Bright as a whip."

I looked the young man over carefully. Thinking in terms of basketball potential, I noticed that he was extremely well coordinated for his age and size. Kids that tall, I had found in the past, almost always were gawky and awkward. I took particular note of Lew's walk. It was easygoing. There was no doubt about it. He looked like a winner. I asked him a few questions. He had no trouble answering them fluently.

"Maybe I can do some school a favor," I said to myself after that brief interview. "Any basketball coach would be happy to get him and in classrooms, he'd make life easier for teachers."

And so, after I had written my story in the office, I lost little time in phoning Ned Hall, the genial headmaster of the prestigious Hill School in Pottstown, Pa. I knew Hall well.

In those days, one of my regular beats each fall was to visit about thirty-five of the east's leading boarding schools and to write daily stories about them. The Hill was one of my favorite campuses.

"Ned," I said, "I've just run across a boy who would make a fine addition to your school. He's a good student, he's real tall, he's into basketball and he's black. I think my story about him and two other youngsters will appear with a three-column picture in tomorrow's *New York Times*. Try to look at it."

"I certainly am interested," the headmaster replied. "The fact that he's developing into a fine player sounds good. Our basketball teams can use some help. But he's also a 98 student? That's what really makes him attractive.

"I'll tell you what," Hall suggested. "Try to get his dad on the phone and see whether the family is interested in sending the boy to the Hill. Our school can help youngsters who may not be contemplating a boarding school because of the expense. Tell his father we're in a position to offer his son free board and tuition.

221

"And if he lives up to all that potential he's shown so far in his academic studies," continued Hall, "I'm almost positive we'll be able to get him a scholarship to Yale as an undergraduate and even to its medical school if that's the way he eventually wants to go."

I was pleased. I thought I might be doing Lew a good turn as well as the Hill School. And so I phoned young Alcindor's father.

"It sure sounds good to me," Mr. Alcindor, who was a policeman on the New York City's subway system, said to me in a friendly voice. "But this is all so sudden. Let me think about it and talk it over. Call me back in two days, please?"

When I phoned him again, Mr. Alcindor told me that the family was still considering the matter. Would I be kind enough to call again in two days? Later that week, I spoke to him again.

"Well," said Mr. Alcindor, "I want to thank you for all your efforts. But we've decided not to accept the offer. And thank the Hill School for us too. Sorry."

I wasn't told and didn't ask the reason for the negative decision. And I never had the occasion to speak to Mr. Alcindor again. I felt I shouldn't pry.

And, except for that little awards ceremony at the Boy's Club, I've never spoken to his son. I nodded to him subsequently at the one or two games I covered while he was a member of the Milwaukee Bucks.

By the time young Lew had started playing basketball two years later for Powell Memorial High School in New York City, I no longer was reporting on nearly as many pro and college basketball games as I was in earlier years.

The reason? I had suddenly become the paper's ski editor. That job did away with the possibility of doing much basketball since both are winter sports.

Lew, the record books disclose, went on to lead his Powell Memorial team through a winning streak that lasted for seventy-one games. Powell's showing during these years, of course, was so impressive that when Alcindor was graduated from high school, he was welcomed at UCLA with open arms.

"Any college in the land would have thought it a gift, wrapped in gold foil, to have gotten this boy," Joe Lapchick, who not only coached the pro New York Knicks but also some strong St. John's University teams, said to me one night at Madison Square Garden. "His mobility and his control under the backboards could make even average teammates look like stars. He's a coach's dream come true."

It didn't take long for Alcindor's high school coach, Jack Donohue to profit from Alcindor's phenomenal play as a schoolboy. Donohue was asked to be head varsity basketball coach at Holy Cross College in Worcester, Massachusetts.

But UCLA, which already had been a power in intercollegiate circles, continued to thrive as a collegiate basketball power with Alcindor wearing its navy blue and gold colors. He was a member of quintets that captured coveted NCAA crowns for three straight seasons, starting in 1967.

Why had his father turned down the Hill School's offer of a scholarship? It wasn't until many years later that I learned the actual reason. I bought a copy of Kareem's highly interesting autobiography *Giant Steps*, which appeared on the best-selling lists during the 1983–84 season. He wrote,

"At the time my family received the invitation from the Hill School, we contacted a family friend, Alexandra Potis, who lived in Pottstown. She recommended we turn down the offer.

"No, no, no,'" Jabbar in his book quotes Ms. Potis as saying. "The Hill School's administrators have made you the offer only because they want you to integrate in their institution."

I was surprised by that revelation. From where did she get that "inside information?" I firmly believe that Alcindor would have enjoyed studying at the Hill School and probably would have become a school hero while he was there. Integration? Hall never, in our conversation, even intimated that such was in his mind.

Even at that, Jackie Robinson, with whom I once had dinner—just the two of us, at Yonkers Raceway—is best remembered today because he, as a Brooklyn Dodger, started integration in major league baseball in 1947. Within two years he was named the National League's most valuable player. He's a hero of his race.

When I first began writing about this episode for this chapter, I wondered whether anyone was going to ask me to prove my story. Looking back through old *New York Times'* files seemed like a difficult and tiring job, Jabbar in his book *Giant Steps* made such an ornery job unnecessary because he wrote:

"Upon graduation from grammar school"—he was six feet, five inches tall by that time—"I had received scholarship offers from any Catholic school and the Hill School in Pottstown, Pennsylvania."

What he probably didn't know that I was the young fellow who triggered the offer from Ned Hall and from his distinguished prep school.

Suffice it to say Jabbar's subsequent feats in basketball probably will remain among the sports' top legends for many years to come. As outstanding as he was in schoolboy and intercollegiate play, he scaled what seemed like insurmountable heights as a professional.

"He began breaking all kind of records early on," remembered John Cirillo, the basketball publicist of the pro New York Knickerbockers. "Kareem kept turning in great performances and kept making them look so easy. His introduction of the skyhook shot alone became a sensation."

Kareem first played pro ball with the Bucks in Milwaukee and subsequently moved on to become a star with the high-ranking Los Angeles Lakers. At the time he retired, he was the only performer to receive six National Basketball Association "Most Valuable Player" awards. He was picked for the league's All-Star teams an astronomical seventeen times.

Some of his statistics? In 1984, he passed the lanky Wilt Chamberlain's professional NBA scoring record. Wrapping up his pro career, at age forty-three, was in itself, a remarkable plateau—an overtime even for a basketball player who at that stage of life has resigned himself to light workouts on the neighborhood playground level.

By the time he put his pro sneakers aside, Kareem had amassed a career total of about 36,000 points. It was a scoring performance that surpassed the league's all-time record for an individual player by an unbelievable 17,000 points. In bidding adieu to the call of the hoops, he had played in 500 more games than any other athlete in the pro league's history.

Kareem's continued amazing feats on the basketball floor kept Joe Lapchick, the fprmer Celtics star, marveling. He knew of my early interest in Jabbar, and he often would turn on his soft smile when he saw me.

"As you can see," he said to me one day. "That Kareem sure is knocking them dead. Too bad you didn't turn coach the first afternoon you saw him. If you had, you'd have been a winner. That kid sure has reached the heights.

"And I'm not joking when I say the word 'heights,'" the ever-popular Lapchick continued. "He really knows how to raise his feet and go up in the air whether he's shooting or rebounding."

Lapchick had every reason to be an expert on the subject of "heights." As a young man, he had played at the center position for the famed touring pro Original Celtics during the 1920s and the early 1930s.

The Celtics, one of the more prominent forerunners of the famous "Harlem Globetrotters," was a pro team that took out-of-town opponents in ballrooms as well as in arenas. Sometimes on a Sunday, here was a team that thought nothing of playing three games in three adjoining communities.

Lapchick was the team's center because he was considered tall. His height? Barely six feet, five inches—tiny for a center by present-day standards. In an era when high school coaches passed up the tallest students because they considered the big boys "uncoordinated," Lapchick had been one of the few exceptions.

"But I was never an Alcindor," he told me with a grin when he was coaching the Redmen of St. John's. "If I had been blessed with his height and his ability, the only thing that could have stopped me in those days would have been a power outage in a gym during a game."

One thing is certain, when Kareem was in his prime, the lights never went out for him.

Another "whiz kid" that I met well before she became famous was Carol Heiss. It was during a figure skating tournament for juniors in 1952. She was a pretty blonde, just barely in her teens, who lived in South Ozone Park in the Queens borough of New York. Her father was a baker.

Carol's story in her early days appealed to me immediately because she was on her way to stardom the hard way. To become a top performer in figures and dance routines on ice, devotees of this sport know that the prerequisite, as in the concert piano or violin fields, is practice, practice, practice!

Carol would rise each weekday morning—virtually at dawn. After a quick breakfast, she would be escorted by her mother to Manhattan. It was an hour's trip on New York's rapid transit system. They would head for the Ice Club with its rink atop the old Madison Square Garden at Eighth Avenue and Fiftieth Street.

"These daily trips each day on the city trains are ordeals," Mrs. Heiss told me early one morning after her arrival with Carol at the rink. "It's particularly hard on my daughter but she loves the sport.

"When we finally get here," she continued, "Carol takes her lessons on a small patch of ice assigned to her teaching pro. Then she practices her free skating routines. After that, she's off to school for a full schedule of classes."

Carol's dedication and great spirit of competition, despite this rigorous daily routine, paid off. In addition to her signal success, at age nineteen, in the 1960 Olympics at Squaw Valley, she also captured world championships in her specialty five straight years, starting in 1956.

Since I was at Squaw Valley to report on the Winter Olympics, along with Gladwin Hill, one of our paper's most versatile writers, I was able to congratulate Carol and her mother personally. We shook hands at rink-side after the blonde stylist had been picked by the judges as the gold medalist.

That same edition of the international classic was the one in which the United States pulled off a tremendous surprise in hockey by upsetting the Russians. The game was easy for me to remember because I'm a late riser.

225

And this game, of all things, started at an unusually early hour—about 7:00 A.M. I think this scheduling was done for live television purposes to attract viewers in the east as well as in Europe. I remember saying to Hill on the day before that big game,

"Sure you don't want to cover it? Here's one game, as far as I'm concerned, that may just as well be held at dawn. If I go, I'll probably start dozing. I usually don't have breakfast until 11:00 A.M."

Maybe Hill customarily ate his breakfasts late too. He showed absolutely no interest in my problem. As it developed, it all worked out to my advantage. Because that game, for me, made history: the Americans scored a big upset over the Russians.

As it happened, I also was present twenty years later when the US hockey team captured only its second Olympic gold medal by again conquering a highly favored Soviet Union sextet.

That second triumph was scored in the 1980 edition of the Winter Olympics held at Lake Placid. The unexpected victory by American skaters triggered a wild night in that usually quiet Adirondack village. Fans emerged from the Olympic Arena seeking places to celebrate—and they did.

As for figure skating, that Olympics' women's gold medal was captured by Annet Poetzsch, a stylist from East Germany. Where was I? At age sixty-eight, trying to keep warm in my motel room which was just about twenty paces from Lake Placid's only traffic light. After Miss Heiss' rise to fame, twenty years earlier, I sort of had lost interest in that sport.

"I'm passing that skating event up," I told the colorful Red Smith, our paper's top sports columnist, who was berthed only two motel units away from me. "I have to be up the first thing in the morning to cover a ski event."

"You're right," answered Smith with his ready wit. "You'd better get your sleep. After all, you're a growing boy."

Equally as heartwarming as Carol Heiss' success story, by a youngster whom I knew early on, was the meteoric climb to the top by jockey Steve Cauthen in thoroughbred horse racing. I spoke to him the very first day he rode in New York, at Aqueduct.

I was walking through the Big A's race secretary's offices, where trainers and jockeys' agents gather just before a day's racing program begins. Lenny Goodman, the friendly, famous agent who had booked mounts in earlier years for such great riders as Bobby Ussery and Braulio Baeza, among many others, greeted me.

"Anything new?" I asked him.

"Nothing," he said with his familiar grin, "but I've got a sixteen-year-old apprentice rider making his appearance in New York for the first time today. I'm convinced he's going to become one of American's top jockeys.

"You're the first writer I'm telling this to," he continued, "if only because you're the only one who seems to stop by to ask, 'what's new?' This kid, someday, and remember I'm telling you now, is going to be a star. He was raised around horses. His father is a blacksmith back in Kentucky."

"You're really kidding," I sort of scoffed. "Your boy rider probably hasn't even begun to shave yet. How can you be so sure? I wonder if I'll still be around when he wins his first race. I've and you've seen it take months for some young riders to make it into the winners' circle."

"Not this boy," Goodman replied. "He's ready to win right now."

I headed for the press box, high atop the track, convinced that Goodman was merely suffering from an overabundance of enthusiasm. I'd heard such tales before. I had listened to some coaches and even fans rave about a young athlete only to find that he didn't pan out.

But it wasn't like Goodman to go bananas over a young jockey. Like most successful agents, when it came to the media, Lenny was inclined to underplay rather than enthuse over a situation.

I recalled, at that time, that rainy morning that I had been on a Pennsylvania Railroad train with Delaware Park my destination. Sitting right in from of me, by chance, was none other than Goodman. With him was the crack jockey Bobby Ussery, who in the early 1960s and thereabouts, was a standout rider, and whose mounts were booked by Lenny.

The two men also were headed for Delaware because Bobby had the mount on a thoroughbred named Needles in the rich Delaware Park Handicap. They were traveling by train from New York because their airline plane had been grounded. It was small wonder. As our car rushed though the New Jersey and Pennsylvania countrysides, huge raindrops were pelting its windows.

"How do you think your horse is going to do today?" I asked Lenny.

"Terribly," he answered. "Bobby and I thought we had a good shot to win the race but only up to the time this heavy rain started. We really don't know how good a mudder our horse is."

How did the Needles do later that day? He won by about a city block. The closest racer to him approaching the finish line was more than fifteen lengths back. As I said, Goodman wasn't one to be overly optimistic.

On the day that I saw him years later, at Aqueduct, enthuse about young Cauthen, I remembered Goodman's pessimism on that Delaware trip. Was he spoofing me about his new young ride Cauthen? He wasn't.

Because on that very first afternoon, the teenage jockey brought home the winner in the feature race, an unusual feat for a new rider.

The next afternoon, young Steve triumphed with two of his mounts. One veteran horseman whom I questioned said to me,

"That new rider sure has a masterful touch with his mounts and a great seat in his saddle."

After only Cauthen's second day at Aqueduct, I went below to the jockey's room to talk to young Steve. Here was a clean-cut looking youngster, a surprisingly well poised one who had ready answers, it seemed, even for fast questions.

"You sure have started things here with a rush," I said to him. "As you know, it's unusual for a bug (apprentice) boy to do that well, particularly at your age. Of course, the weight allowances you're getting for being an apprentice rider is a big help. But even at that, you sure are causing attention."

"Mr. Goodman, my agent, has been getting me good horses to ride," Cauthen modestly said. Modesty, I soon realized, was one of Steve's chief traits.

"One other part of your career that interests me," I continued, "since you're only a teenager, is whether you plan to do anything about furthering your education? Here you are, away from home and away from school."

"Oh sure, my family and I thought about that" was his quick answer. "I'm going to take correspondence courses in English and History. I know it's going to be hard, but I'm going to try."

In the years that followed, I never thought of asking him about those academic plans. It seemed unnecessary because this boy was making it clear that he had his career all picked out. Academia, in his case, just didn't seem too important as he continued to bring home winners day after day with remarkable consistency.

Just before the Christmas holidays that year, he left for his home in Kentucky having been a sensation at Aqueduct. When he returned to the jockey's room in early January, I visited him in front of his dressing cubicle again.

He was busy combing his hair in front of a small mirror about thirty minutes before post time for that day's first race.

"How did you enjoy your vacation, Steve?" I asked. I was interested because I liked him. He was a fine young man who seemed to be handling the praise that had been heaped on him by the media in an amazingly cool manner. There was absolutely nothing uppity about him.

"It was just fine," he told me. "I went home," he said with a smile.

"Did you do anything more interesting than that?" I asked in all sincerity.

"Do anything more interesting?" he replied, his eyes opening wide in surprise. "What can be more interesting than that?"

228

Here was a youngster, I told myself, who was too good to be true. I sort of lost track of Cauthen, thereafter, because I was off to do skiing stories for the paper.

But Steve didn't need me or anyone else to hound him with the possible exception of Goodman. With the latter's help in obtaining "live" mounts, Steve skyrocketed to fame in the unbelievable span of only one year.

In the days that followed his debut in New York, the Kentuckian kept bringing mounts into the winners' circle with unbelievable regularity. A highlight of his 1976 campaign was provided on an afternoon when he triumphed with five of the seven horses he rode. The following year, there were several programs on which he triumphed in six of his rides and four on which he came home first with five.

It was small wonder that at the end of the 1977 season, he emerged as the leading rider at New York's two metropolitan tracks—Belmont Park and Aqueduct. A distant second to him that year was the celebrated rider Angel Cordero, Jr.

Cauthen skyrocketed to the top of that year's jockey standings in New York, even though he was sidelined for a month. He had suffered multiple injuries sustained at Belmont Park's opening day, May 23. When he first appeared on the track after his recovery, he was applauded and cheered lustily by racegoers.

Young Steve proceeded to turn in what was jokingly referred to as a "minor miracle." On that very first day, he won with a four-year-old named "Little Miracle." What was so noteworthy about that? Here was a colt that hadn't come home first in more than two months. With that victory as a springboard, Cauthen had no problem finishing ahead of the rest of New York's jockeys that year.

There was no doubt, on that day, that the teenager had already become a celebrity. Dozens of members of the print and air media had descended on Aqueduct to interview him. He'd had a hectic morning with the press.

After scoring with Little Miracle, in that afternoon's second race, Steve, still showing a slight puff over his injured right eye, was asked by waiting members of the media as he weighed out near the winners' circle, how it felt to be back.

"Just like it always has," he replied in his typical taciturn manner and with a bit of a twinkle in his eyes. "It feels good."

Cauthen had arrived that day three hours earlier than usual at the request of the press. When he arrived, he had been immediately besieged in the jockey's room by a notebook brigade and a host of television cameramen. The turnout of media was so large that it spilled out of the room into the adjoining weigh-in area.

229

Dick Meade, the gray-haired, veteran jockey's valet, also a Kentuckian, amazed by the huge turnout of the press, looked at me and said,

"I've been tending to jockeys here in New York for almost fifty years. But I've never seen the likes of this. I reckon there must be about a hundred press in here right now."

Meade said he could vividly recall when such famed former riding stars as Earle Sande, Eddie Arcaro, and Ted Atkinson were in their prime.

"They certainly rated attention from the press and got it," he said. "But the fuss over them at any time, only is small potatoes to all this ado over Cauthen. You know, I think this kid is on his way to becoming a folk hero."

I remembered that remark as I kept making my skiing rounds. Almost everyone who knew names of important sports personalities of that era seemed to know about Steve Cauthen. Even in my trips to the High Rocky Mountain country and to baseball and football sports areas in the south, I asked people, out of curiosity, whether they had ever heard of this young man.

In almost every instance, the answer was in the affirmative although New York, where Steve was captivating racegoers, was many hundreds of miles away.

Steve eventually moved from the American scene. He went to England to test his ability in a nation where horses race around a track clockwise rather than counter clockwise, as is the case in America. There he sparkled again. He soon became the leading rider among Great Britain's jockeys.

The last time I spoke to Cauthen was at a New York Turf Writers' dinner that is held every August at the plush Gideon Putnam Hotel in Saratoga Springs. Steve was on hand to receive a special award in recognition of his feats as a rider.

He was seated at a table with his parents, and I went over to see him.

"I want you to meet the folks," he said as he introduced me to them. "They're great people."

You know, having gotten to know the young rider, I heartily agreed with him.

I suppose I shouldn't have doubted Goodman when he praised Cauthen on that first day the youngster rode in New York. Because earlier, sometime in the early 1950s, I had been introduced to one of football's greatest stars in the making—Joe Namath—when that former New York Jets' star quarterback only was probably ten or eleven years old.

At the time, I was managing and coaching a semiprofessional women's basketball team, the Arthur Murray Girls, who played against men only, primarily in benefit games. We were in Beaver Falls,

Pennsylvania., Namath's hometown, scheduled to play in the local high school gymnasium.

Just before the game's start, I began chatting with a local football coach. He brought over a tousle-haired youngster to our players' bench to meet me.

"Here's a kid who someday is really going to make it big as a football player, probably as a pro," the coach said to me. "He already can do everything a backfield player should do except fumble," he added jokingly.

I gave that meeting little thought. Just as I had done with Cauthen and even with Jabbar, in my mind, I sold this youngster short.

"Just another case of a kid who's a great athlete as a kid," I told one of my players who had heard our conversation, "but who just won't make it. The competition's too tough. Besides, how'll they ever find him, here in Beaver Falls?"

But that coach in Beaver Falls didn't fill me in with enough details about Namath. For example, it was well known in town that this youngster was hungry when it came to sports participation. Hungry? Joe, it developed, was playing Little League Baseball with boys twice his age when he was six and with a kids' "hit-'em-and-knock-'em-down football league" when he was only eight.

Namath, of course, went on to sparkle at the University of Alabama. And as a pro quarterback, he led the New York Jets to the Super Bowl championship in 1969. The last time I saw him was at the Gulfstream Park racetrack, where he was thumping the drums for that race track's promotion department.

About a decade after I'd met the young Namath, I came upon three young determined ski racers. Although they were still in their lower teens, they had begun to indicate that when it came to tearing down steep slopes and streaking between slalom gates, they were on the best of terms with gravity.

I saw all three at a junior national championship meet in Colorado. It was at a time when nature was not cooperating with Rocky Mountain's skiing retreats. The snow cover on the trails was abnormally thin. One had only to look at the evergreens just below the tree line to realize that the snow gods were shortchanging local lodge owners. For them, a scarcity of snow meant a scarcity of guests.

The three youngsters proceeded to demonstrate that they were able to plunge down steep vertical drops with reckless abandon—on green grass—if necessary.

The trio was made up of Jimmy Heuga, Billy Kidd, and Billy Marolt. Each of them had grown up on the front yards of different American mountain ranges: Heuga in the high Sierras of California, Kidd in Vermont's lush Green Mountains, and Marolt in the rugged Rockies.

They were so impressive in their descents during the championships that I went out on a limb. I prophesied in my story that all three undoubtedly would become American Olympic stars. All three did. They competed in the 1964 Olympics at Innsbruck, Austria, the first of two winter classics held at that mountain-rimmed city.

Kidd and Heuga whizzed down the special slalom courses at the first of the two classics held at Innsbruck to capture medals. Billy carried off the silver medal with a second-place finish while the smaller-sized Heuga, with the third fastest clocking, came away with the bronze award. They were the first American men ever to win medals in Olympic skiing history.

I wasn't in Innsbruck at the time, but I heard the news within an hour after their successes had become official—while in New Hampshire to report on the national collegiate skiing championships on Cannon Mountain in Franconia.

That event having been concluded, the following morning, I joined Al Merrill, Dartmouth College's skiing coach, for the long drive to New Hampshire's Lebanon Airport.

Suddenly, Al gave out a yell as the news report on his car's radio revealed that Kidd and Heuga had won those medals in Austria, an hour or so earlier.

"That's fantastic," exclaimed Merrill who in later years became head Nordic coach (ski jumping and cross-country) for US Olympic squads. "Now perhaps we can start winning some more medals in the next Winter Olympics."

However, that hope proved merely wishful thinking. It took exactly twenty years before Americans succeeded in winning Olympic gold medals—and in Alpine events at that. For finally, in the 1984 edition of the international classic, held in Yugoslavia, Phil Mahre and Bill Johnson captured gold medals in the slalom and downhill events, respectively.

That was a grand showing for a nation, whose men, until that year, had failed to bring home a gold medal for the United States.

What the United States evidently needs for its men, in both the Nordic and Alpine phases of the ski sport, are whiz kids—whizzers like Jabbar, Cauthen, and yes, Kidd and Heuga.

CHAPTER 23

Yo Ho! Where the Trade Winds Blow

Any sailor who knows the difference between a cutlass and a crow's nest knows that the Caribbean Sea is located between Central America, the West Indies, and South America. Those that do know are probably well aware that these troubled waters, long ago, provided a happy hunting ground for pirate ships flying the black skull and bones flag.

Whenever I've been on a cruise ship that's dropped anchor off the island of Hispaniola, which houses the nations of Haiti and the Dominican Republic, I often find myself thinking of such buccaneers as Captain Kidd, Bluebeard, and yes, Long John Silver. And I can almost imagine hearing the commands as their ships weighed anchor.

"Ready about. Helm's a-lee. Tack and sheets. Mainsail haul. The wind is breezing up and the glass is falling. Careful now, men, we may have to ride out a gale of wind."

But how about pirates in the twentieth century? In April of 1983, I was on the scene of a scary incident that had all the earmarks of a corsair raid. The location? In the Caribbean just off the mouth of Costa Rica's slow-flowing Rio Colorado.

The crew? Three men and a boy, dressed in ragged khaki shorts and tattered shirts, captained by a man who was described as "a grizzled old sea dog." The vessel? A fifty-foot iron fishing trawler with a few jagged holes in its sides. It flew no flag.

Out on that Caribbean, just a mile or so offshore, were three American sports fishermen prospecting for giant size tarpon in two 17-foot

233

"johnboats." To their shock and utter amazement, they were approached and taken captive by this villainous-looking crew.

The oldest among the three anglers was Harry Kime, a seventy-year-old retired manufacturer from California, who had just previously undergone quadruple heart bypass surgery and who was a dedicated sports fisherman. Could it be that he and the others were going to be held for ransom?

What other reason could there be for their capture? It all smacked of days of old when rich maidens were taken from sailing vessels by buccaneers and held until they received pieces of eight or the equivalent from that girl's wealthy parents.

I had arrived at the Rio Colorado a day or two after this hair-raising capture. I had gone there, to the plush Casa Mar Fishing Lodge, to try my luck with the big tarpon. The tarpon there, I'd been told, weighed in at as much as 100 pounds.

I arrived to learn that Kime and his guide Tomas, instead of prospecting in the waters at the mouth of the Rio Colorado as they usually did, had elected, instead, to seek the tarpon in the Caribbean itself. Kime had asked his guide to head north along the shores of the sea.

"Some of those Americans who have been fishing at the other camp down the river," Kime reported to his guide, "tell me that there are acres of tarpon rolling and jumping out in the Caribbean itself. We could find some extra excitement out there."

Extra excitement? Within two hours, the accomplished American angler found himself worrying about whether he was going to be held for ransom. And because the men who had captured him wore tattered remnants of military shorts, the thought also crossed his mind that they might be Nicaraguan Sandinistas, and that he and his two fellow Americans had been picked up as possible spies.

He was perplexed. Kime was a familiar figure around the lonely Rio Colorado which flowed though Costa Rica's rain forest. He had been traveling from California to the Central American country for years to hunt tarpon. His base also was the Casa Mar Lodge, on the northern banks of the Rio Colorado. Always, such trips had provided only pleasure.

Sports fishermen, in five other similar aluminum skiffs—all seventeen-footers with outboard motors—also, it seemed, had heard the tale about the "acres" of tarpon, and they too had headed for the open sea. But after two hours of searching in vain, they all decided to head back to the river.

"Looks as if we were told wrong," Kime said to his Spanish-speaking Tomas, who had a working knowledge of English. Kime grinned and then thought to himself, "I should be old enough to know that the grass doesn't always grow greener next door. I should have stayed on the river."

He certainly should have. Because as the five small skiffs were heading back to the Colorado, Kime noticed that his small craft, which was astern of the small five–aluminum boat fleet, was being approached by a rusty-looking trawler.

Tomas was making good time heading for the river's mouth when shots from a 50-caliber machine gun, interspersed with bursts from smaller automatic weapons, were heard coming toward them from the rapidly approaching big iron boat.

Kime, veteran sportsman that he was, realized that any protection his small boat offered was virtually worthless since its gunwales were less than a foot above the water line. He stood up, raised his two hands as high as they could go, and shouted, "Surrender! Surrender!"

Since three of the other small sports fishing boats were ahead in the far distance, the gunmen on the trawler directed the rest of their warning shots around Kime's craft and one occupied by two other tarpon-minded fishermen, David Donaldson, forty-five, of Homewood, Illinois; Luke Dallis, thirty-seven, of Greenville, Michigan; and their guide Adrian.

"Who are these guys?" Kime asked Tomas. "Pirates? In all my years fishing here and in many other places around the world, nothing like this ever has happened to me."

His guide, although just as surprised and as worried as Kime, tried to allay the fisherman's fears by shrugging and trying to laugh it off.

"Maybe my mother-in-law, she has sent these men after me," he joked.

But any further idea about making light of the situation was quickly dissipated as the creaking old trawler drew alongside the small craft. A brief conversation in Spanish ensued between a member of the trawler's crew and Tomas. Finally, tow lines were thrown out from the trawler.

The two skiffs were towed for about fifteen minutes before the crewmen took the Americans and their guides on board. Not being able to speak Spanish, the sportfishermen relied on the guides to tell them what was happening since the latter were in constant conversation with the crew.

"What are they saying?" Kime asked Tomas.

"I think they are talking about shooting us," was the reply. "They are saying we were fishing in Nicaraguan waters but, as you know, that isn't so. The Nicaragua border is miles away."

Suddenly, they saw a youngster pointing a burp gun at them.

"En seguida," (quickly) said the unkempt looking captain. "We have places to go and we must get there quickly."

The crewmen finally began trying to load the two small aluminum skiffs on board with a squeaky winch. They were careless. Out into the open sea went seat pillows, fishing rods, Kime's special medication, and even eyeglasses. It was thought by the captives, perhaps, "all that stuff" had been dumped into the sea on purpose to make it look as if their boats had capsized and they had drowned.

"What do you want of us? What did we do? Where are you taking us?" Kime finally asked the swarthy-looking captain. "Are you taking us to jail?"

The Spanish-speaking captain remained mute. Actually he didn't understand a word Kime said.

"I'm worried," Kime told Tomas, after noting that in addition to the youngster's burp gun, there also were two 50-caliber guns mounted near the bow. Tomas, also scared, blurted out to the captain,

"Please don't shoot us. *Tengo ocho hijos*—I have eight children. There will be no one to support them if I die."

He received no further answer as the trawler began making a 160-degree turn to the starboard to head up the Nicaraguan coast. It was while the captain was busily engaged at the wheel that Kime found time to take another look at the iron craft. Noting how slowly the weather-beaten boat was moving, he said in a grim tone to one of the other Americans, "we're on a crawler rather than a trawler."

"It was in even much worse shape than even I had originally thought," Kime explained to a reporter later. "It was rusted beyond belief. Near the middle of the deck was a jagged, gaping hole about three feet in diameter. It certainly looked to me as if we had been captured by pirates, and maybe we actually were going to be held for ransom."

Kime finally concluded, however, that the group had not been taken by pirates but rather by seamen who had close ties to the Nicaraguan army. Because when he could lie down in a little room off the pilot house, he noticed a liberal supply of mattresses on which were stenciled "National Guard of Nicaragua." Alongside, in wooden crates, were six full cases of ammunition.

"It looked to me as if we were on a disguised hunk of junk that really had been set up to be a little warship," he said later.

As a result of this discovery, Kime and his fellow captives now began thinking that, yes, they had been picked up as possible spies.

"Do they really think we're American spies?" Kim asked his fellow captives. "If they do, it doesn't make sense. After all, we were still in Costa Rica's waters when captured. And spies wouldn't be sailing around in little aluminum skiffs without any protection."

Nevertheless, the group proceeded to receive the full treatment as if they might be involved in espionage. After a ten-hour sail up the coast, they arrived at the Nicaraguan community of Bluff, the site of a Nicaraguan military installation. Kime was examined by a physician who found that the American had normal blood pressure and that his (lados) lungs were "normal."

"Normal," Kime told his companions. "I'm in terrible shape. Maybe I should start claiming insanity."

The physician then interrogated him, asking, "Why are you here?"

"My answers apparently didn't satisfy him because he finally shrugged and had us all taken across the harbor to the city of Bluefields," Kime explained. "There, at a small hotel, we were fed small hamburgers about a half-dollar in size. Guarding us was a soldier with a machine gun.

"After a brief night's rest, we were awakened at 5:00 A.M. I figured that it might be firing squad time. Instead, we were taken to a small airport where we boarded an old Soviet built plane that evidently had once been used for military parachute jumping. We were accompanied by three armed soldiers. Once we took off, even they began questioning us. We were flown to Nicaragua's city of Managua.

"This thing is really getting serious," Kime remarked to his friends. "Managua is the capital of the country. What did we ever do to wind up here? They really must consider us important spies."

Ushered into a room in which an intelligence officer was seated behind a desk, Kime was asked, "Why have you come all the way from America just to fish," he asked the septuagenarian, "and where is your base on the Rio Colorado?"

"Because the tarpon fishing is so good down here," Kime replied.

Kime said he was a little relieved that the officer kept asking questions. He felt nothing "bad" could happen to them if the Nicaraguans were still talking.

"Before you knew it," Kime added, "the officer began talking politics. He wanted to know why President Reagan wanted to attack Nicaragua and why he had sent spies to try and cause trouble?"

"I am not a spy. I am a Republican," Kime answered, "and I voted for Reagan. But if he attacks your country without cause, then he's wrong, just like you are if you attack us."

The Americans and their guides were ushered to a car and off the group went again under guard. When Kime noted that the automobile went speeding past a highway sign that read in Spanish "Leaving Managua," he and his companions became perturbed again. They again thought that perhaps they were being taken to a secluded spot to be shot. Nothing had been said to give them hope.

"But we evidently had been cleared," said Kime. "We were driven to the Costa Rica border where we were turned over to that country's police. Now assured of our safety, we concluded that the higher officials in Nicaragua had concluded that the captain of that piece of junk who captured us had been over zealous."

Donaldson and Davidson, the other American anglers, were off to the United States the next day after their ordeal that had lasted for about thirty-six hours. Their vacation time at their fishing lodge had expired. Kime? Despite his heart condition and his age, he was back on the Rio Colorado the next morning in search for tarpon.

The entire incident, in the next few days, resulted in an international "naval" victory for Costa Rica even though that nation has no navy. At that time, it had only three patrolling gunboats, manned by policemen.

Three days after Kime and his group had been released, one of the gunboats was sent out to sea, by appointment, to meet the iron trawler that had been involved in the capture.

"We're here to return the small fishing boats and whatever fishing gear we could salvage," a representative of the Nicaraguan government told the police colonel in charge of the Costa Rican gunboat. "I also have release papers here that I would like you to sign."

The police official refused to sign them.

"These papers read that the Americans were taken in Nicaraguan waters," he pointed out. "We know that this is not true. I can sign them only if, instead, you change that statement to read 'captured in Costa Rican waters.'"

The change was reluctantly made and so Costa Rica was able to sail off with its moral victory even though almost all the fishing gear, plus Kime's glasses and medication, had been lost at sea.

"I've been fishing for more than sixty-five years," Kime told me that first morning after his release. "And I've never been kidnapped before.

"Of course, these are different times from when I first began dipping a hook, at the age of six," he concluded with a grin. "That was on the Sac River near my home in Arkansas' Ozark country. I was only angling for run-of-the-mill catfish then.

"Trying to take the big tarpon, I guess, makes the risks a different kind of ball game."

On a fishing trip, also where the trade winds blow and where pirates once roamed, I met Captain Austin Hodge, a seventy-one-year-old salt. In his day, he was best known for his sailing rather than for his angling.

This old-timer was considered one of the most famous seafaring men in the Dutch Windward islands. He lived on the Caribbean's Dutch-French island of Sint Maarten. I found his background so captivating that in 1972, I wrote a story about him for *Holiday Magazine*.

Hodge's home was on the Dutch side of the popular tourist island. In his younger days, he had been an adventurer. It was said he could have survived with a diaper pin for a fish hook and a sturdy branch of a tree as a weapon.

He had skippered disabled schooners in the roughest of Caribbean seas, lifted heavy casks that required the strength of three men, and could cook over a fire he had created with a piece of metal and stone. He was a man for all seasons.

When I met him he had more or less retired to the porch of his seven-room concrete home to watch the Caribbean fill up with cruise ships. Although a septuagenarian, his appearance gave strangers cause to wonder why this sturdy, youthful-looking, muscular man had seen fit to quit the sea.

By that time, Captain Hodge had spent what he called "a full life." He had sailed the nearby waters of the Caribbean and the Atlantic countless times as a seagoing mailman. He had skippered a ferryboat and operated one of the most popular guest houses on his side of the British West Indies. He had even put in stints as cook, waiter, and "chief bottle washer" at such well-known American outposts as New York, Connecticut, and New Jersey.

"What did I like doing best?" the tawny, leather-skinned blue-eyed captain answered in his soft island patois. "I liked it all. Early in life, I decided I never would work at anything I didn't enjoy. As a boy, I walked the beaches searching for shells and turtle eggs. As a teenager, I played cricket with a bat often carved from a piece of fence board.

"And when I became a man, I went to the United States to see what I was missing. I've been back on the island these past forty years, and I'm glad I'm here because I decided I never would have been happy in America."

There were many on the island who maintained that the captain was a walking advertisement for strength—that he could lift a 100-pound box of fruit as easily as a baby lifts a toy balloon, and that he could sail through a heavy storm to such neighboring Dutch islands as Saba and St. Eustatius, with his bright blue eyes closed, controlling the tiller with no more than a fingertip.

When such boasts reached his ears, an animated Hodge would protest in all the languages he spoke— English, Dutch, French, Spanish, and the island's Papiamento. "It's only idle chatter," he told me.

But the Captain's reputation was not based on idle conversation. Through the years, as a skipper, he had weathered tempestuous squalls that made his craft—as large as fifty-foot sailboats—"spin like tops." He had repeatedly inched into harbors at night during tropical storms with only a kerosene lamp as a landmark and in channels only slightly deeper than the draft on his boat.

"They do not lie, those people who speak in awe of Austin Hodge's feats," a fish dealer along the island's main drag, Front Street, told me. "He's turned in feats of strength at sea in emergencies, such as tossing a heavy anchor overboard that four of his seamen couldn't move.

"And though he no longer sails, the good sisters of St. Joseph's College on the island still refer to him as 'Our Captain.' You see, there was many a time he ferried the nuns to safety to the islands of Saba and 'Statia.'"

I found just listening to the modest Hodge spell binding. He maintained that little had happened at sea through the years to surprise him. Fierce storms that he had been in? He shrugged them off by saying,

"That is when the sea is mean, it is no playground—that even a pelican with its tiny brain knows something of its moods. To sail on the sea, a man should be gifted with a compass in his head."

The son of a shipwright—his father was born in 1878 on the neighboring English island of Anguilla—the Captain trod his first deck shortly after he learned to walk. The elder Hodge, anxious for companionship, frequently would take the toddler to sea with him on short trips. By the time the youngster was eight, he owned his own little sloop—a twelve-footer.

"When I was fourteen," the Captain told me, "an importer with an office in Marigot, the capital on the French side of Sint Maarten Island, came into my father's place. He asked if he knew someone who could sail across 'the channel'—to Anguilla—to deliver a letter. In those days there was no other fast way, no radio, no telephone.

"'Of course I know someone,' my father replied. He pointed to me and said, 'There's the best sailor on this part of the island. If he can't make that eight-mile sail without getting your letter wet, no one can.'"

The trip was one of the first cross-channel voyages for the young one, and this one was for pay. Soon he was carrying letters and passengers in both directions. He was laughingly referred to as a "one-man telegraph office and postal service."

"I liked the States," Captain Hodge told me, "but I missed the sea. And when I returned to Sint Maarten for just a visit in 1930, I stayed here. I helped operate the local radio station but always was ready to trim a sail and often did. Then when the job offer came for me to captain our forty-three-foot government motorboat, the *Trixie*, I grabbed it."

Although the *Trixie* cruised about on power rather than with sails, Captain Hodges enjoyed making his official trips among the local islands for "the service of passenger and mails."

Came the year 1946 when his official boat had to be repaired because of engine trouble. He was asked to skipper the government's sailing schooner *Aurora* as a substitute. The *Aurora* had no auxiliary engine.

"On one of my early trips with her, Governor Papp ordered me to start out on my regular tour of the islands immediately—to lose no time," Captain Hodge recalled.

"'The mail service has been held up too many days because of the trouble with the *Trixie*,' he told me, 'and now we must do everything in a hurry.'"

"But this was one time that speed was not within my control," Captain Hodge continued. "When we lifted anchor for that voyage, there wasn't a breath of wind. It was oil-calm weather. For three long days, I remained within swimming distance from my starting point. With the orders as they were, I waited out the wind in our harbor. It took me eight days to finish that round-the-islands trip—a journey I usually completed in one day with the *Trixie*."

In sharp contrast was the voyage he took in 1947 on the two-masted *Blue Peter*, a new government boat that boasted a small motor. He arrived on the island of St. Kitts on schedule, and his four-man crew, as usual, went ashore in the small tender. The only one who remained aboard was Alfred Gumbo, a fourteen-year-old boy who was learning "the ropes."

A huge storm blew up at about 11:00 P.M. The crew was unable to return because of extremely rough weather. During the turmoil, the *Blue Peter*, with its little motor, conked out, was pushed aground by the tide and heavy winds. Hodge and the youngster, nevertheless, managed to get the boat afloat.

When the storm prevented them from returning to the St. Kitts harbor, they rode out the blustery winds all night and limped into St. Eustatius. There the captain picked up another crew, returned to St. Kitts, got his regular men back aboard and continued his rounds of the islands, as if the entire voyage had been routine.

During our conversation, Captain Hodge evinced an interest in visiting the new hotel at which I was stopping—the Concord of Sint Maarten, which had just opened. During the visit, under starry skies, the Captain marveled over the hotel's gardens and the size of its lobby. He was impressed too that it had been built on coral rocks that jutted out into the Caribbean.

While walking on the hotel's long promenade and looking over the side at the sea's boiling waters, he remarked, "You know, you can catch fish right off this walk."

As we were leaving the hotel's premises, I asked him what had interested him most about that resort.

I felt certain that he was going, perhaps, to single out its large, well-appointed dining room, the lobby's graceful, winding stairway, or maybe its busy colorful gaming room. I should have known better.

"I was impressed by everything I saw," he said with a smile. "But one thought keeps crossing my mind as I leave. The hotel here, with all its outdoor lighting . . . what a great landmark it makes for a sailor at night."

Lights? There's no doubt that two men, standing helplessly in the Caribbean, on the overturned side of their small sports fishing boat, would have been relieved if they could have seen lights during their five-day ordeal at sea. Their plight was caused when the motor on their twenty-foot inboard conked out.

I saw them while a passenger, in 1989, on a 10-day cruise aboard the Holland American liner *S.S. Rotterdam*. The stranded men were spotted from a distance. Their capsized boat was bobbing in the sea swells about fifteen miles southeast of the island of Grenada, yes—on waters once frequented by pirates of old.

History tells us that sailing ships flying the flag of the Dutch West India Company, which had been founded in 1621, sailed this same region and engaged in piracy. They captured the island of Curacao, which is about ninety miles south of Grenada. Much more recently, Grenada became the subject of international focus—in June of 1985—when US troops with a token force from six area nations invaded it as "liberators."

Even a Hollywood film director on location couldn't have staged this modern-day scene with the two men any better; a rescue at sea with desperate men being tossed about, waving their hands over their heads as our big ship approached.

Watching the helpless pair from vantage points along our ship's rails was a cast of hundreds of passengers—in a way, unpaid supernumeraries—wondering what the two bobbing individuals were doing out there, all alone. Most of the tourists aboard believed they were being greeted by the two individuals, as possibly a Grand Chamber of Commerce promotion. Our fellow passengers began waving back.

But they soon stopped. It became obvious to them that the men were in desperate straits, trying to keep their footing on that small overturned hull with a great deal of effort. Some of our passengers moaned in disbelief as the huge liner, weighing an estimated 38,000 tons and being 748 feet in length, skimmed right past the waving pair as if it were in a race to the finish line.

"You mean we're not going to stop and pick them up?" asked one of our passengers. "Or is the scene out there just for our entertainment? If it is, then it's a neat piece of work. I've seen fake hold-up men in action for the entertainment of sightseers in action on a movie set in Tombstone, Arizona. It had gunfire and all. But this sure is different."

It was different because within a short time, the ship began making a U-turn. Its bow soon was directed toward the overturned craft. Once near it, a motorized tender, manned by a few members of the crew, was dispatched. Within fifteen minutes, the rescue had been completed. The overturned little boat was abandoned to drift over the swells, perhaps, to never-never land.

"If this was back in the days of the buccaneers," observed one male passenger who had climbed out of our ship's small outdoor swimming pool to watch, "I might think we were being set up. I've seen movies in which pirates, back in the seventeenth century, ambushed unwary merchant ships by sending a few decoys out in a boat and then charging in from behind a neck of land with their own ship to make a capture."

But this was no movie. We were on the open sea. There wasn't another vessel to be seen even on the horizon—anywhere. Some of the gawkers along the rail were heard fretting about the length of time it had taken the *Rotterdam* to come about to help the two stranded men. Capt. Jan W. van der Noordt, the pleasant-mannered veteran commander of the *Rotterdam*, explained it all.

"Once we noticed their plight, we stopped as soon as we could," he said. "We were doing almost twenty knots. Getting a big liner like this to slow down and come about takes time. After all, a ship is not like an automobile. It has no brakes."

As a newsman, I was interested in obtaining more information. I asked whether the captain would see me. He graciously consented, in his office, near the ship's bridge.

"In the forty years I've been to sea, twelve of them as a captain," he told me, "I never have been involved in such a rescue." Then he gave me some added details.

"Those two men set out to sea, they say four or five days ago, eager to test a new motor in their small boat. But as soon as they got a few miles from shore, their motor failed. And so they kept drifting.

"They told me they were native Grenadians, and that their names were Hugh Greenwich and Steve Winsen," continued the captain. "They explained that while they had been adrift for five days, that it only had been the night before that their boat had been overturned by a passing tramp steamer.

"'We saw that tramp steamer approaching us, and we began waving at it, to veer off,' Winsen had explained to me," said the captain. "'But those aboard never saw us. When we finally realized that it was going to smash into us, we jumped overboard. We were unhurt. That steamer's big wake, however, capsized our small boat. We had no choice but to climb back onto it although it was now upside down.'

"As for those two people who are now aboard," explained Capt. Van der Noordt, "our physician reports that Greenwich has glazed eyes and was in a stupor, a condition probably caused by drinking large quantities of sea water. As for his companion, he's suffering mostly from a low-grade fever."

As soon as the *Rotterdam* dropped anchor off Grenada, the two men were hustled ashore, alone, on a tender. And once my wife and I were on the island, we visited two old friends from Connecticut who wintered in Grenada.

I told my friends the story of the rescue. I said that I planned to stop by the local police station so that I could make some further inquiries because I planned to write the story for my paper, the *Palm Beach Daily News*.

"But it will be just a waste of time," they said to me. "The chances are that the police will know nothing about the incident yet."

They were correct. I spoke to the lieutenant in charge of the police desk. It was then at least four hours after we had landed. I told him that I wondered why the families involved had not reported the two men missing. He shrugged.

"It's not unusual for people on our island to set out in their boats and to remain at sea for four or five days," he replied. "Men growing up here know the sea. They know how to take care of themselves."

Having seen those two frightened men on the overturned boat and the rescue, I was convinced that these two men, in no way, could have taken care of themselves. They were lucky to have survived.

When I returned to Palm Beach, I wrote the story of the rescue. It ran about one to two pages long. Then I mailed a copy of it to the Holland American Line's headquarters on the Pacific Coast.

About two weeks later, I received a phone call from a young woman representing the steamship line. She told me that her company would like to reprint the story in its own newspaper for the information of its staff. I gave my permission, asking only that a copy of their newspaper be sent to me when the story was reprinted. The promise was made graciously.

But I never received it.

"I'd say your story was never used," an old friend who is a specialist in private investigation work suggested when I told him the story.

"Putting a focus like that get-around might give some rascals ideas," he said. "Just think, setting up a decoy overturned boat on the Caribbean and then having the rescued men on it help in staging a hi-jack of the big steamer . . . and on what once was pirate infested waters! What a story that would make!"

CHAPTER 24

Hope Springs Eternal – Drumbeaters Hope Springs Eternal

If you would keep your fate in hand,
Five things observe with care;
Of whom you speak, to whom you speak,
And how and when and where.

Every year, be it during the start of the pro baseball, football, or basketball seasons, there always are sure to be some owners and coaches, nurturing hopes of championships, even though it is generally agreed that their teams are far short of the necessary manpower to be a winner.

It took the Chicago Cubs, who were National League champions in 1945, all of thirty-nine years to recapture a pennant. The Braves, when they played in Boston starting from 1901, only gained National League honors twice—in 1914 and 1948—before that team's franchise was moved to the greener pastures of Milwaukee.

Still there were many years in between when owners of those two clubs thought that they were fielding a team capable of winning championships. George Steinbrenner, as principal owner of the New York Yankees, with what often seemed justification, believed that his teams had the capability to win pennants just about every year. As might be expected, they didn't.

And just like the Ike Falk story, there always have been items dealing with lesser known figures than major league baseball owners who have tickled sports goers. There was George Marshall, the one-time owner of pro football's Washington Redskins. He helped add flavor to the sport by sending his team's big marching band dressed as Indians to games in New York whenever the Redskins played the Giants.

Back in the 1950s when the Brooklyn Dodgers were still playing at Ebbets Field, a quartet known as the "Phony Symphony" would pound away at their instruments in their field level box seats, to keep the crowd alive. In deference to the sportswriters and fans who delighted in referring to the Dodgers as The Bums, the Phony Symphony would hammer their musical instruments while wearing battered top hats and derbies.

And then there were those other "phonies"—gate crashers—always ready to accept the challenge of beating the price of a ticket by talking their way past an admission gate or perhaps finding an unguarded exit in which to enter a sporting event. For most of them, it was a challenge. I once saw a young man climb over the high center field fence in Yankee Stadium to gain a free admission. Even if some of these freebie seekers were thwarted on any given occasion, there was always "next time."

The most famous gate crasher of all was One-Eyed Connolly. He was so good at giving ticket takers the slip, that it was said he was going to be able to talk his way into heaven. He attended many important sports events without paying the price of admission.

He came into focus in the post-World War I years. Wearing a patch over one eye and a rumpled jacket, no tie, he could be seen seated at ringside of important world championship boxing matches. I ran into him once walking just behind Jimmy Walker, then the mayor of New York City, acting as if he were a member of "His Honor's" party.

"Any sportswriter my age remembers the One-Eyed guy well," Jimmy Dawson, the famed boxing expert once told me. "We all knew at ringside that he never bought a ticket. He usually sat in a vacant seat up front.

"If someone came along later with the usher to claim the seat," Jimmy explained, "Connolly would look for another vacant one up front and sit in that seat. As for World Series games, they seemed a pushover for him. You usually would have no trouble finding him because he'd be sitting in one of the ball park's best seats, behind one of the dugouts."

Also getting away with what seemed the impossible was one of America's top self-acknowledged confidence men, Italian-born Guido Orlando. I ran into Guido several times, once at the New York Athletic Club, in post-World War II days. He got his start, in a way, because of sports.

At about the same time that Connolly was coming into prominence as a gate crasher, Orlando started his career of being a successful "scoundrel."

Among the accusations leveled at him as he engaged in his career was that through the years, he had "befuddled" bankers in the midst of a Congressional investigation, promoted "patches" of California sand into a financially successful real estate bubble and one day, had tied up traffic for hours on New York's busy Times Square—all with his characteristic brainstorms.

He was brought to the United States in July of 1917 at age eleven. Within a few months, he was appearing in saloons in his new home of Bellaire, Ohio, and environs, selling newspapers with the latest baseball scores. To get the sympathy from the bar loungers who wanted to help out "a poor kid like that," he would appear in worn knee britches and bare feet.

"I would also sell papers to passengers on trolley cars while the cars stopped on street corners," he related in a book he authored in the early 1950s with the help of a ghostwriter, titled *Confessions of a Scoundrel.*

"If they gave me a nickel or a dime, I would make believe I was digging in my pockets for change," he wrote. "The trolleys, of course, would take off before I could find it."

Within a year, he was ordering guitars by mail from the North Shore Novelty Company of Chicago and peddling them to schoolmates.

"I joined the school's orchestra to be in better contact with the boys in our band who were studying music. But I couldn't read a note. Yet I played before school audiences and was able to make a profit by doing it. It was the first really successful bluff I ever threw."

And so a career was launched. One of Orlando's biggest "triumphs" was scored just north of New York Times Square at the large-sized Capitol Theater. Aimee Semple McPherson, a well-known evangelist of her day, had drawn only tiny audiences in the opening days of a show that she was staging.

Major Bowes, the manager of the Capitol, enlisted the aid of Orlando in seeking more action at the box office. Guido proceeded to hire a bunch of actors and then rented about twenty policemen's uniforms at the Eaves Costume Company. The next morning when Aimee went on for her first performance, there they were, a lot of cops milling around in front of the theater.

Soon a crowd formed, curious to learn why there were so many policemen in front of the theater. Before long, bumper-to-bumper automobile traffic became the order of the day on Broadway in the Times Square area.

"Real police appeared," wrote Orlando in his book. "I told them that this was all a publicity stunt. But those legitimate cops hung around too, and the crowd got bigger. I phoned the newspapers and told them people were fighting to get to the theater to hear Aimee. By the next afternoon, because of the front-page spreads in the newspapers, I had to fight the crowd myself to get into the theater. At the box office, there was a long double line of people waiting to get into the Capitol to hear Aimee."

During the 1930s, I got to know the slow-speaking Abie Cohen who earned a meager income as a delivery boy for Brooklyn sports' promoters. Although careless in appearance, he somehow managed frequently to be photographed with sports celebrities. Recently, I discovered a picture of him in the superbly done "Baseball Hall of Fame 50th Anniversary Book," on page 127.

Abie, who is not identified because the photographer evidently didn't know who he was, is shown posing in a full-page photo that includes none other than Babe Ruth and Lou Gehrig. Five men are in the photo. Two of the men are legitimate. They were there to make presentations of silver loving cups to the two baseball legends, Ruth and Gehrig.

The picture's caption makes no mention of where it was taken. But I know. It was snapped at Dexter Park, once the home of the semi-pro Bushwicks, located on the Brooklyn–Queens boundary of New York City. How do I know? Because I was there for the exhibition game played that afternoon between the Bushwicks and "Babe Ruth All Stars."

Abie was wearing his best Sunday suit topped by his familiar gray felt hat on that afternoon. He was a sports hero worshipper who managed to get into that photo with Ruth and Gehrig by offering to carry the trophies from the press box to the field.

Suffice it to say, Abie didn't pay to get into that ball game at Dexter Park that afternoon. He'd got in, of course, free of charge. Every time I saw him he had an unlighted cigar stub dangling from his teeth.

"Why are you so interested in being photographed with celebrities?" I asked him one Sunday night when he appeared at our Brooklyn–Queens section of the New York Times to deliver some boxing photos.

"I dunno," he answered, humping his shoulders. "I think, I think maybe it's because I read about them in the papers . . . the papers . . . so much. They are famous. Maybe if people . . . they see me in these pictures . . . maybe they'll think I'm famous too."

While I kept meeting up with winners and sinners, I also kept running into winners and losers. And they had nothing to do with gate crashing or celebrity seeking. They all had one common denominator—"zeal."

Walter J. Ferentino, a milkman with a horse-drawn wagon delivery route in the Corona section of New York City's Queens County, Queens, proved to be a luckless loser. And then there was the highly imaginative Andy Furman, who, I think, as of this writing, can still go either way.

Furman's profession is sports public relations. I first met him when he was doing publicity for the professional Fort Lauderdale Striders soccer team in Florida.

It was obvious from the start that he operated on the belief that nothing was impossible when it came to getting free space in the newspapers. Imagination? In my experience, he's had no peer when it comes to offbeat, zany ideas.

"He demonstrated his imagination the first time I met him," remembers Allen Finkelson, a vice president in charge of public relations at Florida's flourishing Pompano Park harness horse track. "He phoned me one afternoon and said, 'I have a great idea. How about one of our pro soccer players racing against one of your harness horses down your track's stretch as an added attraction to one of your programs?'"

"Who are you going to have run for you? Superman?" Finkelson asked. "Do you really think you have a player who can hold his own against one of our horses? Our trotters and pacers can do a mile in two minutes!"

"I sure have" was his instant reply. "You'll be surprised."

"I wasn't surprised," Finkelson candidly admits. "It was absolutely no contest even though we sent out one of our slowest horses hoping to provide for a close, interesting finish. Our horse won by about a city block.

"Disappointed over that fiasco, I returned to my office," continued Finkelson. "Suddenly this Andy Furman comes bursting in. He wants to use the phones for long distance calls to the wire services and to report on this 'race of horse against man.'

"'This story isn't worth telling to the outside world,' I said to him. 'Your soccer player, as just about everyone expected, lost by such a big margin that he might just as well have been chained to the ground. The wire services won't be interested. Now, if your player had beaten our horse, that would have been a story.'

"'It's still a good story,' Furman insisted. 'You'll see. I'll place it.'

"And he did," said Finkelson, who by that time had been a highly successful publicity director for at least three decades. "In fact, I was so impressed by what this guy did in getting the media to take his story that I immediately phoned friends at Monticello Raceway in upstate New York. I recommended Andy for the publicity job there. He was hired."

What Finkelson didn't know was that before coming to Fort Lauderdale, Furman had previously tried to promote greyhound racing in New Jersey and basketball at Oral Roberts University in Tulsa, Oklahoma. At Tulsa, he disappeared from the scene quickly after heralding the arrival of DePaul University's Blue Demons basketball team with a unique freebie offer.

"All Satan worshippers will get in free to see this game" was the announcement he made. That one effort ended Furman's stay in the Sooner State.

In Fort Lauderdale, in an effort to bolster drastically sagging attendance for his Striders soccer team, he came up with another promotion scheme which he called "Phone Book Night."

His idea called for him to phone people listed in the telephone directory and to invite them, as guests, to a soccer game. He soon gave up that plan when he realized that he might be embarking on a lifetime's work in thumbing through the thick book. His scheme, it developed, produced few acceptances from the telephone company's customers.

Once he arrived at Monticello Raceway, Furman demonstrated that he had lost none of his excogitation. Among his promotions there was a "Funeral Night," followed shortly be a "Leonid Brezhnev Night."

Leo Doobin, who managed the racetrack, didn't like the funeral idea from the start.

"It was much too morbid," he explained. "Furman had invited local morticians to Monticello, and in their honor, planned to raffle off a free burial and casket. The man who won it got all upset when he realized the whole thing was a spoof. We had to pay him off with a lifetime track pass."

To get space in the ink and air media for his Brezhnev promotion, Furman announced that he had sent a wire to the Soviet premier inviting him to come to the track as its guest.

"However," the cable, which Furman said he had dispatched to Moscow, read, "you are welcome but don't bring any Russian race horses with you." He explained this part of the message by pointing out that he merely was catering to President Carter's feelings at that time about not having American athletes compete in the 1980 Summer Olympics in Moscow. Everyone chuckled.

The tireless publicist ended his stay in Monticello when he announced that the track would stage a "Ku Klux Klan Night." The "attraction" called for fans to come out to see white garbed members of the Klan "enjoying a night of horse racing." For members of the Klan, he publicized the following message:

"Wear your white sheet and get in free."

Doobin, as might be expected, was horrified. Monticello Raceway is in an area where lots of blacks reside. Nearby, are resort hotels that cater to thousands of Jewish people.

Had Furman's inspiration been carried out, members of the local police force were convinced a riot would have resulted.

"I wasn't supporting the Klan or anything like that," Furman explained when called on the carpet by Doobin. "I never went through with it."

Naturally, he couldn't. Doobin fired him soon after learning of Furman's latest inspiration.

And so the publicist moved on to his next job—at Kentucky's time-honored Latima track, a thoroughbred plant located a few miles south of Cincinnati. It was here that Furman came up with a "Marriage Night" to be held in the track's Winner's Circle.

But when Furman was unable to get a couple interested in having its marital vows taken before a racetrack crowd, he offered himself and his fiancée as principals in the ceremony.

"I let everybody in free who brought me a gift," he reported after the wedding nuptials had been completed. "I got a rabbi to perform the service as well as a big crowd of 5,200 spectators to watch me take the plunge. Somebody must have liked the idea."

The last I heard of Furman was that he was working at radio station WLW, in Cincinnati. But he still was right in there, up to his elbows, trying to promote. In 1985, he was turned down after applying for the job of publicity director for the Pittsburgh Pirates of the National Baseball League.

In November of 1989, he surfaced with the idea of bringing a National Basketball Association franchise to Cincinnati. To promote his idea, Furman estimates he sent at least 500 pieces of mail to Dudley Webb, the prominent Lexington, Kentucky developer. Webb finally responded with a phone call.

"Are you the guy sending me all these letters?" Webb asked.

"Yes, sir," Furman is alleged to have said quietly.

"Let's get to work then," Webb replied.

Webb then put Dick Robinson, a senior vice president of his company, in charge of that project. The latter reported that he was definitely looking into the idea.

"Dudley Webb is not the kind of man who goes through motions," Furman thereupon gloated to Rick Bozich, the sports columnist of the *Kentucky Courier-Journal* in Louisville. "He wants an NBA team in his area. I'm the dreamer, he's the money guy. Now the dream is focused.

"Everybody told me I was crazy when I started sending out all those letters telling people we needed a big-league pro basketball team here," Furman explained. "And I was crazy. But every new idea is probably crazy in the beginning."

For Walter J. Ferentino, the New York City milkman, the year 1940 was described by Lou O'Neill, then the sports editor of the *Long Island Daily Press*, as being "unbelievably crazy."

Ferentino, back in the days when the Sheffield, Borden, and Renken milk companies among others, were offering home delivery—having their bottles of milk delivered by horse and wagon. Ferentino was one of the most experienced milkmen in the county.

Since almost his entire working lifetime had been spent calling out "giddyap" and "whoa" to horses, he was convinced that he was well qualified to be an excellent judge of horseflesh.

"After all," he once said to me, "I've been driving them for more than twenty-five years."

Because milk deliveries usually were completed before noon, Ferentino found plenty of time to attend the races at metropolitan New York's thoroughbred race tracks. Such cavalry grounds as Aqueduct and Jamaica were only a few miles from his Queens County home in Corona. But like most horse players, he lost many more bets on the horses than he won.

Having seen hundreds of thoroughbred horses race through the years, Walter had one burning desire: to own one.

"I don't have much to spend," the milkman told the ever-friendly local sports editor Lou O'Neill during a visit to the races, "but I'd like to buy a thoroughbred. If you hear of an auction sale in which you think horses will go cheap, let me know."

Ferentino should have kept his mouth closed. It was that request that eventually got him into deep trouble.

Because as that winter was turning into spring, the colorful O'Neill phoned him.

"I remembered your request about owning a horse," the sports editor told him. "There's going to be a dispersal sale early next week at Belmont Park. Some of Alfred G. Vanderbilt's Sagamore Farm's racing stock is scheduled to go on the block. You might go out there and watch it to get some experience."

Ferentino was willing, eager, but cautious. He was convinced that any Vanderbilt horse offered for sale was going to be way out of his pocketbook range. After all, Sagamore Farms was just about to thoroughbred racing what J.P. Morgan was to banking.

"I went to that sale just to listen," he told me weeks later. "But as they kept bringing those colts and fillies out, I began listening more carefully. Some of that stock was going for small prices."

And then out came Sagamore Lady, a well conformed, two-year-old filly whom it seemed was perfectly mannered. It developed, though, that there must have been something wrong with her. No one seemed willing to make an offer for her.

"Before I knew it," said Ferentino, "the auctioneer got the bid down to $50 and I raised my hand. To my utter surprise, I got the horse. I felt that if there was anything wrong with her that I could cure it. After all, I'd been close to horses all my life."

As it turned out, Ferentino should have kept his hand in his pocket instead of raising it. It brought him nothing but problems and expenses. For starters, enthused because he now was a race horse owner, he put the filly in an indigent trainer's care prepared to pay the feed bill and other necessary expenses. He even purchased green and white jockey silks. That's when Lou O'Neill phoned me.

"I sort of feel sorry for this guy," Lou said to me. "But I think he's going to make an interesting story. Just think, a milkman with limited means becoming the owner of a filly from the prestigious Sagamore Farms."

It did make an interesting story. I eventually sold it to *Esquire Magazine* but not until after additional distressing events had developed.

Ferentino's trainer, it developed, took a lot of time trying to get Sagamore Lady into shape. Indeed, it wasn't until late that following August that he told Ferentino that he was going to enter Sagamore Lady in a race.

"I think we have her back in good health," the trainer reported. "The Saratoga meeting is about to close. So, I plan to start her when Belmont Park opens in the next ten days or so. We might get lucky."

Ferentino was ecstatic. But luck on that first day the filly ran was noticeable by its absence. She finished a dead last. However, she did display the least bit of late speed in that five-eighths-of-a-mile race.

Ferentino took that closing sequence as a promising sign. Since he previously had told some of his milk route customers that he had become a race horse owner, he now saw fit late one September morning to leave a note attached to their milk bottles. It read:

"My horse is racing again tomorrow at Belmont Park. It's her second start. I think she has a good chance. It's worth a good bet."

Suffice it to say, Sagamore Lady finished last again. And in two subsequent races at Jamaica, she fared no better. She trailed the fields.

Perhaps the most serious aspect of this thoroughbred's dismal finishes was that Ferentino's milk customers, because of his morning reminders attached to the milk bottles, had continued to bet and lose. Some of them changed their milkman.

By this time the fun-minded Dan Parker, the esteemed sports columnist for the *New York Daily Mirror* had learned about the Corona milkman who was not only losing at the races but also losing customers. Always ready to provide his readers with a laugh, Parker wrote in his well-read column:

"The name of Ferentino's stable should be called the 'Rigor Mortis Stable' and his jockey's silk colors instead of green and white should be 'black and blue.'"

There came a moment of decision for Ferentino. Now overwhelmed by feed and training bills, he finally concluded that Sagamore Lady could not cope with the high-quality competition at New York's tracks. He told his trainer that he was going to rent a horse trailer—that he was to take Sagamore Lady to the Pascoag race track in Rhode Island.

"I can make a killing there," he said. "My filly has such a poor record that no one at that track will bet on her. It will make her odds go way up. And in Rhode Island, she'll be racing against inferior horses."

Pascoag? Anyone who ever had placed a bet with a bookmaker knew that racing oval, tucked north of Providence and just south of the Massachusetts line, was considered the Devil's Island of all race tracks. Only the slowest and least expensive race horses in the land raced there.

Ferentino revealed his plans to his milk customers three days before he left for Rhode Island.

"This is it!" he wrote on his notes to them. "We're going to win big up there and at a fancy price. No one in Rhode Island knows anything about us."

He spoke the truth, at least in one respect. Because on the day of the race, Sagamore Lady was ignored by that track's spectators in the betting because no one there ever had seen her run. And as had been expected, she went to the starting gate as a long shot. And deservedly so as it developed because she finished dead last again.

When Ferentino returned to his milk route two days later, he found at least three notes from neighboring households attached to the empty bottles he picked up. The three messages were scrawled on the past performance record of Sagamore Lady as printed in the Daily Racing Form. One of them read:

"If you have the nerve to leave another memo for us about your great horse, please consider us as another one of your ex-customers. We suggest that you get smart and sell her."

That's exactly what Ferentino did—and for only $25.

CHAPTER 25

Winners and Sinners – Art Rooney, etc.

You have to be lucky, plucky, and smart
To be a big winner despite a slow start
Once you are there; right up at the top,
Is when to keep plugging, not when to stop.

Winners and Sinners was the name of a small publication conceived and written by Ted Bernstein, once an important editor of the *New York Times*. He was a highly regarded grammarian. Each month, for the benefit of the news department, he would issue a two-page mimeographed sheet on which he would point out outstanding headlines and good lead paragraphs as well as poor ones.

His critiques proved so popular, that often in making my rounds of schools and colleges, faculty members would ask me if they could be put on the mailing list to receive them. The name of his little paper comes to mind after all these years only because I've become privy to my share of winners and sinners.

It was Bernstein who helped me have my first book published in 1972—on skiing. He was an advisor for Quadrangle Press, then a *New York Times* property. I told him about an idea I had of putting together a ski directory and with it, a sizable introduction.

He got me the go-ahead in a surprisingly short time. It was the most advanced book of its kind in its day. In it was just about everything dealing with ski areas—coast to coast—with the exception, I used to jokingly say, of the birthdays of owners who owned those more than 400 ski areas.

I have a winners and sinners list of my own. It's made up mostly of winners, people whom I found unforgettable, such as Art Rooney,

Lowell Thomas, Ned Irish, and Tommy Deegan, among others. All four started from humble beginnings. Oh yes, I shouldn't forget another winner, Ike Falk. This was a guy in a class all by himself. His plugging never brought him financial prosperity, but it did bring him—he was devoted to baseball—a lifetime of pleasure.

But to get to Rooney. He was that lovable fellow who owned football's Pittsburgh Steelers. He prospered as a team owner. But his stand-out characteristic was "'preciation."

He never forgot those newsmen who had reported on the Steelers in that team's early history, in the early 1930s, at a time when the Pittsburgh team was the perennial doormat of the National Football League. That was in an era in which the Steelers proved one of the league's most consistent clubs. They always finished last.

Good old Art would take these early defeats in stride. Actually, he had no reason to do otherwise. After all, in agreeing to accept a league franchise in 1933—for only $2,500—at the urging of his friend George Halas of the Chicago Bears—he had merely converted, at Halas's suggestion—his Pittsburgh semi-pro football players, who were being paid only a few dollars for Sunday games into a full pro squad.

"After all," he told me in those early days, "we can't be expected to do much winning in this big pro league because we don't have anyone even remotely resembling an All-American. Some of the fellows never even went to college. But we'll get better even if it takes a long time."

It took a long time. And although the Steelers played extremely poorly in their early years, Rooney retained his customary happy and optimistic attitude. He became popular with newsmen because he was so genial, easy to talk to, and last but not least, because he had that Will Rogers's philosophy of "never meeting a man I didn't like."

Even when the Steelers became a football power many years later and went on to greatness (and Rooney became a multimillionaire), he, unlike some other sports magnates who had struck it rich, remained his friendly self. He often made it a point to visit his sportswriting friends, in the press box, whether it was at a football game or a baseball game at Pittsburgh's Forbes Field or later at Three Rivers Stadium.

"You know, Mike," he said early one fall back in 1978, while I was reporting on the annual college football game between the University of Pittsburgh and Penn State, "my pro team probably is going to win its first divisional championship in our history this year. It would make me feel ten years younger if it turned out that way."

It did turn out that way. And three years later, the Steelers won their first Super Bowl championship. To give a fitting touch to that memorable occasion, the team awarded the game ball to Rooney. During the next five seasons, Art's team went on to capture three more Super Bowls.

It was during those joyous years, in particular, that Rooney, one day, came late into the baseball press box of the Pittsburgh Pirates who were then entertaining the New York Mets. He greeted all the New York writers that he knew.

Then just before he was ready to leave, he turned to me and said,

"Why don't you come with me to my box? It's on the third base side. I want you to meet six young ladies. They're bright ones."

"Young ladies," I thought to myself. "That's for me"

Hastily adjusting my necktie, I walked past the home plate side of the stadium with him. He ushered me into his box. Sitting there were six nuns of varying ages. And as Art had said, they were bright. All of them were well tuned in on baseball.

Yes, the phrase about Rooney that stands out in my mind like a lone, graceful-looking royal palm tree in a desert, was the long memory he had for sportswriters, even those who had retired. It was common knowledge that two ailing members of that scribes' clan, Lou Effrat of the *New York Times* and Harold Weissman of the *Daily Mirror* and later the publicity director of the New York Mets baseball team, were phoned long distance, regularly, by good old Art who would call to enquire about their health.

Even several years after I had retired from the *New York Times*, he kept in contact with me. I've had a postcard, which I received from him in early 1986, pinned on a wall facing my bed a few years before he passed on.

On one side is a caricature of Rooney with his ever-present cigar in his mouth. The sketch was done by that well-known artist Le Roy Neiman at a football dinner in New York in 1972. Rooney's message on the card?

"Mike—I expect to get to Palm Beach during the last week that the horses are running (at Gulfstream Park). Call and see if I am there. We will go to dinner. I would like to go to the horse track with you." And then humorously, he added, "I'll get rich with your figures."

By "figures" of course he meant my handicapping—my ability to pick winners. He was kidding. Because, through the years, I, like many others, haven't been too successful at it. To this day, I keep telling people that I haven't won a bet since the War of 1812. Actually, that's not exactly true. I've won at the day of the races, but rarely. Art knew that I, like most sports writers, was a poor handicapper.

One night, while he was entertaining my wife and me at the Palm Beach Kennel Club, which also belonged to his family, he asked me how I was picking my selections for that night's program.

"My system is simple," I replied. "I'm only betting numbers. The numbers I'm picking tonight are the three that your handicapper has picked for each of the races on the track's program. I'm using them, in reverse, hoping to get a bigger price for the trifecta should my numbers finish one-two-three in the order."

Art smiled.

"Has that system ever worked for you?" he asked.

"Almost never," I replied. "One reason is that I only buy one $2 ticket instead of spending more for a lot of different possible combinations. But there's always that first time."

As it developed, that night's races didn't provide it. I failed to cash a winning trifecta ticket all night. "And so what else is new?" I thought to myself as my wife and I left the track for the drive along the ocean to our apartment.

I didn't learn of Art's death until about a week after he had passed away. I believe I was out in Arkansas helping to publicize an important greyhound racing event. One of the sorriest things in my life was that I never did get to his funeral. He was like a God.

Art left five handsome sons. I got to know two of them better than the rest, Tim and Pat. Both are just as pleasant-mannered as was their dad. Tim as head of Yonkers Raceway in New York was of extreme help to the members during my five-year term as president of the Metropolitan New York Harness Writers.

Pat Rooney as well was as personable as their father. Pat surprised me recently by telling me he was taking up croquet, a particularly popular sport in the Palm Beaches. Why the surprise? Because he had the youth and the build of a football player.

Lowell Thomas became one of my favorite personalities during my later years at the *New York Times*. A native of the mining town of Cripple Creek in Colorado, Lowell worked hard to gain prominence. I first met him at the Lake Placid Club, when on occasion, he would broadcast his nightly coast-to-coast news reports. George Carroll, the club's pleasant executive secretary and his close friend, introduced us.

Thereafter, Lowell, busy man that he was with his motion picture newsreel broadcasts, book writing, and his proprietary interest in the novel three-dimension film productions, would occasionally find time to contact me. It usually would be because he had come up with an idea connected with skiing.

The day I'll never forget was that morning when he showed at the Brodie Mountain Ski area in the Berkshires of Massachusetts in a station wagon. At the back of it were about five pairs of skis, including the new type "Shorties." They were about thirty-nine inches long.

"My friend Cliff Taylor who used to teach skiing up in Vermont, in Brattleboro, asked me to try these out," Thomas said to me. "He maintains they're the greatest development in the sport since the rope tow. He insists it'll make winter skiing easier, particularly for a fellow my age."

I was a little surprised because Thomas had impressed me as a purist when it came to skiing gear. I recalled a picture I had in my files that showed him, as a war correspondent in World War I, holding a pair of skis upright that were probably more than a foot taller than he was.

And so, on that day, Lowell went out on Brodie's slopes and tried them. He said he liked them. But the last time I skied with him in Colorado—back in the 1970s—he was using his regular five feet-plus skis. He had soon learned that "Shorties" only made sense for beginner's slopes. And Lowell was no beginner.

Ned Irish amazed me because he struck it rich after starting out as a sportswriter for the *New Evening World*. He came up with the idea of staging college basketball double headers at Madison Square Garden. When I heard about it, I thought it was just a foolish idea.

Through those earlier years, I had reported on college basketball games played at New York University, St. John's, Long Island University, and City College of New York. Their games, until Irish appeared with his idea, had been played in campus gymnasiums. Crowds of 1,500 had been considered banner ones.

"It sounded ridiculous to me," I remember telling my boss Joe Gephart. "Why, I was at the Garden a few years ago to report on a game played by the Original Celtics, one of the greatest pro teams of its day. The attendance? It was less than 2,000. How could Irish expect these college teams to be a better drawing card?"

But Irish, with astute maneuvering, began staging college double headers at the Garden that drew crowds of more than eight times the number that the Original Celtics had attracted. It was generally known, however, that many of the fans who turned out had wagers with bookmakers on these games. Members of this large group, as might be expected, were among the loudest rooters, even though in many cases they were not particularly interested in the teams at play. Before long, Irish was importing collegiate teams from the Pacific Coast and Midwest to oppose local New

York quintets. And he did so with a minimum of expense. These squads, on their way east, also were being booked to play games en route to the Garden in cities to the west, thereby having other promoters share and guarantee traveling expenses.

Strike it rich? I know he did—because one day when I phoned him at his home number, a strange voice answered the phone.

"Hello," I heard a man on the other end of the line say, "This is Mr. Irish's butler. Can I be of service to you?"

Tommy Deegan's rise was just as sensational. I first met him when he was the sports correspondent for the *New York Times* and *Brooklyn Eagle* for Bushwick High School of Brooklyn. Later, he became our sports representative at Fordham University in the Bronx. He was handsome and one of the neatest dressers I ever met. It seemed obvious to me, though, in those early days—in the early 1930s—that every dime he ever earned was important to him.

We both traveled on the BMT Jamaica elevated rapid transit line to reach our homes in Brooklyn. I would feel so sorry for him that on the few trips I made with him, I would insist on treating him to the ride, shoving two nickels into the turnstile slots while motioning him to follow me through the gate. He never objected.

About two years later, in the mid-1930s, we dated two girls and took them to Coney Island. Among our bits of nonsense on that occasion was to have our picture taken in one of those broken down "art galleries" on Surf Avenue. Imaginative young journalists that we were, we improvised. We had the girls sit in a prototype of a touring automobile while we mounted its running boards, crouched, and peering ahead as if we were plainclothes police chasing bandits. I still have that picture somewhere.

Tommy Deegan? He subsequently became a staff sportswriter for the *New York Times* to start what I always considered an Horatio Alger success story. After a short stint on that job, he left to take over the direction of Manhattan's swank Fifth Avenue Association. Before I knew it, he had become the president of the huge Chesapeake and Ohio Railroad system.

None of this, I guess, should have surprised me. Tommy had a striking personality and a winning smile. If someone told him a tale that was supposed to be funny, he would start chuckling as if it had been conceived by one of the world's greatest wits. People, particularly tycoons, it seems, like to have their jokes appreciated.

On the other side of the coin—way on the other side—was that little rotund, eccentric Ike Falk. His success story was almost unbelievable. It was one that dealt with a buoyancy of emotions rather than with the pocketbook.

Ike was employed in the *New York Times* "Morgue"—a department in the business of filing away old clippings. The latter were indexed for use by our reporters and rewritemen seeking background material on persons whose names might previously have cropped up in the news. Ike gets into my winners' category, sort of through the back door.

A $30-a-week clerk during the World War II era, he was a rabid New York Giants' baseball fan. One "memorable" night in 1936, when he should have been on the job filing old clippings, he began his annual chore, on company time, of course, of checking the scheduled games for the approaching National and American Leagues baseball seasons.

For him, it was for good reason. As each season approached, he would sit down one night—or maybe two or three—and pick out the games he thought he might be able to attend during the oncoming season, without conflicting with his job in the Morgue.

Remember! At that time, night baseball had yet to be introduced to the major leagues. And so, Ike usually would choose eight or ten afternoon games that he hoped to be able to see, some of them on weekends when he had days off.

He would stop to speak to me often as he passed from the Morgue to the newsroom to deliver clippings. Simple soul that he was, I liked him and once wrote a full-length story about him for *Argosy Magazine*. He was a good fellow who became the paper's largest donor to its Blood Bank.

Ike would only get angry whenever someone poked fun at some of his unusual but harmless mannerisms, such as talking to himself while munching a sandwich and walking down the hall, all at the same time. Oh yes. He also would see red if someone—even in jest—referred to his New York Giants as being a "lousy" team.

"Right now, I'm hoping to see a dozen games this season," he said to me one night while I was punching away at my typewriter. "I'd like to see more. But it costs $1.10 to sit in the grandstand. That's expensive, particularly since sometimes I have to leave before a game is over in order to get to the office on time."

Ike, a roly-poly graying man, who barely had reached the five-foot mark in height, often would be good-naturedly kidded by staff members during the course of an evening. After all, he did walk like a duck, and handicapped by a mouth of false teeth, he sometimes sounded like a duck when he spoke. But he didn't look like a duck. Besides, ducks don't clean their eyeglasses with their neckties while they're waddling.

In late winter, staff people entering the Morgue at night to seek old clippings for backup material on that day's breaking stories, would see the somewhat eccentric Ike writing down the dates on individual index cards for each of New York's baseball games—contests to be played at home that season by the Giants and the Yankees. They'd kid him. Ike's labors, to them, seemed like such a great waste of time.

Ike paid them no mind. He insisted that, for him, indexing the ball games made lots of sense. In deciding to see games, he was being picky. He just didn't want to attend games in which his esteemed Giants were scheduled to play against such poor players as the Phillies or the Boston Braves. The Brooklyn Dodgers, the St. Louis Cardinals, or perhaps the Cincinnati Reds? That was different. Those were among the clubs he wanted to see his beloved Giants beat most.

Early one evening, he came shuffling up to my desk, excited.

"I've been checking every game that the Giants and Yankees are to play at home next season, and I've found a mistake in the schedules. They both have home games scheduled for the afternoon of August 20th—the Giants at the Polo Grounds and the Yankees at the Stadium right across the river. There's something wrong.

"I've just told the men in our sports desk about the mistake because these two teams never play at home at the same time. But they laughed at me.

"One of them told me, 'You're nuts, that it was impossible,' and that I had better wipe my glasses and take another look."

Any New York baseball fan, of that era, knew that the Giants and Yankees would never be playing on their home grounds on the same afternoon. The reason? The two ball parks were only separated by the narrow Harlem River and were no more than a few thousand feet apart.

For both these clubs to play on the same day in New York would have been the equivalent of having two abutting motion picture theaters offering the identical film at the same time. Ticket sales would be split. Even Ike knew this Giants–Yankee date conflict represented a bad business situation.

"Are you sure you're right about this conflict in dates?" I asked Ike as he riffled through his index cards right in front of me.

"Absolutely" was his reply. "I was so surprised. I've checked it out five times."

"If you're so sure," I said to him, "why don't you write to the National League offices here in Manhattan and find out about it? The chances are that if you've discovered the mistake, so have they. But write! There's no harm in letting yourself be heard. Maybe it is a mistake."

Ike was right. It was an error. And because he had saved the National League office embarrassment by finding it out well before that season's start, he was rewarded with National League Season Pass #180 valid for ALL games played in ANY of its cities. The pass was made out to "Ike Falk and One," a gift that was signed by Ford C. Frick, the league's commissioner. Falk received a similar one each year for as long as he lived.

His passes can probably still be found in one of the glass cases at Baseball's Hall of Fame in Cooperstown, New York. Falk was delighted, each year, to contribute them to that popular sports shrine which is located about 175 miles northwest of New York City.

It was in that tastefully designed red brick Hall of Fame complex that Ike made one of his classic remarks. Seen peering with nose almost on the showcase that contained his annual passes, he was cautioned by a New York sportswriter who knew him well.

"You'd better be careful," the writer joked. "The museum's curator is apt to put you under glass too as another baseball curiosity."

"He can't do it!" replied Falk with a confident wave of his hand. "I have a return trip ticket on the bus to New York."

As might be expected, once he became a regular recipient of his free pass, Ike, who had always sat behind home plate at home games, became a well-known figure at the Giants' stronghold—the Polo Grounds. It was small wonder. Fans, from time to time, would find themselves craning their necks to determine whether they had a stray cow in their midst.

What they were hearing was Ike strenuously shaking a raucous, clanging cowbell so realistically that it seemed only a cow's neck could be the motivating power. Falk picked his spots in ringing the big bell. If a Giants player made a single, double, or triple, Ike would reach for a small bell and shake it enthusiastically.

But if one of the Giants hit a home run, Falk would grab the cow bell and bedlam, of a sort, would follow. He would rattle it with such vigorous movements that it seemed that his store teeth possibly would be shaken loose from their moorings. As a climax, he would throw the bell into the air and let it drop with a noisy clatter.

The first season, with his pass, was a wonderful one for Ike. But he ended up with a problem on his mind.

"I've been able to make just about every game that the Giants played at home," he told me one night in November. "But do you realize that my pass went to waste every time the Giants played in Pittsburgh, St. Louis, Cincinnati, and Chicago and three other National League cities? And here

I am, stuck in New York with a good pass and no chance to use it for any of those out-of-town games."

It was obvious to me that Ike intended doing something about it. And he did. Within two years, as night baseball was introduced to the big leagues, he almost squeezed his pass dry. Thanks to the advent of play under lights, one season he succeeded in attending as many as 114 games.

He accounted for most of this big number by turning out every afternoon at the Polo Grounds when the Giants were at home. If he was on his day off, he might be seen rushing to Brooklyn to see the Dodgers play, at night, on their home diamond at Ebbets Field.

That season, Ike started his vacation on the same day that the Giants began a road trip. When they left New York, he left with them; only he traveled by Greyhound bus and the players by Pullman train. And when his favorites trotted onto Pittsburgh's Forbes Field the next day, there was Ike behind home plate shaking both bells with all his might.

On that one trip, Falk saw the Giants play the Pirates four times, and then, when the New York team left for games farther west, not wishing to part with any more traveling expenses, he remained in Pittsburgh for the rest of his vacation to watch the Pirates in action against what he referred to as "lesser" teams.

Early every season, Ike would announce his predictions for the winners of the American League as well as the National League pennant races. He was always wrong. I remember that before the start of the 1941 season, he departed from his usual custom of picking the Giants for first place. He predicted that they would have a poor season because of the lack of batting strength.

He proceeded to explain what he expected: that each of the top three Giants pitchers would win at least fifty games among them.

"As for the rest of the Giants' pitching staff," he told me one day in April, "such players as Bill Melton and Carl Hubbell as well as two or three others will win at least ten games each."

"But, Ike," I said to him, "that adds up to enough games to make the Giants the pennant champion."

"So much the better," said Falk, strolling off down the hall with a jaunty air.

That season, of all things, it was his "hated" Brooklyn Dodgers who captured the National League pennant with 100 victories.

"This has been a bad year" was Ike's observation on the day the Dodgers clinched the pennant. "No wonder the Allies are having a tough time in Europe."

CHAPTER 26

Wrapping It Up – Millionaire Living

Success is failure turned inside out—
The pleasant path to erase all doubt
And so we come to the end of the trail
After years of waiting to end my tale.

Bill Corum, the one-time famous star columnist of the *New York Journal*, was on his way home from Cincinnati in 1940. He was in the train's drawing room following the end of the World Series between the Reds and Detroit Tigers, in a talk-fest with other sportswriters. The conversation, over assorted drinks, finally got around to careers.

"That's a subject I've thought about a lot lately," said one gray-haired writer. "Talking about careers, I'm told that Lefty O'Doul, as manager of the San Francisco Seals, was happier being with a minor league club than he ever had been in the bigs. I always felt the goal of every ball player was to get to the big leagues and stay there."

The discussion boiled down to what type of job each of the writers would have chosen if given a chance to start all over again.

"There's no doubt in my mind about my choice," finally offered Corum. "I never wanted to be a millionaire. I just wanted to live like one—or be a sportswriter."

Grantland Rice, the famous columnist, in reminiscences he put together in the 1950s, backed this feeling up with a tale he told about Toots Shor, the well-known West Side, New York City restaurateur.

"Shor was watching a group of sports reporters after a Baseball Writers' party," recalled Rice. "It was 3:00 A.M., and as he watched them carve their initials in his bar, he remarked to a customer,

"'Look at them. It's all so misleading. There's not a millionaire in that bunch. They just live like them.'"

As I worked for the *New York Times*, my attitude about my job was similar. Once I was out of the city, "toiling" for that esteemed journal, I was on an all-expense deal. Just think—being reimbursed for plane and train tickets, hotel and meal bills and stopping at top hotels—say at Sun Valley, St. Moritz, Lake Placid, Los Angeles, Chicago, London, and so on.

I never regretted my decision to sacrifice a possible law career for sportswriting. My wife, Cecilia, who attended a three-room schoolhouse in a community of 300 in Vermont, before going high hat and matriculating at New York's Barnard College, often had remarked, "How could you blame my husband for choosing the career that he did? Why would he want to go into a courtroom and fight and argue for a client when all he had to do was to go to a ball game, a horse race, a country club, or a ski area in the Alps which he enjoyed? That's what many people who are lawyers and doctors look forward to doing on their days off. His only job was to write about what he saw in the exclusive surroundings of a press box or a ski chalet."

One of the big plusses in the business, I soon found, was the pleasant associations made with men and women in the sporting world. Among my most enjoyable memories are the short boat trips I made to meet incoming sports celebrities down New York Bay who were arriving on ocean liners from Europe.

"You'll have to get up at four in the morning to cover this story," I recall having John Rendel, the boss's secretary, tell me early on the eve of my first such assignment. "The Immigration cutter will take you aboard at the Battery, off Whitehall Street. And you can't be late. That boat will not wait even if Uncle Sam is on his way."

These assignments all were highly enjoyable. And why not? As the cutter puttered from the Hudson River down Upper Bay to meet the arriving steamers at our Quarantine, the immigration officers and I would sit down for a five-and-ten-cent limit poker game that might last forty-five minutes.

Once alongside the huge liners—such as the *Manhattan*, the *United States*, and the *Ile de France* —all of us would ascend a narrow stairway and make our way to our respective destinations. The customs people would start checking out baggage while I would head for my celebrity—a tennis player, a golfer, or maybe a boxer. After that, it would be breakfast in the ship's first-class dining room as a guest of the steamship company.

When on the road on a sports assignment, I often would receive plush treatment if only because I was with the *New York Times*. It wasn't unusual to be ushered into a suite—at no extra charge—rather than just a plain old room in a hotel.

Because of the nature of the business in which sports assignments are made at the last moment, I often would phone for a room reservation to ski areas when their housing was all sold out. I recall phoning Aspen's Housing Bureau in Colorado's Rockies one Thursday afternoon. It was on the eve of a busy racing weekend in that old silver mining town.

"We don't have a vacant room in town" was the reply. "All the hotels and motels are booked solid.

"Just a moment," she said after I had identified myself. "Let me see if we can't do something for you. I will call you back in about fifteen minutes." In ten minutes my phone rang.

"We found something," she informed me. "There is no room at the regular lodges, but we've arranged to have you stay in a private home. You will be staying there as a guest. There will be no charge and a lady will meet your plane at the airport to chauffeur you."

A lady, about twenty years my junior, was there right on schedule. As we left the airport, I looked at the car's gas gauge. It was almost empty. So I had her stop at the nearest service station to fill up. When we reached her home, it turned out to be a comfortable place with turn-of-the-century furnishings.

When it developed that her husband was not at home, I invited her to dinner that night. We were joined in the restaurant by two of her friends. After eating, we all returned to her house. Tired from my all-day journey from New York, I excused myself and went to sleep. When I returned to my Long Island home after a two-day stay in Aspen, I sent her an ivory-handled Victorian engraved silver fish set as a gift for her hospitality.

It was rather routine to receive unexpected courtesies in covering sports assignments. I've been on many an elegant, big sports fisherman boat out on the ocean prowling for 500-pound swordfish or 700-pound blue tuna—as a guest and not as a fisherman. I've dined at many of America's top sports clubs—such as the New York AC, the Penn AC, the Denver AC, and the athletic club in Tulsa, among others. I've been on US Coast Guard planes over the Atlantic reporting on the goings-on of the time-honored Newport-to-Bermuda yacht race. I've been squired around in chauffeured cars by government tourist or Chamber of Commerce representatives in such countries as France, Austria, Italy, Switzerland, Ireland, Scotland, Hong Kong, Taiwan, and many states in America.

I've watched ski jumping tournaments while sitting close to Norway's King Olav and shaken the hand of the Prince of Wales—Prince Charles—after watching him play polo in Palm Beach. And I've played poker, once one of my favorite pastimes, with many a well-known sports personality.

Yes, poker was part of many a sportswriter's scene, and not only on those small immigration boats. I also found these games of chance in progress, in those early days, almost everywhere I went. For example, poker was routine in the press box at Roosevelt Raceway on Long Island after the pacers and trotters there had called it quits for the night.

"It looks as though we'll have to cut out these night games," Nick Grandi, the track's publicity director finally told us one day. "It's producing bad blood. It seems that one of the writers has been borrowing money from the others and not paying up. In fact, he can't. He's in hock."

There's no doubt that Grandi's decision to have the games stopped had been made with reluctance. After all, he had been the one who had gone to all the trouble of having a poker table, with a plush green covering, ordered and installed for our pleasure.

Probably the poker games I enjoyed most were the ones played during the road trips I took with the New York Yankees baseball team. Taking part in the friendly, low-limit card games which were usually held in a complimentary suite were such well-known personalities as Elston Howard, Frank Messer, Bill Kane, Phil Pepe, Bill White, plus a few other writers. We'd get together in the team's hotel about an hour after the completion of that night's ball game.

The pleasant-mannered Howard had been one of the Yankees' mainstays as a catcher and outfielder for a decade starting in the mid-1950s but was now a coach. Messer and White were two of the club's three broadcasters; Kane was the road secretary while Pepe was the *New York Daily News* writer. Bill White, who was a major league player for thirteen years and who starred at first base for the St. Louis Cardinals, in 1989, became the National League's president.

Playing with White, Howard, and Kane was a delight. The repartee by this trio, filled with friendly humor, made even losing feel enjoyable. Joining us on occasion was Whitey Ford, who had once been the Yankees' outstanding southpaw pitcher and amiable Phil Rizzuto, the third of the club's announcers, who had sparkled as the Yankees' shortstop some thirty years earlier.

The one poker game experience I remember best, however, was the card playing session that was held during a trip that basketball's pro New

York Knickerbockers were making to Boston to meet the Celtics. The card game, at that time, was a totally unexpected one because the team and the press originally had been scheduled to fly from New York's LaGuardia to the Beantown city, a one-hour trip by air. When we arrived at the airport, we were told that all flights had been canceled minutes earlier because of the weather. A hurried call to the New York, New Haven & Hartford Railroad revealed that the team could still get to Boston in plenty of time for that night's contest if we hurried back to midtown Manhattan's Grand Central Station. We made it just in time.

Within fifteen minutes after that train left the New York terminal, a high-low poker game was in progress in one of the team's drawing rooms. It was a game in which two winners split the pot, the man who held the high hand after seven cards had been dealt and the player who held the low hand.

I had played seven-card, high-low poker many times. But these fellows were engaged in a variation of it with which I was not familiar—"Criss Cross poker," they called it. Joe Lapchick, the Knick's head coach, who had once been a member of the fabulous touring Original Celtics; Frankie Blauschild, the team's publicity director; and Lennie Lewin of the *New York Daily Mirror* were among the players.

"Want to get into the game?" Blauschild asked me as the train hurtled through such suburban New York towns as Pelham, New Rochelle, and Mamaroneck. "We could use another player."

"Not me, at least not yet," I replied although I felt, as a poker lover, a strong desire to join them. "In the past, I've played in such crazy games as One-eyed Jacks Wild, Deuces Wild, Spit in the Ocean, Last Hole Card Dealt Wild, Baseball, Merry Widow, Jacks or Better, or just plain Stud. But until today, I've never seen Criss Cross played. Let me watch for a while."

It was while the train was approaching Stamford, Connecticut that I finally asked to be dealt a hand. I realized that seven-card Criss Cross was almost entirely luck because the seventh and last card dealt—the wild one—could change the game's entire outcome.

To put it simply, this was one afternoon in which I enjoyed a rare experience—that of not being ABLE to lose. I kept sharing winning pots at about an unbelievable rate, about three out of every five games as the train breezed past New Haven, New London, Providence, Taunton, and points north. By the time we had reached North Station in Boston, I had won about $400 and was cashing checks for those who were losing.

Was Criss Cross really a game of pure luck? Absolutely! I found that no skill was necessary. Even when I had poor hands after four or five cards, the next two placed before me made me a winner. And so, I was well loaded with greenbacks as I watched the Knicks play the Celtics that night.

We were slated to leave Boston for New York by air the next morning but again found ourselves on a train. Low visibility again had grounded planes. And as I had expected, the Criss Cross game was resumed almost as soon as the train's wheels started rolling.

"How about it?" Blauschild asked once we were well underway. "You probably were the only winner on the trip up. Are you going to let us try to get even on the trip down?"

I had anticipated this invitation as soon as I learned that our flight back to New York had been canceled. As a frequenter of the pari-mutual windows at the race tracks, I had often heard the lesson of the turf preached—"quit while you're ahead." And so, I decided to take my time in getting back into Criss Cross competition. Maybe I'd wait until we were thirty minutes from New York and then join the play so that some of the boys could regain some of their losses.

"Not right now," I told Frank. "I have some important reading to do. But I'll join you later."

What important reading did I do? Because I consider myself a Civil War buff, I had taken a hardcover book from my home dealing with Abraham Lincoln's generals. I dug it out of my suitcase and began reading what I had read many times earlier that General Pope had been clobbered by the Confederates at the Second Battle of Bull Run.

But actually, I couldn't wait to take part in the game. And I didn't wait until we were nearing New York. I got back into it by the time the train was passing through Providence—only about thirty minutes from Boston. I was welcomed by all. But they all may have soon had a change of heart. Because again I began winning with what must have seemed to them as amazing regularity.

Suffice it to say, by the time we were back at New York's Grand Central Station, I had added another $300 to my coffers. At least two of the players owed me money they didn't have, and I had about three new personal checks in my pocket. As it developed, I never had occasion to play Criss Cross again if for no other reason than that whenever I did travel thereafter with the Knicks, we never again were grounded.

I once was on the scene in Yonkers, just above the New York City line, when I saw almost sixty women golfers grounded—at least temporarily. They were members of the Westchester–Fairfield Association who had descended on the historic St. Andrew's Golf Club for one of their weekly tournaments.

It was at a time when many women players across America had begun to wear Bermuda shorts—apparel that came down to just above their knees—as they made their rounds over tees and fairways.

But these Westchester–Fairfield women barely had gotten into the front door of the clubhouse when they were told that St. Andrew's did not permit play in that "type of getup."

"It's a hard-and-fast rule here," they were told by the club's manager. "All I'd have to do is let one of you ladies out on our course with those 'briefies,' and I'd be out tomorrow looking for a new line of work."

Officials of the women's association who, as usual, had arranged that year's schedule in advance for play at a different club each week, were aghast. About half their 100 players were decked out in shorts and prepared to play.

"I can't believe it," said one of the association's officials. "We've been playing in shorts at all of the other clubs and no one's made a fuss." The club's manager remained adamant. St. Andrew's had been named, back in the late nineteenth century, after the famed club in Scotland. And ever since 1889, when the Yonkers links had begun hosting players on its then six-hole course, the "proper apparel" club rule had been adhered to—to the letter. The lady golfers discussed the problem in a fast get-together.

"We have no choice," a member of the women's group said to the players who had appeared in Bermudas. "I suggest we rush over to the club's pro shop and see whether they have any women's skirts for sale."

"Hurry is the word," said a lady golfer. "I've just come from the pro shop. They only had about a dozen skirts for sale. It'll be first come, first served, providing you can find your size."

The tournament was delayed and played, but only after the operator of the pro shop had made desperation phone calls to other golf courses within a twenty-mile range asking whether they had any golf skirts on their racks.

Play got underway on schedule for those who had arrived in skirts. But for those who had to buy skirts, they finished an hour or two behind time.

"Another golf skirt!" lamented one of the late starters. "That's the last thing I needed. I've been giving the ones I have away because it's much more comfortable to play in Bermudas."

The question of what represented ladylike apparel for the women kept surfacing all through the 1940s and in the decade that followed. I remember during a Ladies PGA tournament at the Concord Hotel in the Catskills, asking that the great playing pro, Patty Berg, cooperate for a gag photograph.

"What do you want me to do?" said the red-haired, ever pleasant Patty who had been to women's golf in earlier days what Babe Ruth had been to baseball. "If such a picture will help the sport, I'm ready."

"As you know," I told her, "some fuss is being made over the short skirts players have been wearing. I have a tape measure. I wonder whether you would consider measuring how far some of the skirts of some of the players are above their knees?" Patty, affable as ever and eager to get women's golf as much exposure as possible, agreed. And so off she went to the first tee with four players to be photographed.

"As you can see, the skirts that our girls are wearing are in good taste," she grinned as she came off the tee having done her measuring chore. "And they won't get in our players' way in trying to cope with par."

And the skirts didn't, as Hall of Famer Betsy Rawls in winning the tournament did a superb job in coping with the difficult course.

Difficult? That was the path that Thomas E. Dewey found himself traveling during the presidential campaign of 1948. He was beaten by Harry S. Truman in a major upset. It was unsettling.

One winter's afternoon, Dewey subsequently barely was able to keep on his feet when he tried to take up skiing. My friend Lowell Thomas phoned me a few days after Dewey, New York's one-time governor, had tried the sport. "Since his home was near mine in Pawling, New York," Lowell told me, "I had been after Tom to try skiing. But he was reluctant. He kept telling me he was too old for that sort of thing. That it was okay for me because I'd been doing it for years.

"To my surprise," Lowell continued, "he phoned me one morning and said he was willing to give it a shot. Inwardly I groaned. He had picked the worst possible day. The usual January thaw had taken place followed by the usual freeze-up. It would have taken an ice skater, let alone an expert skier, to have coped with that afternoon's conditions." But since he had urged the governor to try the sport so many times, Thomas decided he couldn't back out. With the temperatures having dropped back to well below freezing and the outdoors apparently at its wintery best—ice and all—how was he going to explain to Dewey that a postponement might be in order?

And so off they went. Thomas, at home on skis, nevertheless took the precaution of asking Jim Parker, the local ski pro, to accompany them. But as might be expected, Parker could not do the impossible. The surfaces were so glassy that Dewey was sent sprawling repeatedly. "We all emerged alive from that outing," Thomas told me. "And chances are the Governor and I will remain friends, but I think only if I make sure not to discuss skiing ever again when I'm with him."

Topping it all has been life with the *Palm Beach Daily News*—"the Shiny Sheet"—in that exotic land of poincianas, pelicans, palm trees, and mansions. The *News*, with its relatively small circulation, caters to people, who for the most part, live close to Worth Avenue's exclusive shops and the Atlantic Ocean. The paper is part of the Cox Communications chain.

The paper's nickname is well deserved. The *News* is printed on glossy magazine-type paper, much stiffer to the feel than run-of-the-mill newsprint. Its readers, it seems, way back when, complained. They maintained that they preferred reading a paper that didn't leave ink on their hands. The *Palm Beach Daily News*, unlike the *Times*, doesn't.

"Our coverage should be on sports in which our Palm Beach people are interested," Mrs. Ash, the publisher, told me on the day she agreed to have me join her group as a freelancer. "Our readers play a lot of croquet. They're interested in thoroughbred horse racing and, of course, there's always polo, golf, and tennis."

"There's more than enough here to keep me busy," I replied. "And freelance is just great. At this stage of the game, I'm not interested in a 9-to-5 job. I just want to keep busy."

And I have kept busy. I've written four or five articles each week and they haven't been short ones, usually about 800 words each. I write my pieces on a word processor that I have at my ocean front apartment. In the summertime, I write a weekly column from my place in Vermont.

Our news staff, while small, is a conscientious one. And just as in the case of large metropolitan dailies, the air in the office becomes tense just before press time which technically has been at 5:00 P.M. That closing time is hours earlier than at papers in the big cities.

But I'm still succeeding in beating the deadline whether it's with polo stories at the Palm Beach Polo and Country Club, croquet at the Breakers Hotel, golf at the PGA Resort in Palm Beach Gardens or horse racing at Gulfstream.

The closest brush, however, I've had until now with the deadline—of all things—dealt with our paper's crossword puzzle, a *New York Times* syndicated feature that "the Shiny Sheet" prints daily. A problem surfaced at about 4:15 one afternoon.

"The answers to our previous day's crossword puzzle have been mislaid," I heard Ellen Koteff, who was then our managing editor, lament to a staff member. "Lots of our readers will be looking for them tomorrow morning. If we don't have those answers in our paper, there's sure to be plenty of complaints."

"Maybe I can help," I volunteered. "I think I possibly can pick up the answers by telephone."

Being familiar with the necessary procedure because of my years with the *Times*, I phoned its syndicated office in New York and was able to get the full cooperation of a staff member who knew where to look. She, thereupon, dictated the necessary words while I filled in the blank spaces in the puzzle that had been in our paper that morning.

Because of the pressure of time, the answers were rushed to the composing room and appeared in the Shiny Sheet the next morning with the scrawly, printed letters that I had jotted down so quickly.

Do you now? I believe it was the first and only time, in all my years of working crosswords that I was able to fill in all the blanks.

After almost a decade with the Shiny Sheet—in this, my second career—I've had just as good a time as I had with the *New York Times*. And I'm covering just about the same sports that came my way in earlier years.

In the Palm Beach area, I've encountered Donald Trump, the Prince of Wales, an annual participant in the area in polo; Jack Nicklaus, Gary Player, and JoAnne Carner, among others in golf; jockeys Angel Cordero and Eddie Maple in thoroughbred racing; and lots of baseball stars during the spring training season. I have just reason to feel content. Originally, I wanted to be a baseball player. Sportswriting, I guess, was my second choice. Was it a good one? Am I content about the decision I made? All I have to do is to remember what actor Telly Savala, who was then starring as a television detective in "Kojak" once said to me. We were at New York's Belmont Park.

On hand to make a presentation in the winners' circle I was introduced to him as "the *New York Times* sportswriter."

"Boy!" he blurted as he shook my hand in his firm grasp. "Would I like to change jobs with you!"

Michael Strauss 1926, 13 years old

Michael Strauss 1935

Michael Strauss 1965

Michael Strauss with renowned clown Emmett Kelly

Michael Strauss of the New York Times with the tools of his trade

Mike, Nixon and the Yankees 1969

Mike with Pittsburgh Steeler's owner Art Rooney

Michael and Cecilia Strauss 55th Anniversary, 1993

Michael Strauss and Donald Trump, Mar-a-Lago, Palm Beach,2001

Michael Strauss in the press box, 1975-

Michael Strauss with Palm Beach Daily News

INDEX

Made in the USA
Middletown, DE
03 January 2019